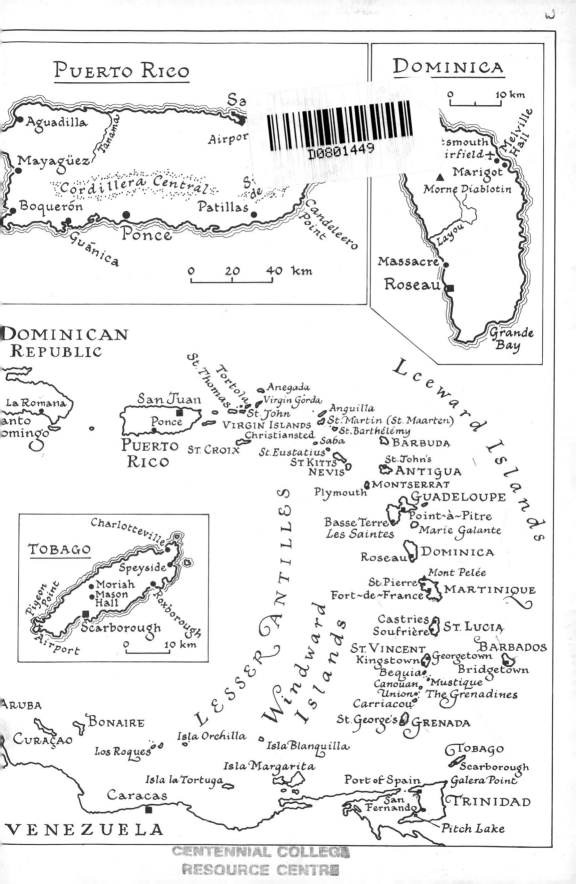

PUERTO RICO

Aguadilla

Mayagüez

Cordillera Central

Boquerón

Guánica

Ponce

Patillas

Sa

Airpor

Sa de

Candeleero Point

Tanama

0   20   40 km

DOMINICA

0   10 km

tsmouth irfield

Melville Hall

Marigot

Morne Diablotin

Layou

Massacre

Roseau

Grande Bay

DOMINICAN REPUBLIC

La Romana

anto omingo

San Juan

Ponce

PUERTO RICO

St. Thomas

Tortola

Anegada

Virgin Gorda

St. John

VIRGIN ISLANDS

Christiansted

ST. CROIX

St. Eustatius

Saba

Anguilla

St. Martin (St. Maarten)

St. Barthélémy

BARBUDA

ST. KITTS

NEVIS

St. John's

ANTIGUA

MONTSERRAT

Plymouth

GUADELOUPE

Basse Terre

Les Saintes

Point-à-Pitre

Marie Galante

Roseau

DOMINICA

Mont Pelée

St. Pierre

Fort-de-France

MARTINIQUE

Castries

Soufrière

ST. LUCIA

St. Vincent

Kingstown

Bequia

Canouan

Union

Carriacou

St. George's

Georgetown

BARBADOS

Bridgetown

Mustique

The Grenadines

GRENADA

Iceward Islands

LESSER ANTILLES

Windward Islands

TOBAGO

Charlotteville

Speyside

Moriah

Mason Hall

Roxborough

Scarborough

Pigeon Point

Airport

0   10 km

ARUBA

BONAIRE

CURAÇAO

Los Roques

Isla Orchilla

Isla Blanquilla

Isla Margarita

Isla la Tortuga

Caracas

Port of Spain

San Fernando

TOBAGO

Scarborough

Galera Point

TRINIDAD

Pitch Lake

VENEZUELA

Touch the Happy Isles

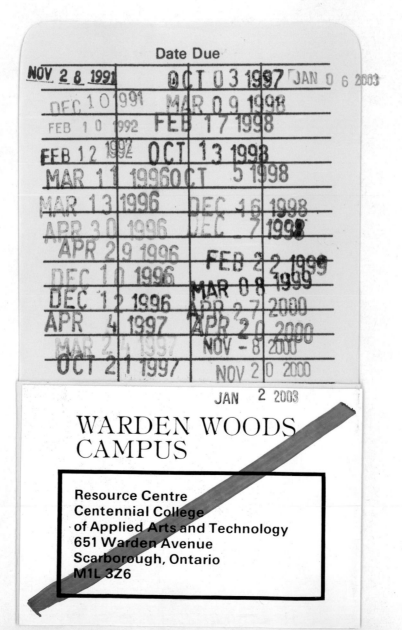

Also by Quentin Crewe

A CURSE OF BLOSSOM
FRONTIERS OF PRIVILEGE
GREAT CHEFS OF FRANCE
INTERNATIONAL POCKET BOOK OF FOOD
IN SEARCH OF THE SAHARA
THE LAST MAHARAJA

Touch the Happy Isles

A JOURNEY THROUGH THE CARIBBEAN

Quentin Crewe

MICHAEL JOSEPH
LONDON

First published in Great Britain by Michael Joseph Ltd
27 Wrights Lane, London W8
1987

© 1987 by Quentin Crewe

Endpapers by Peter McClure
Line illustrations by Jonathan Heale

British Library Cataloguing in Publication Data

Crewe, Quentin
    Touch the happy isles: a journey through the Caribbean.
    1. Caribbean Area—Description and travel—1981–
    I. Title
    910′.091821   F2171.2
    ISBN 0–7181–2822–2

Photoset by Wilmaset, Birkenhead, Wirral
Printed and bound in Great Britain by
Billing and Sons, Worcester

ACKNOWLEDGEMENTS

The author and publishers are grateful to the following for permission to reproduce copyright material.

Aitken & Stone Ltd, London — *Old Patagonian Express* by Paul Theroux

Jamaica Institute of Social and Economic Research, Kingston — *Report on the Rastafari Movement in Kingston, Jamaica*

John Murray (Publishers) Ltd, London — *The Traveller's Tree* by Patrick Leigh Fermor

Come, my friends,
'Tis not too late to seek a newer world.
Push off, and sitting well in order smite
The sounding furrows; for my purpose holds
To sail beyond the sunset, and the baths
Of all the western stars, until I die.
It may be that the gulfs will wash us down:
It may be we shall touch the Happy Isles . . .

TENNYSON, 'ULYSSES'.

For Sabrina

Contents

Acknowledgements

First and foremost, I must thank Hamish Goddard, my companion and helper on the long and complicated journey which formed the basis for this book. For a young, energetic person, the task of looking after someone in a wheelchair for six uninterrupted months is necessarily exhausting and extremely limiting. Never once did Hamish complain without good reason; never did he put his own interests first, leave me in the lurch or unexpectedly abandon me even for ten minutes. He plodded through hours of activities which held nothing for him. He sat through interminable conversations which bored him. He drove without mishap over the most terrible roads for prodigious distances. And at the end of it all, he thanked *me*. Of course, he did lose the car keys every day, leave behind my notebook, my clothes and even, on one occasion, three bottles of extra special rum, but no one could ever have had so delightful, patient and sympathetic a travelling companion.

In writing a book of this sort, one is grateful to all the people one meets on the way who, to a greater or lesser degree, help one to build a portrait of a place and I am thus indebted to all the people mentioned in the book. Some, I realise, may not be so pleased to be mentioned. (One person, about whom I had been far more agreeable than he deserved, happened to see a part of the draft and wrote a whining letter of complaint, denying all he had said to me.) I hope that most of them will accept this as my thanks.

Many others, who gave me much of their time or showed us great hospitality or helped in other important ways, do not necessarily appear in the book. I would like to thank most particularly the following people: Brian Alexander, Ninoska Bonelly, Sir Giles and Lady Bullard, Kenneth Diacre, Sally and Robert Dick-Read, Valerie and Maurice Facey, Lord Glenconner, Alan Godsal, John Gold, Robin Hanbury-Tenison, Gordon Harris, Lennox Honychurch, Lydia Howitt, Sheila and Ken Kennedy, Jacline Labbé, Lyton Lamontagne, Earl Levy, Sue McMannus, James and Celia Milnes-Gaskell, Desmond Nicholson, Reginald Oldham, William Otway, Esteban Padilla, Simon Parkinson, Wenda Parkinson, Alton Peters, John Pringle, Annabelle Proudlock, Jim Rudin, Monica Tamberg, Jill Tattersall, Viviane Vieux, Marina Warner, Sally, Duchess of Westminster, Simon Winchester and Victoria Winlaw.

Finally, I would like to thank those who have helped with the making of the book: first, Alan Brooke, for his unending faith, optimism and encouragement, then Roland Philipps for sage guidance and most especially Margaret Robertson for her placid and intelligent help in preparing the manuscript in bizarre and even mildly farouche circumstances.

1

Trinidad

FIRST IMPRESSIONS AND AN OLD HERO

The excitement of any arrival is tinged with fears. What are you doing there? Is it true that you will surely be mugged in the street? Can the exchange rate be right? Will there be a hotel room? A man on the plane had said there was no hope of one. But it is mostly: what are you doing there, when the immigration man so clearly doesn't want you? In Trinidad the immigration men look especially fierce.

Then other things take over. Driving through the dark, the noise of the frogs seemed louder than the plane had been. Landing in the tropics, I find I have always forgotten the exact feeling, the distinctive smell, and that rich thickness of the air. Hamish, in the back of the taxi, asked what the little lights were. Fireflies. He didn't believe there were such things. Then he fell asleep. How could he fall asleep when he had never before left Europe?

The taxidriver was quiet, talking in almost accentless English about such things as Sunday drivers and telling me that all private number-plates on cars began with the letter P. Taxis are vast wallowing American cars of great age – their numbers began with H.

Other forgotten things: those premises with wire mesh over them

1

rather than roofs. (Are they intended for creepers which never get planted?) The cluster of flags and bunting round second-hand car dealers, an Americanism this. The epiphytes and orchids growing on telegraph wires. How can they take enough sustenance from the air to grow ten inches tall?

Then we were in a traffic jam, the Trinidadians returning to Port of Spain after a Sunday outing. We might have been back in England, were it not for the warm, thick air and the frogs, which continued to make a noise even in the industrial outskirts of the capital. In the dark, it was hard to see much of the town as the power was cut. Strange castellated shapes and pointed gables of fairy-tale houses surrounded what seemed to be a park.

We arrived at the Kapok Hotel, a name which had nothing to do with the stuffing in their mattresses, but rather with the large silk cotton tree growing by the entrance. The Chinese owner, I was told, built half of the hotel with the help of an architect. Having paid the architect, he then built the other, mirror half with no architect, thus getting a hotel of the size he wanted for half the fees he would have had to pay. This was our first encounter with the entrepreneurial ingenuity which informs so much of the Caribbean.

At dinner, I began to wonder whether the whole idea of a book about the Caribbean might not be a mistake. Nearly everyone in the hotel was white. At a table nearby an Englishman was booming on about the Duke of Bedford, relating improbable stories about him and the Duke of Windsor. Beyond were some Americans talking about money and elections. One girl kept agitating about whether her telephone calls would come through. They were all carrying their own world with them, confident that it was the right one and quite unaware of the one they had moved to. Would I ever find a real Caribbean?

I felt rather depressed, but we walked out after dinner. Small knots of young men stood at street corners or sat on the steps of houses. What of all the talk of mugging?

'Orright man,' said the young men.

'All right,' we said. It is a comforting greeting.

A long journey of many months is somewhat like reading a book, perhaps even more like writing one. The first page is the hardest. In reading, you are suspicious of the quality; you must get accustomed to the author's style, to the typeface, before you can feel at ease. In writing, it is a matter of flailing and floundering until you are back in practice. So it is with a journey. There is the *angst* of Palinurus about arrivals; the worry, too, of the unfamiliar. There is also the craft of travel to be brushed up. It takes a few days before the packing and unpacking become as automatic as doing one's teeth, and yet more days until one's passport number, and its place and date of issue, trip off one's pen onto those tedious forms as easily as does one's date of birth. A traveller, as opposed to a holiday-maker, must re-school his patience with officialdom, exaggerate his politeness, use more imagination about other people's lives.

Once the traveller becomes engrossed, when he feels almost part of the place he is travelling through, as a reader identifies with the characters in a novel, it becomes a delight. The *angst* vanishes, the unfamiliar seems natural.

Trinidad was very much the first page.

The girl at the hire-car desk was called Amalia. She was pretty and flirtatious, perhaps to divert attention from the condition of the cars. Two of the tyres on the car we were offered were worn down to the canvas. We made them change them for slightly less worn ones. Then the spare was flat; it had to be repaired. And there was no jack, so they gave us one from another car. I wondered what the hirer of that would do.

A car was of little use in Port of Spain. The streets are narrow and steep and jammed for the greater part of the day with traffic which remains motionless for ages and then rushes in alarming surges, taking no account of the equally packed crowds of pedestrians. There is a great sense of energy about the town, but I felt Port of Spain was unfriendly and uncaring. It is an ugly town for the most part, the weather-boarded houses having been replaced by dim concrete buildings. Only round the Savannah, the park I had noticed on our way in, are the buildings interesting – wild gingerbread mansions next to crazy Victorian, Scottish-baronial castles, strangely jumbled fantasies which, tangled together, make a totally surprising, but entertaining collection.

The people in the streets are almost as curiously assorted as the buildings round the Savannah. The mixture of races must be as complete as has been achieved anywhere in the world. Quite apart from the variety of European immigrants, ranging from Spanish through British, French, Portuguese–Jewish, to Corsican, there are Negroes,

Indians, Bangladeshis, East Indians, Chinese, Amerindians – indeed almost every known race mixed and intermarried in the grandest hotch-potch. Oddly enough, this has not produced people of any particular beauty. Whereas on other islands, especially Martinique and the Dominican Republic, the women are possibly the most beautiful in the world, and the men, in Martinique at least, are reasonably handsome, in Trinidad the mixture has not worked as far as looks are concerned. The people have a slightly sinister air about them, so that I found myself thinking often of the brutalities of Michael X, the murderer of <u>Gail Benson</u>.

There also appeared to be an inordinate number of lunatics wandering in the streets. A cackling woman leered at me, muttering something quite unintelligible save for one repeated obscenity; a man danced by, grinning maniacally, with a lavatory seat round his neck; and there were numerous people, literally barking mad, who yapped as they wandered with pointless urgency through the markets.

I wonder whether Europe was like this once. I seem to remember that when I was a child, there were more demented people on the street. In particular, I remember a woman whose penetrating bark could be heard above the traffic noise from the Ritz to Piccadilly Circus. If by chance one were on a bus with her, the journey was made hideous by the awful wait for her next ear-splitting yap – so loud and sudden that, even knowing it was coming, one jumped in startlement. Perhaps we have drugged such unfortunate people into silence.

There was little of the spontaneous warmth I had expected from people's accounts of the Trinidad carnival – despite the 'Orrights' of our first evening's walk. Hamish's brief shorts, printed with red cupid bows and the words 'Hello Darling', provoked some response. The girls blew kisses at him and the boys just laughed, with mocking hostility.

A little tragicomedy was being performed at the Town Hall. The city had commissioned a flood report from a firm of engineers, but had failed to pay the engineers' bill. The engineers sued and the bailiffs were busy removing the Town Hall furniture. It was evidence of the decline in Trinidadian fortunes since the fall in the price of oil. The politicians had assumed that the bonanza of Trinidadian oil would last forever. The city paid up in the afternoon and the bailiffs brought back the furniture the next day.

*   *   *

By that time I had wearied of Port of Spain and was exploring the island. My first objective was the Pitch Lake. The earliest record of this deposit of natural asphalt is in Sir Walter Raleigh's diary for March 1595. Evidently the asphalt at that time had overflowed from the lake and, when he landed near Point Galba in southern Trinidad, Sir Walter found it on the beach. It was, he said, 'most excellent good' for caulking his ships.

The next English sailor to take an interest in the Pitch Lake was Admiral Lord Cochrane, my childhood hero and a vague family connection. In the story I was told by elderly relations, Cochrane acquired the Pitch Lake and brought large quantities of asphalt to England. He was given permission to asphalt Westminster Bridge for the opening of Parliament. Alas, the day was extremely hot and the asphalt melted. The carriage wheels and the hooves of the horses all got stuck in the gooey bitumen. No one wanted to hear any more about asphalt. The Admiral, on the other hand, was as sure as ever that one day it would be recognised as the best material for road surfaces. As he lay dying (elderly relations being fond of such phrases), he made his heirs swear never to sell the Pitch Lake. In the feckless manner of heirs, they naturally sold it for a pittance.

All was not quite lost, because the purchasers had bought only the main lake and had not bothered with a little pool not far away, which they thought was of no significance. The Admiral's great-granddaughter, whom I remember as an old lady of prodigious age, went out to Trinidad in her youth to look at what remained of Lord Cochrane's property. She found that, if she extracted asphalt from the little pool, the level fell in the large lake. The Trinidad Lake Asphalt Company had to buy the little pool for a huge price.

The drive to the Pitch Lake was largely through flat country on a large highway leading to San Fernando. The hills lay to our left rising out of the plain in a long bluey-grey ridge, but I could not make out the trinity of peaks which prompted Columbus to give the island its name. After San Fernando, the country became more agreeable, hillier and with lusher vegetation. The small villages were prettier, with wooden houses – often on stilts to discourage the termites – instead of the atrocious concrete villas which the Indians, in particular, prefer. The Indians, who account for nearly half the population of Trinidad, are inclined to live near the larger towns rather than in the countryside and, as we went inland, the number of houses with little shrines and clusters of prayer flags in their gardens diminished considerably.

Old books describe the Pitch Lake as almost a place of horror: dark, flat and forbidding. It was not nearly as bleak as I had expected. One becomes aware of the lake some couple of miles before one sees it, for the air is filled with the smell of sulphur. As soon as we arrived at the lake itself, we were surrounded by importunate guides offering to take us down to the edge and to guide us through. They expanded, with much mime and gesture, on the dangers of venturing near the lake alone: 'You gone in three seconds on a wrong step'; 'Leave the car one minute on what you think the safest ground, one minute all gone.' We agreed to take one called Winston as a safety measure.

The lake lies below the road, which suggests that the level has gone down many feet since Raleigh's time, when it overflowed, and also makes one doubt the rolling-eyed assertions of the guides that it is bottomless. It does, in fact, lie twenty-nine feet below sea-level. When I say 'in fact', it is with some hesitation, because the Ministry of Information paper from which I learnt this also gives the composition of the asphalt: 'An examination . . . shows that it is extremely uniform in composition. Celloidal clay 30%, Bitumen 54%, Salt water 3%, Mineral matter (ash) 36%.' Any substance with a composition which adds up to 123% must arouse some doubts. The document also says that the lake covers 40.4 hectares and is 76.2 metres deep.

In the sunshine, with frigate birds ('chicken hawks' said the guide) overhead and other birds flitting in and out of the reeds and the water hyacinth, the lake looked rather pretty. The pathways through the lake had a spongy quality and, if one paused for long, one's weight made a deep impression on the ground. I was glad then of the guide.

All round were small, bright greeny-yellow pools. If one bent down and touched them, the sulphur scum sprang away from one's finger revealing crystal clear water underneath.

On the far side men were working, extracting great dripping lumps and loading them into a skip. 'Thousands of tons a day,' said Winston. Three hundred tons, says the Ministry leaflet. I saw two skips loaded in half an hour.

When we left, I discovered that Hamish, not yet accustomed to the currency, had amiably given the guide what he asked for, which was twenty pounds. I could hardly complain, for the day before I had bought a camera and the Indian trader pressed on me some rolls of film as a present. It was not until much later that I found it was out-of-date stock, which made all the photographs a rich Prussian blue.

The saddest part of this visit to the Pitch Lake was that there was no sign of a smaller lake or pool which could have provided the opportunity for the ingenious revenge of my elderly Cochrane lady. The guide denied that there was any such pool. The pamphlet makes no reference to another pool. In the village of Cochrane, five miles away, no one had even heard of the Admiral. Nonetheless, all these were manifestly unreliable sources of information. I shall continue to believe the family fables.

We asked the young men in Cochrane how to get to Siparia. Patrick Leigh Fermor had written in his *Traveller's Tree*, forty years before, of a Black Virgin entirely clad in leather. She stood above the altar of a church, founded in the eighteenth century by Franciscans from Aragon. The young men advised us to go a long way round, but mentioned a far shorter way through the oil fields. 'Better not that way, man. If you go that way you spend the night.'

We decided to risk it. We followed a pipeline. Soon the little huts and dwellings fell away and we were in thick tropical forest. Every so often we would come across one of those oil pumps which look like huge birds pecking mechanically at the ground. They look odd enough in the fields of Texas or the sands of the Arabian desert, but here, working away quite alone in the dripping, engulfing forest, they have an even weirder quality, like some primeval creature. The pipe still ran beside the road, with many branches off it down smaller roads. Occasionally there were warnings about smoking but otherwise no sign of people. Then our road dwindled in size and all at once no one road was more important than any other.

Each road had a number. For a while we followed number one, imagining that it must be the most important, but it became little more than a mud track. There seemed no logic to the numbering. I thought of Alice in court. 'The King . . . called out "Silence!" and read out from his book, "Rule forty-two, all persons more than a mile high to leave the court." . . . "*I'm* not a mile high," said Alice . . . "Besides, that's not a regular rule: you invented it just now." "It's the oldest rule in the book," said the King. "Then it ought to be number one," said Alice.' There was no number forty-two.

We debated which way to go. There was a rusty, iron tower, fifty feet high, so devoured by creepers that it was barely distinguishable among the forest trees. Should Hamish climb it and see whether he could spy out the way? It was not safe enough. 'You will spend the night,' they had said. The forest with its jungly noises and the lonely pecking machines was eerie but in some way not in the least frightening. I wondered how the conquistadores or Raleigh and his sailors had ever explored such an island and mapped it. Hacking a way through this forest must have been tedious, unbearably hot and dangerous, particularly with the threat of hostile Carib Indians.

A wonderfully beautiful, turquoise-blue butterfly skipped down road 256. It was roughly the right direction and was a pretty omen. We followed the butterfly and soon reached houses and a road. Siparia, when we reached it, was a dreary little town, lacking all character. The Catholic church was quite modern, dedicated to La Divina Pastora. Above the altar was a garish cloth woven with a Shepherd Christ. In front of the altar was a group of schoolchildren, practising evangelical hymns and quite giving the lie to the notion that all black people are musical.

In one aisle, I found a black Madonna. She did not date from the eighteenth century and was unfortunately dressed in clouds of white organza. Hamish, whose father is a robust canon in the Church of England, had never been in a Catholic church and was intrigued to learn that you can light candles to saints. He lit one to the Black Virgin, while I speculated on the colour of the statues. Jesus on the Cross was white and so was John the Baptist. There was only one black saint, who I supposed was St Augustine.

What became of the leather-clad virgin, I do not know. She was, according to Mr Leigh Fermor, thaumaturgic and possessed the faculty of homing if removed from her shrine. It may be that the hurricane of 1963 which flattened eighty per cent of Trinidad proved too much for the powers of this image.

We drove back along the coast to Port of Spain, past all the oil refineries and then by a confusing series of tiny roads. Trinidad has few beaches, compared with other Caribbean islands, and the ones that I saw were not very appealing. On this coast, it was hard to reach the sea, as the land became marshy wherever we approached, so we wandered through canefields near the Caroni swamp, in the hope of seeing Scarlet Ibis on their way to roost. We ended in a rubbish dump where, instead of Ibis, we found a thousand vultures looking like swollen, black fruit, hanging on the trees or fallen on the ground.

Trinidad seemed to be composed of disappointments. Later I was to wish that I could go back there and have another go at it, but I do not feel that it would have made much difference. V. S. Naipaul wrote, twenty-five years ago, of the search for an identity by the peoples of the Caribbean. He was writing at the time of the failure of the West Indian Federation. Most of the islands, for better or for worse, have in the intervening years found a very definite, individual identity. There has developed also a very distinct Caribbean character, which is not to say that there is any hope of the islands agreeing collectively on any single point, any more than the Arab nations could all agree on a common policy.

The one island which seems to me to have been left out of this new development is Trinidad. The huge oil revenues raised Trinidadians' standard of living beyond the wildest hopes of the people of any of the other islands, for very little effort on their part. The admiration for foreign, in particular American, products – food, cars, language and every other aspect of western culture – is still stronger in Trinidad than in the other islands. But, at the same time, the old-fashioned 'back to Africa' stance, that has virtually faded away in the rest of the Caribbean, also remains quite strong in Trinidad.

Now that the oil revenues have failed, Trinidadians find themselves thrown back to the beginning – angry, disillusioned and betrayed – while most of their northern neighbours are getting on more simply with the enormous problems of being St Lucian, Dominican, Anguillan, Jamaican or whatever.

2
Tobago
AN ABUNDANCE OF WEATHER

It was raining when we landed in Tobago. There seemed to be such a *lot* of weather. The skies of the Caribbean can hold so much incident. Taking the blue as a background, there can be, in one corner, huge piles of cumulus like a knickerbocker glory; in the centre, scattered nimbus and some wispy clusters; to one side, a black, black block, sweeping down, seemingly to suck up the sea. The rain falls in thimble-sized drops. In a moment it soaks, but one doesn't mind. People come in from the rain laughing. Soon it clears, and the land steams in the sun.

We set out to find Galera Point, where Norman Parkinson, the photographer, lives. 'Don't ax again for Galera Point,' said the first man I asked, 'ax for where Parkinson live.'

As soon as we set off, I was amazed for the first time, as I was to be amazed again and again, to see how different two islands, only a few miles apart, can be. Each of the next sixteen islands, with the exception of Barbados, was to be visible one from the other, yet each was to be so distinct from the last that, were I now to be suddenly transported unknowingly to one of them, I would surely be able to say which it was within minutes of arriving.

10

What will grow on each island does not differ, but what is grown, in what proportions, and on what sort of land, varies enormously. The combinations of coconuts, bananas, sugar cane, spice trees, citrus fruit, pineapples, grass, cacao, yams and all the rest are endlessly varied and every combination gives a new appearance to the landscape.

Tobago, in any case, is not as mountainous as Trinidad and is generally more fertile. The open spaces, with grazing cattle, and the groves of coconut palm, lend a calmness which was wholly lacking in those parts of Trinidad which we had seen. Scarborough, the capital, is both cramped – because most of it is on a steep hillside – and indeterminate, shooting off in different directions, seeking the easiest places on which to put buildings. It has a few pretty, wooden houses and a fine Assembly Room, the rest being modern concrete or stucco.

Parkinson's house proved to be on the other side of the island. The road climbed steeply up and down, through pretty gullies filled with tall bamboos. A bird which looked like a European roller, all pink and vivid blue and grey, sat on a telegraph wire. A man told me it was called a mott-mott. After a small village, we came out of the hills, high up above the sea. The house sat across the bay, half-way up a promontory. We could find no one, so had to return by the hill road and start to look for a guesthouse or small hotel. The maps in Trinidad had been hopeless, little pen-drawn sketches, which bore hardly any relation to reality. Apparently, all maps of Trinidad and Tobago were withdrawn in the seventies, in case the guerrillas got hold of them.

Tobago had a better map than Trinidad, perhaps because they are more interested in tourism. It listed hotels and gave descriptions of them with numbers as map references. I liked the sound of number twelve and found twelve on the map. We drove to the spot. No hotel. After hunting for an hour, I discovered another twelve on the map, on the far side of the island. So we tried number nine, described as a beach hotel. It was way inland, nowhere near the map reference and very gloomy. We ended up in a modern hotel near the airport, owned by some Indians who had put it up, but then evidently decided that that was all they needed to do. The room smelt. The water was cold. The food was inedible.

In the morning, Parkinson's son, Simon, telephoned. It was our first experience of the impossibility of doing anything on a small Caribbean island without everyone's knowing of it. A friend of a man from whom I had asked the way had told Simon that a man with a wheelchair was looking for him.

Simon removed us to a charming, small hotel with only eighteen rooms, called the Kariwak. This kind of hotel is so much the most sensible kind of establishment for the Caribbean. Tourism is now the largest industry for most of the islands, but mass tourism, particularly on the smaller islands, is both unsuitable and damaging. Moreover, it is doubtful whether the locals benefit from it.

All tourists alter whatever they have come to see simply by being there. A pretty fishing village is no longer a fishing village if a 200-bed hotel is built in or near it. It is what the travel agents call a 'resort'. The whole way of life of the village is changed. It may be that the hotel gives jobs to the youth of a fast-growing population, but it may also corrupt them. (There was almost no island on which we were not offered cocaine.) In order to cater for the unadventurous tastes of the average package tourist, enormous quantities of familiar foods are flown in from the United States. A vast percentage of the foreign currency brought in by the tourists goes straight out again to pay for these imports. Most of what is left goes out also, under special agreements entered into by governments to encourage foreign investors.

Then, to attract customers, governments have to borrow money to build bigger airports. A helicopter pilot, called David, was staying in the Kariwak: 'I lie in bed in terror,' he said, 'listening to the agonised whine of that full backthrust, when the DC9s land on the runway. It is only 6,000 feet long.' With a long enough runway an island becomes what the travel agents call a 'destination'.

David told us about the hazards of flying for the oil rigs and how they have to wash the helicopters three times a day with fresh water, to get off the salt from the eternal trade winds. Other people drifted in and out, often interesting me with stories and theories which I was later to hear in exactly the same form about each island. 'Tobago planters were once the symbol of wealth; "rich as a Tobago planter" was a common saying in the eighteenth century.'

'The people here are much more beautiful than on the other islands. Because Tobago was so rich, the planters could afford to buy the best slaves: Ibo, Hausa and Fulani. So we have the best-looking, tall people, whereas on the other islands they had cheaper slaves, from further south in Africa.' This kind of theory was just as likely to be postulated by a black person as by a white one and rarely bore much relation to observable fact.

12

Tobago was enchantingly lazy after Trinidad. We sat in the bar of the Kariwak, drinking superb rum punches and chatting with the streams of people who used the place almost as a club. Little, yellow-breasted banana-quits flitted in and out, settling on the rims of our glasses or on the sugar bowl. The French name for them is *sucrières*. Most of the time it rained and the barman ran out of rum punch, not because he was short of ingredients, but because, he said, he would never serve it until it was at least two days old.

We made agreeable expeditions with Simon and his mother. The first was to their house. On the way, we stopped at the rum shop in the village of Moriah, which Parkinson uses as his office, while he waits for the telephone he applied for eighteen years ago. Henry des Vignes, the owner, had just done the place up after a fire. Carved over the bar was a motto, 'He who doth whatsoever is righteous, so shall he prosper.' Selling drink to the public must be righteous, for Henry has surely prospered. On his shelves were a huge variety of bottles – startlingly bright cherry brandy, Peardrax, Kola Tonic, Vat 19 and six or seven other kinds of rum. Henry asked me what I did. When I told him, he shouted to a girl at the back of the shop, called Inez. She was about sixteen, dark, very lame and rather cross-looking.

Henry pointed at me and said, 'Here is a writer from England. One of the best writers, so I've heard.' He had heard nothing, but he had a point to make to Inez. 'So, you see, if you have not one thing, you may be talented. If he had had the use of his legs, probably he would have had no talent.' Inez looked unconvinced; and I was none too sure myself, but thought it well to look as if I agreed. All West Indians are absolutely direct about matters which we regard as personal. It is refreshing, but inclined to be coupled with that tedious tendency to think all people in wheelchairs are mad and dumb. 'Where does he like to sit?' they would ask Hamish.

Parkinson's house made me wonder whether fashion had always been so ephemeral. It was so easy to date, with its sunken-floored living-room, its vast, upright louvres, stained glass window, green dining-room, white bedroom with a white, fretworked tester, a large Sidney Nolan, some Beatles jokes, a John Ward portrait of Wenda Parkinson. The house seemed to belong to a forgotten age. It also made me wonder at its relevance in a Caribbean island. In the dining-room stood a wonderfully kitsch figure, which the Parkinsons called Mr Winchester. It was a larger than life-size blackamoor, with huge leather boots and a Napoleonic hat, holding a staff, draped with an order and carrying a sword – the last two being additions of Parkinson. Apparently, he originally used to stand outside a brothel in New Orleans. Pinned to his staff would have been ribbons inscribed with the names of the available young girls. Figures like this were the usual advertisement outside brothels, but now the only other example known is in the Smithsonian.

The locals, many of them, are terrified of Mr Winchester and won't come into the house. Others have seen him walking in the district, a foot above the ground. 'When you see them walking a foot above the ground, then you know,' said an old man in the village, with arcane knowledge of these things.

In a way, we still colonise the islands, taking with us our strange ideas and tastes. Yet Norman Parkinson has done much for Tobago. When the worst hurricane of recent years struck the island, he endeavoured to raise money for the relief of those who had lost their crops. He also started a scheme for making sausages, called Porkinson's Bangers. It was intended to benefit small-holders, who might keep two or three pigs. When the scheme was well under way, the government removed the subsidy on imported pig feed and raised the controlled price of pork. The scheme, which was thriving, promptly foundered.

We ate a delicious lunch – *coq au vin* – and drank Pichon-Longueville Lalande, 1971. Outside the rain poured down. One of the villagers, Bruce, came in and sat with us. Simon asked him to tell us what a hurricane is like. In the vivid language of a Glendower, matching the violence of a storm, Bruce conjured up the wind and the rain. I looked behind me. A river of brown water was cascading down the marble steps. Gradually the house filled with water. The swimming pool, a few minutes before a clear blue, was now a mud pond.

Contractors, working on the road above the house, had diverted a drain. The water came pouring down the steep slope of the drive and through the house.

When we got back to our hotel, I re-read the notice which spoke of water economy. How could it, when it rains so much?

With engaging boastfulness, Tobago claims that Pigeon Point has one of the ten best beaches in the world. In reality it is grey and drab but, such is the power of bold assertion, it is a rather fashionable place for a picnic lunch on Sundays. There I met A. N. R. Robinson, who, Simon assured me, would be Trinidad and Tobago's next Prime Minister, a prediction which proved correct. He is the leader of the National Alliance for Reconstruction, who form the main opposition party. He is also the leader of the Tobago House of Assembly, which his party controls with an overwhelming majority of eleven to one.

Caribbean politics are pleasantly informal. There is none of that self-importance which is so provoking in lesser African countries. Admittedly, the eastern islands are tiny, often with a population smaller than that of an average English county. Nonetheless, they are countries and an island with a seat in the United Nations is likely to have a very different perception of itself from, say, Shropshire or Westchester County. It is a measure of West Indian amiability that, in all but the largest islands, the politicians, however good or bad, are nearly always easily approachable and friendly.

Ray Robinson is a short man, with a plumpish face and slightly greying hair. He has a quiet manner, but gives the impression of having a perpetual undercurrent of wry humour. He trained originally for the bar, but then went to Oxford to read politics and economics. Under Trinidad's most famous Prime Minister, Eric Williams, Robinson held the post of finance minister, but resigned over the issue of corruption and the handling of the Black Power movement. His wife Pat is an economist who studied at Columbia University, a stylish, outspoken woman, yet lacking any false sophistication. They were an interesting couple, unexpectedly different from each other in that he was from a Methodist family from Tobago and she was a Catholic from Trinidad.

We sat on the beach munching hamburgers while Ray expounded, with unaffected precision, his views on the predicament of the Caribbean.

'We have three possible courses. We can surrender to what amounts to the colonialism of America. We can follow Cuba. Or we can try, once more, to create some kind of loose federation or something which has not yet been tried. Whatever kind of association it is, it must be political, not just economic.'

Ray entirely rejected the Cuban solution: 'Really, there is no doubt but that we are Western.'

His attitude to the United States displayed an element of bitter resentment. He told a story of the United States having given money to Jamaica to build a factory to produce an artificial fibre. On the day that the factory opened, according to Ray, the United States banned the importation of the fibre. Pat Robinson, too, became enraged about

15

America. It happened to be the time of Reagan's visit to Moscow.

'How dare the Americans trivialise the things which matter most to the rest of the world? Did you see that rubbish about Mrs Gorbachev's clothes? Style Wars they called the comparison between her clothes and Nancy Reagan's – as if Star Wars was some sort of game.'

Ray had a keen sense of history, quoting from Joseph Chamberlain and other politicians and authors.

'The Caribbean is a unique place. It is very fragmented yet it has a fabulous *short* history. The South Seas, by way of comparison, has been the same for thousands of years, with the same people living there. We had the Amerindians, and the archaeological sites now discovered in Tobago are the oldest in the Caribbean; still, it is not the same. The fragmentation is even greater than you would think, for historical reasons. In colonial times, it was quicker to get a letter from Tobago to London than to Port of Spain. We had almost no contact with Trinidad.'

The afternoon drifted on and the conversation became more gossipy, Ray laughing over the bailiffs at the Town Hall, at the same time being horrified that such a thing could happen. I told him that it was just as likely to happen in New York or in Liverpool.

He was funny about a man who had bought an estate on Tobago, complete with a large herd of cows, in which he took no interest, allowing them to roam wild. His neighbours shot and ate them. And we talked of the puzzling case of the cabinet minister who had been shot in the leg in his own bedroom a few days before.

Ray, I decided, belonged to a new class of Caribbean politician, or perhaps was a hangover from the first group of distinguished men who gained independence for their islands. He had an air of incorruptibility and a measured wisdom, softened by his twinkly humour.

Back at the hotel, Diane, the most beautiful of the beautiful waitresses, came to chat. She was twenty-one and had got four O-levels. She thought English was her best subject and asked whether I had read *Great Expectations*, which she judged to be a good novel. Her ambitions were precisely the same as those of almost any English girl of her age. She proposed to work for two years in order to save enough money to go round the world. She asked how I had spent the day. When I told her, she said: 'Robinson is a snob, probably just out to make more money than he has got already.'

*   *   *

At eight-fifteen every morning, on the radio, come what are known as 'the deads'. First, there is an advertisement for Adams Funeral Parlour – 'curcheous and sympathetic'. Then follows organ music, which fades but continues gently in the background while solemn announcements are made.

'Jane Mackintosh, better known as Miss Iris, passed away on the twenty-fourth of November at 11.42 in the morning. She was grand-mother to John, Arthur, Marion, William and seven others and great-grandmother to forty-three and friend of Peter Matthews.' Everyone is always better known as someone else. 'Mr James Coa, better known as Spanish.' In the newspapers similar announcements just put 'B/K as . . .'. The rites according to which the deceased will be buried are usually included. Sometimes the complexity of relation-ships and friendships leaves one dizzy.

'Daisy Albertina Brathwaite, better known as Aunt Daisy, died at her residence 109E Coffee Street, San Fernando, on twenty-fourth of November at 9.25 am. Sister of Evelyn and Winnifred Baily, better known as Teacher Baily. Grandmother of Ferdi and Barry Brathwaite (of Canada), Roger Caesar, and the Findleys, Junior Caesar, Fitzroy Fleming, Ossie Williams, the Popplewells, the Leibas, the St Georges, the Phillimores, the Macleans, the Rileys, the Baileys and Mrs Edna Walker. Funeral takes place on Wednesday, twenty-seventh of November at 3.00 pm from St Paul's EC Church and thence to the Paradise Cemetery.'

The announcements end with the phrase: 'Relatives and friends are requested to accept these as intimations.' Of immortality, perhaps.

In Paul Theroux's *Patagonian Express*, he says he is embarrassed by conversations about colour. I rather enjoy them, as I enjoy any conver-sation which involves people's deepest feelings, subjects which engage the profoundest thought in one's interlocutor.

Gerry Llewellyn came to bring me some prints of photographs that I had taken of the Parkinsons' flooded house, to help them with any argument with the road-builders. Gerry was born in St Vincent. 'There is little opportunity here. I was a teacher, but I decided to make my hobby my profession and now I am a photographer for the paper here.'

We talked of Naipaul and the questions of identity and colour. Gerry was black, quite dark, a powerful-looking man, certainly not of Fulani ancestry to judge from his features.

17

'I'm a West Indian,' he said. 'I don't believe in all this stuff about being an African. I'm Welsh and Scottish, my grandmother was a Macintosh. Roots! Mr Botha is an African, and Nasser, and Gaddafi.'

Gerry pointed to his skin. 'This colour doesn't bother me. I have a friend in Jamaica – a black, black nigger. He's married to an octoroon. They've got twins – identical but one is pure black and the other pure white. So what does that say about roots?'

A friend of Gerry's sat with us. 'You remember that girl Rita? She was black and married a black and they had a blue-eyed white baby. Colonial ladies would come to her in the supermarket and pat the baby. They'd say, "You must be proud to be nanny to a beautiful baby like that." And she'd say, "I'm not the fucking nanny, I'm his mother." '

We drove up the coast to Charlotteville. The land became steeper as we went north, so that the road climbed and fell, with each of the promontories enclosing a succession of bays. In every bay there were echoes still of old plantations, with . glimpses of lawns under the luxurious spread of Samaan trees. The gold and green leaves of cacao trees shone in the dappled sun of the coconut groves. The names of the villages conjured up pictures of early settlers from the north of England – Roxburgh, Kendal, Mount St George, Speyside, Hope. There is always a Hope on every island, a reminder of the evanescent nature of human expectations. (I even remember a tea plantation in Assam called Hope.)

At Speyside we imagined that the people looked cross, for among Tobagonians (never Tobagans), the villagers here are said to be the discontented descendants of escaped slaves from St Vincent – and memories are long in the islands.

Charlotteville is a fishing port, nestling in a wide bay, made up of surprisingly few small, wooden houses for its population of 2,500 inhabitants. Behind it, the hills rise sharply, cutting the village off from the rest of the island and making it as remote and different from Port of Spain as a Hebridean island is from London. We had a drink in the rum shop, where the fishermen refused to believe that Wenda Parkinson could have a Trinidad and Tobago passport. For them, white people were outsiders. The year before, they said, a white girl had come from America to Charlotteville, as they are inclined to come, for the fishermen are vast and muscular. For a while she lived with one of the villagers. One day when he was out 'banking', as they call fishing, several others went and raped her. She ran away screaming. The police came. No one was ever charged with anything. The girl was deported.

We ate our picnic, sitting on a bench down a lane just across the bay. A notice by the beach said: 'Keep a clean scene'. Under a bush near the notice lay a goat and on the bush sat a vivid blue tanager. Beyond the beach, the fishing boats creaked in the water. For the first time, I felt that I was in a place that one could recognise as being the received idea of the West Indies.

After lunch we called on Charles Turpin, who owned 1,200 acres of land round Charlotteville. He thought the suggestion that he could be a distant connection of the highwayman was somewhat tenuous, although Dick Turpin's family did come from the West Indies. He preferred the idea that there might be a connection with the pirate, Ben Turpin. Charles's family have probably been in the West Indies for a couple of centuries, but they came to Tobago only in the 1870s from one of the other islands. His mother, an old lady dressed in velvet and lace, lived in a house up the hill, where the bath sat in the living-room, as it was too big to be taken up the stairs.

Charles confounded all the xenophobic attitudes of the fishermen. He was a most likeable man, whom you would never think of as English. He is, for example, far more West Indian than any white Kenyan is Kenyan. He is concerned for the prosperity of his country and, unlike white people who think of England as home, he enters into the spirit of attempts to improve the nation, in no way resenting, for instance, the TT$20 per acre tax on all land. 'It makes you have to work it.' Much of his land is forest and too steep to be farmed. So he wants to turn 650 acres into a wild-life sanctuary – for iguana, wild pigs, armadillo, a species of very small deer, and agouti. The rest of his land, he believes, should be farmed as a co-operative with all the workers or, at least, as a partnership with some of them. His neighbour, a financier from America, I was told, grumbled when the government took away two of his 1,500 acres of land to make a look-out point and a little shrub garden for passers-by.

When we got back that evening, Gerry came to say goodbye, as we were leaving the next day. He brought with him a boy of fourteen, who was no relation, 'just a friend'. The child quizzed me about the Indian Mutiny, as he saw I was reading Christopher Hibbert, discussed pre-Arawak shards, wanted to know the exact connection between Latin and

Spanish, and demanded an explanation as to why Graham Gooch, who had played cricket in South Africa, had been included in the Test team. The boy considered it to be a grave error.

He also believed, as did almost everyone I spoke to, that, while a Caribbean Federation was a good idea, Tobago should be separated from Trinidad, no matter what the economic cost.

3

Grenada

THE AFTERMATH OF THE INVASION

At Grenada, one lands at the new 'international' airport, built with Cuban and Russian money. The runway stretches across some marshy land and is long enough for almost any aeroplane to land on. What purpose so large an airport can have had is questionable. Grenada has not got enough hotel beds in the whole island to accommodate all the passengers of a jumbo jet. Suspicious-minded people, therefore, formed the opinion that it was to be the base for a Cuban invasion of Trinidad.

After the American invasion or, as the euphemists have it, 'intervention', the work on the airport stopped. So the arrival section is an ill-equipped hut, while the departure part is grandiose and ugly, although I liked the notice over the snack bar saying 'Pay first system', as if this were a new, stylish concept in catering. I have heard since that the arrival building is now complete and working well.

I later found that the land near the airport was a pleasant place to go to see the sunset and to watch the elegant, pure white cattle egrets coming in to roost for the night. Cattle egrets are comparative newcomers to the Caribbean, having appeared in Trinidad for the first time, as far as I could establish, in the late forties. They gradually

21

worked their way up through the islands and eventually reached the United States. These egrets originally came from Africa and must have been blown across the Atlantic in a storm. On the smaller islands, they all nest in one place and, from five o'clock onwards, fly home in groups, like commuters heading for the station from all over a city. In the early morning, they set off again, some of them punctual risers and others sluggards. How do they decide which ones shall attend the nearby cows or horses and which shall have to fly twenty miles or more to the other end of the island? And does each bird return to the same cow each day?

We rented a holiday apartment, an ugly place with the barest essentials, but run by a large, friendly woman called Carmen. One of the problems for travellers in the Caribbean is that there are so few hotels of a middling kind. There are luxury hotels, which cost hundreds of dollars a night, or there are dumps with bedbugs and no water. On the smaller islands, one can find very simple two-bedroom apartments which cost, say, $75 (US dollars) a week.

In the morning, we went into the main town, St George's. The approach to the town brings one over a hill and the first sight of it is from above. The prettiness of it came as almost a shock, after the drabness of Port of Spain and the scrappiness of Scarborough. Actually, what we were seeing was only one half of the town. This half lies in a bay, one side of which is now a marina and the other side the harbour, known as the Carenage. The harbour is surrounded by old warehouses, built of stone and red brick, several of the old buildings having fishscale tiles on their roofs. The bricks were brought from England as ballast in the sailing ships. Behind the warehouses, pretty eighteenth-century houses pile up until, on the top of a ridge, there stands the parish church. The other half of the town tumbles down the other side of the ridge. On that side are the shops and the market square, while on this side are the commercial offices, and also the better restaurants.

The pitch of the roofs is steeper than one would have expected from their date. They look no later than Queen Anne, but none of the buildings is older than 1790. The original town, built by the French, lay round what is now the marina, but was then a freshwater lake. They moved the town to the harbour side in about 1750. Three disastrous fires in the late 1780s, after the British had finally acquired the island by the Treaty of Versailles in 1783, led to a decree, promulgated in 1790, that all buildings must be made of brick or stone and must have a tiled roof. The variety of the building work makes the pretty houses even prettier, some half stone and half brick, some with brickwork of Flemish bond, some more ordinarily English. About a hundred years ago the British dug a tunnel under the ridge to make it easier for horsedrawn vehicles to get from one side of the town to the other. It is now part of the complicated one-way system that does remarkably little to relieve the eternal congestion.

We wandered round the town, rather uncertain as to the attitudes we might expect to meet. The people in the streets looked quite different from the people of Trinidad and Tobago. I noticed that several of the shops were owned by those known throughout the Caribbean as Syrians, no matter if they are Lebanese, Egyptian or of any other middle-eastern nation. But, predominantly, the people are black. It was hard to pin down, but I was conscious of a kind of awareness, even wariness, in people's reactions. Considering that there was a cruise ship in the harbour, there were curiously few tourists around. Perhaps they still hesitate to go ashore in Grenada, fearful of meeting a communist.

For lunch we went to the long beach known as Grand Anse. We avoided the Grand Hotel, with its imported fast food, and tried instead a rough bar and restaurant, used, on the whole, only by locals. It was built with uncut stones, some of them painted white to jolly up the forbidding grey appearance of the place. A young man tried to sell me a hat, which he had woven deftly from palm leaves. He had once asked an older man to teach him how to do this, but the man had refused. So he had just sat and watched from a distance, as the man wove hats for the tourists off the cruise ships. Thus he learned. And he started to weave for the cruise passengers. As he was young and good-looking, he won all the custom away from the old man; which was, of course, why the old man wouldn't teach him in the first place.

I said I did not want a hat. 'But I'm hungry,' he said. So I asked him to eat with us. He was called Michael and was, I should guess, about eighteen. He talked about politics – as everyone else did on Grenada. He had not liked the Maurice Bishop regime, because he enjoyed life on the beach and fun. In Bishop's time, everyone had to dress drably and soberly, and no tourists came because they were frightened. Beach life was no good then.

Michael was too young to have been given a gun. So many of his older friends had had guns. They could walk around town with a big automatic gun and impress people. Now they can only talk.

23

'Those two,' said Michael in a loud voice. 'They would like those days to come back.' He pointed at two men at another table, who had dreadlocks gathered up under striped, knitted hats. 'They had guns.' The Rastas were perfectly aware that we were talking about them. They even smiled, slightly wolfish smiles, I thought, and went on with what Michael said were their plots. It spoke well for the liberal attitude of the present government, I felt, that erstwhile gun-toting supporters of the Marxist revolutionaries were free to air their views in public.

He had eaten a good chicken stew, albeit one that had made my mouth feel like a nuclear meltdown. In return for his lunch Michael insisted on giving us a hat and a woven fruit bowl.

In the evening, we called on a couple called Belizaire. Mr Belizaire was a St Lucian by origin, but he worked as a civil engineer for the British, who moved him round the Caribbean. His wife came from an old, distinguished Grenadan family and, when he retired, they settled in St George's. They lived in a large house above the town, built in the fifties. It was next door to Government House. Just in front of their gate was a roundabout, put there by Sir Eric Gairy, Grenada's first Prime Minister. They rather liked it because, in his day, it was lit and that deterred burglars. When the Americans invaded, they found themselves in the firing line, in the battle for Government House. 'It was a war, conducted in our garden,' said Mrs Belizaire, with a certain measure of pride. She expressed great contempt for people who went away during the hard times or had to leave the island 'because of their nerves'.

But the dangers were very real. The People's Revolutionary Army, they said, had a tank concealed behind their house. It was probably an armoured carrier rather than a tank. 'The Americans spotted it from the air and told their troops in Government House. They were using corner-turning missiles, which roared round our house,' said Mr Belizaire. The boys manning the tank all knew Mr Belizaire and were well aware that he would be on the side of the Americans, but they seemed to bear him no ill-will. They made jokes and asked him for some juice to drink. There was little left in his fridge. 'I asked them if Coke would do and they were quite satisfied.' Eventually, their tank was blasted to pieces.

I loved wandering round St George's. The harbour was a delight, with its rather tatty, beautifully-shaped, old schooners, in among the freighters. Something was always happening and the frigate birds soared overhead. There were few reminders of the austere times under Maurice Bishop and of the 'war'. The shelled and burnt police station, in the market part of the town, and Maurice Bishop's shattered office, on the opposite side of the bay from the harbour and Fort George, are the only physical evidence of the troubles. Brass band music pom-pommed out from the present police quarters, whenever I passed it. At the same time, in every little encounter, there was always talk of what it had been like.

Jim Rudin, an American of mixed African, Amerindian and East Indian descent, runs a small art gallery, named after a spectacular tropical tree – the Yellow Poui. He had a fairly difficult time under the People's Revolutionary Government, but survived because government visitors from communist countries such as Romania, always wanted to take home examples of art. Jim's gallery occupied the first floor of an old house on the ridge between the two halves of the town.

The standard of painting was not very high. Perhaps the best was a 'naif' painter, an old man from the adjacent tiny island of Carriacou. He signs each picture with his full name – Mr Canute Calliste. His appealing style was reminiscent of Lowry, though his subjects were often connected with death. Under each painting he writes the title: The Whale is dead; The Dead are berred in Carriacou; Steduns fleeing from death. This last was not a record of an actual incident but a flight of Mr Canute Calliste's imagination.

While I was in the gallery, a woman from the Commonwealth Institute in London, who was organising an exhibition, was asking some of the artists what their needs were. A number of them spoke of tools – fine brushes for the painters, chisels for the sculptors. But it soon became plain that what they really wanted was contact with other artists and the chance to see their work. Stanley Coutain, a chunky young man in a maroon shirt, was a sculptor. I had noticed an imaginative, half-abstract carving of a bell-tower, which he had done.

'I have seen nothing but photographs. I have never seen a Henry Moore.'

It was, somehow, as moving a cry as if he had said he was hungry. They longed for exhibitions to come to Grenada. They wanted to be taught. Only one had had any training. Dennis Samuel had been to the School of Art in Jamaica, where, it seemed to me, he had learned more about politics than he had about art.

25

One might be tempted to think that they might develop more interestingly on their own, so enthusiastic were they. Going round the gallery, I saw that this was not the case. One painter from Trinidad, whose name I have happily forgotten, was producing stuff with all the meretricious tricks of a Tretchikoff. Others were lured up sad alleys by photography and advertising and strip cartoons and tourist taste.

Originality, however, will always look after itself. Stephen Williams, a young man with gentle eyes and a soft beard, came over to me and said, 'I believe in ghosts and phantoms,' rather as one might say, 'I read more biographies than novels.' It wasn't a matter, really, of belief, but of choosing an available path to follow. He told me that he looked at clouds and saw shapes and animals and people. Then he wove them in palm leaf, somewhat like mats. He said he preferred his works to be seen lying flat, at any rate at first. Later, if people wanted, they could hang them on the wall. But he implied that, when hanging, they assumed a different and, in some way, more limited character. As he left, he gave me a sort of Black Power salute. Then he went, as he put it, 'back to the country,' a matter of ten miles or so.

It was time for us, too, to go to 'the country'. Our first expedition was to Dougladston plantation, an estate belonging to Sir William Branch. We drove up the West coast from St George's. In the valleys which ran inland from the sea, the forest looked almost artificial. Wonderful greenery tumbled from the high cliffs of rock, like unrolled bolts of cloth in a draper's shop.

The country here was far more densely populated than Tobago had been. We passed through a succession of villages. In each of them there were young people hanging about, doing nothing. Often, they would shout at us. Usually their accent was so strong that we could not understand what they said. Sometimes we could. 'Hey, white man,' or even, 'Hey, white bastard.' At first, I found this disconcerting. Then, once, we stopped and said to our abusers, 'Yes?' and waited, smiling, as we hoped, quizzically.

'Well, you know man. You know how it is, man.' And we would all laugh. It was, broadly speaking, just a thing to shout; it was not really informed by hatred or venom. At least, that is what I chose to believe, but Grenada was the only island where this happened.

Of course, once we had stopped and made friends, they wanted a lift.

Where to? 'Worve,' they said. I looked at my map. I could not find Worve. Was it far? 'Not so far,' they said. Which could mean either one mile or fifteen. We drove on till they stopped us. 'It's Worve,' they said. It had not crossed my mind that that was how Gouyave was pronounced. It was here that Patrick Leigh Fermor had seen the announcement of a sweepstake of which the first prize was a free funeral for the ticket holder or for any friend or relation.

At that time, in the days of high prices for cacao and nutmeg, Gouyave was a prosperous place, although it was primarily a fishing village. It benefitted, too, from a lively smuggling trade. The fine clapboard buildings are now very tumbledown and decaying, many of them derelict and deserted. It has a rather eerie atmosphere and a sorry reputation for alcoholism. The fishermen, back from the sea by noon, have little to do but drink all afternoon and evening.

Sir William was in the yard of his plantation. We had arrived quite unannounced, because the telephones were out of order. Nevertheless, he greeted us warmly and appeared delighted at the opportunity to show us around. He led us up into a long wooden shed. As soon as one went through the door, one's nose was aflare, first with a violent vinegary smell, then a brewery one, then spices.

Sir William was a cheerful, red-faced man of some age, perhaps well into his seventies. Showing people round his estate was obviously one of the major pleasures of his life, and one could not help but be drawn into a greater than expected interest in spice-growing. The long shed, Sir William said, was the drying-room and is called the boucan – the word from which was derived the name buccaneers, who lived on dried meat and dried fish.

Sir William explained that there were three paying crops: nutmeg, cacao and banana. I had never seen a nutmeg in its original form. It looks a little like a small apple, but more precisely round, and evenly coloured. This fruit, which ripens about nine months after the tree flowers, falls and bursts open of its own accord. It is easy to harvest, as all you have to do is to pick it up off the ground. This must be done daily because, if left even for only one day, a fungus attacks it.

Inside the fruit is a brown nut, encased in a red, plastic-looking, unevenly shaped net. The brown nut is the nutmeg and the net is mace, the same fruit producing two quite separate spices. The nut can also be crushed and distilled to produce nutmeg oil. During the Second World War, the price of nutmeg reached a level that it has never equalled since, because the oil did not freeze at high altitudes. No other oil had been found, at that time, for aeroplanes, which were beginning to reach greater heights than ever before.

Nutmeg came to Grenada in 1813. Sir William warmed to the tale of its introduction.

'There was an ex-naval planter, Mr Cantine. After the collapse of sugar, he sailed the family windjammer off to the Far East, in search of trade. In Penang he found that they drank rum, lime and sugar, just as we did, but they grated nutmeg on the top. Mr Cantine smuggled back some seedlings and some nuts.'

Sir William told the story with an abundance of detail about the dangers of smuggling spices from the east and the tell-tale brown stain the nutmeg made on Mr Cantine's white uniform.

'When he got back, Mr Cantine gave a party at which, he said, he was going to surprise the island. At least two hundred people came from all over, even those with malaria, because they had heard that the surprise was a new drink.

'Everyone was given a glass of rum, lime and sugar and they all said, "What's this? It's what we always drink. He must be up to his mischief." Then two maids came and grated nutmeg into every glass. They took a sip. "Ah!" Then another sip and they all looked at one another. "Oh, yes." Another sip. Then another glass and a next one and a next one and a next one. And the men made mistakes with other men's wives and the wives made mistakes with the other wives' husbands. And the next day, they had a sore ride home in their buggies. And that's how we have drunk it ever since.'

After the drama of that story, the processing of the cacao nut was less absorbing. Sir William cut open one of the large green fruits. Inside were many small nuts in a sweet, milky substance, which was pleasant and fresh to suck. These contents, as I understood it – which was not always easy on account of Sir William's broad Grenadan tones – were left to ferment. Hence the vinegary smell. Grenada produces a tiny proportion of the world's production, but, he claimed, it is the best, because of the carefully controlled temperature of the fermentation at 45° Centigrade. Therefore it is used in the best confectionery.

Sir William also grows bananas, an obvious enough business, but I was impressed to hear that he got eighteen tons to the acre, when many producers are content with seven or eight. The banana is surprising also in that it bears a useful amount of fruit only six months after planting.

Apart from the paying crops, Sir William grows cinnamon, rich green bay leaves, cloves, all-spice (*Eugenia pimenta*), tonka nuts (used for scenting snuff), ginger, a little coffee and, finally, the calabash. The fruit of these last look wonderful when growing, so perfectly round and shining green, as if they had been polished. They always appear much too big for the tree they grow on. There is nothing useful in the fruit, except the hard shell which, when dried-out, makes a perfect all-purpose vessel. In describing this, Sir William began to croon gently to a calypso rhythm:

> You can drink from it,
> You can eat from it,
> You can wee in it,
> You can two in it,
> You can even wash your feet in it.

After we had seen the workings of the plantation, Sir William asked us to come up to his house and, on the way, told us that the estate had belonged to a Mrs de Freitas, for whom he and his brother had worked. Nearly twenty years ago, she gave the two brothers the opportunity of buying the 263-acre estate at a reasonable price. The People's Revolutionary Government confiscated a third of the land, but he got it back when the new government came to power. 'The PRG said we and our kind were exploiters.'

Certainly, the workers' houses on the estate were very poor and had no electricity, but his own house was far from luxurious. It was a beautiful wooden house, a perfect example of an old colonial plantation house. The rooms were large and high. On one side there was a broad, enclosed verandah, with beautiful floorboards and sloping, Grenadine shutters. The house was sparsely furnished except for the vast dining-room, which was filled with racing trophies. We sat on the verandah on thirties chairs with wooden arms. There was little else there, except for two fine wood-carvings and some plates with English cottages painted on them. There were also masses of large lizards scurrying after mosquitoes.

Lady Branch was a chatty, voluble person, who always started to speak long before anyone else had finished. She gave one an impression of power and laughed immoderately at her husband when he forgot to put the nutmeg into the rum punch he made for us. When that was put right, it was indeed one of the best punches I have ever had, made with Barbadian rum and fortified with a few drops of the extremely strong local spirit.

As we drove away, down past the litter of derelict vehicles which destroyed the prettiness of the valley below the house, I wondered at the legacy of colonialism. The view from the house must once have been spectacular, down the valley, along the river to the ocean beyond. Now, the trees and the forest are all grown up, obscuring everything. In Mrs de Freitas's day, it must have been a wonderland.

It is not that the islanders have rejected all that the plantation owners stood for, as the racing trophies on the Victorian sideboard bear witness. It is the selection which is intriguing. One looks with amazement at the spruce policeman in his white helmet and white gloves, directing the traffic on the top of the ridge in St George's. He is so much smarter than any European policeman. But the abandoned carcasses of cars lie beside every road. Beautiful houses decay while hideous ones are built. Many pomposities are preserved, while many practicalities fall apart.

Far more appalling than what the local population may neglect, to my way of thinking, is what white investors do to the islands. We went through steep little valleys to the east coast and to a small, pretty peninsula. At the entrance to the peninsula, there was a barrier with a hut for someone to man it. It is fair to say that there was no one there and the barrier was open, but the principle – and usually the practice – was to irritate me throughout the Caribbean. How can anyone want to live in a place with guards at the entrance? If it is dangerous to live there, then it is a silly place to choose. If it is not, it is pointless.

In reality, security is not the point of these barriers. If one is white, the man in the hut nods you through without question. It would be a bizarre assumption to make, in a predominantly black country, that all whites are honest. Security has become a euphemism for white privilege. Of course, a black person could buy a house within the confines of these places and, indeed, some blacks do, but in doing so, they are subscribing to a contempt or distaste for their own people.

The houses on the peninsula were mostly hideous bungalows in the Japanese–Scandinavian style. They had over-prinked gardens, with improbable lawns, vulgarly dotted with flowering shrubs. It felt as if Purley had been miraculously transported to the tropics. The whole thing was the creation of a British architect. His own house was a concrete affair of no interest, except for an amazing tree, which was planted only twenty-five years ago. It was a *Ficus benjaminus*, its branches twisting and curling in and out of themselves, rising to forty feet and spreading over a huge area.

The architect was a mildly embittered man. He thought that the British were disliked in the Caribbean, partly because they would never have done what the Americans did in Grenada. 'The British ignore the Caribbean and count for nothing in it,' he said. I wondered at his own commitment to the Caribbean when he told me that he had left the island during Maurice Bishop's rule, though he came back at Bishop's suggestion on being told that, 'it would be wise to do so.' There was a lot of talk about how 'these people' do only four hours' work a day and lay only twelve blocks, when they should lay thirty. Perhaps, I thought, they would work eight hours a day and lay thirty blocks if they were paid as much as the workers who set these happy norms.

It seems extraordinary to me that people should go to a Caribbean island and expect everyone to behave as if they were in the Home Counties of England or the east coast of America. And, as if that were not enough, make every endeavour to change the very landscape, so that it no longer has any connection with a Caribbean island.

The proper country was very beautiful, wild and far more mysterious than the forest in Trinidad. Setting off to cross the island at a more northerly point, we climbed through the dark woods, full of mahogany trees. Beside the road, on the hillside, were banks, sometimes fifty feet high, covered in brilliant green, fern cushions. The centre of the island was covered in thick mist and, in memory, it felt chilly and forbidding. In reality, it was dankly warm. So thick was the mist that we could not see the Grand Etang, a lake in the crater of an extinct volcano. It was a comfort to drop down towards the east coast, taking little roads through groves of nutmeg and cacao. It was a matter of a very few miles, but there was a different spirit about the people. They were gentler and better-looking. We passed the old airport, Pearls, where wrecked Russian and Cuban planes still stood on the potholed runway and goats munched beneath a notice saying, 'Only passengers beyond this point'.

We stopped to look at a huge Seventh Day Adventist church at Mount Rose. It was an odd building, built of small, irregular stones. It must

31

originally have been the parish church. It had pleasant Gothic windows, but its square tower was marvellously ugly, topped with a smaller round tower that, in turn, was capped with a circular cone. Some schoolgirls crowded round us. We asked them if they knew the date of the church. They didn't. 'Why you don't watch the notice?' said one girl, whose name was Shirley. Hamish went to look at the notice.

'Is he your son?' they asked me. It was a question I was asked every day by somebody. So intense is family feeling throughout the Caribbean that many people would not believe me when I said that we were no relation to each other. 'You are lucky to have so good a son, you should not have a joke about it.'

When Hamish came back, with no news from the notice, one of the girls said, 'He would do for you to be marrying, Shirley.'

'Don't be broad,' said Shirley.

They thought we were Americans at first. When we had told them we were English, Hamish asked whether they liked Americans or English best. 'Oh, Americans,' they said. Then they added, out of politeness, 'But the English are often very nice.' It was a change from the west coast cries of 'white bastard'.

A little further on, at Tivoli, we came across another vast church. Again, it had five huge Gothic windows on each side, but this time the tower was much too small for the body of the church. There was a crooked avenue of trees, one of which was burnt and dead, maybe struck by lightning. Oddly, the avenue ran parallel with the church, but led nowhere. The whole scene was reminiscent of an English village, with a large green spreading out before the church.

Tivoli played a distressing part in the recent history of Grenada. It was from here that a number of Maurice Bishop's former supporters tried to escape in a boat, sailing to Black Rock, with the intention of going on to St Vincent. Bishop heard of their flight and sent a coastguard cutter to capture them. They were brought back, tortured and killed.

At the extreme north-east corner of the island, we came to Levera beach, a lonely, unspoilt place. There were a few houses hidden away but, at first sight, it appeared completely deserted. Big Atlantic breakers came pounding in over the sands. The sea beyond was dotted with little islands: Sugar Loaf, Green Island, Sandy Island, Mouche Carree, Ile Ronde, Les Tantes, Ile de Caille, London Bridge, Kickem Jenny and, we hoped, faintly in the distance, Carriacou, the home of Mr Canute Calliste.

Our map showed a road following the shore. There was something that looked like a bridge across a stream not far ahead. 'Let's go for it,' said Hamish, and he drove madly down the beach. After a hundred yards, the car sank deep into the sand and stopped, leaning at a horrible angle towards the sea. There was no question of pushing or rocking the car out. We had seen some people working in the coconut plantations, a couple of miles back down the coast. Hamish left me in the car and set off to enlist their help.

I watched the tide creep closer. Every so often, an extra large roller would send a platter of water right up to the car, and the wheels would sink deeper with an ugly lurch. An hour went by and I began to think I would be engulfed by the sea. Then a young man called Nigel came. I explained that I was waiting for help. 'No problem,' he said, 'they will come.'

At last Hamish returned with a Land Rover, belonging to some local government office, and, after much digging, we moved a few yards. More digging. Nigel, who had joined in the work, suddenly gave a shout. He had found a gold watch. We all looked amazed. Then one of the other men recognised it as his. It had fallen off in the first lot of digging. 'No problem,' said Nigel, handing over the watch with no resentment at this reversal of fortune. Finally, we got out. The men who had brought the Land Rover surprised me by asking, almost apologetically, for exactly the sum I had intended to give them.

The charm of the people at this end of the island was most striking. How can it be that, in an island twenty-one miles long and twelve miles wide, with a population of only 110,000, such marked differences can occur? On some islands, one can trace idiosyncracies back to an historical event, but I could find none for this division of Grenada.

The way back took us through Sauteurs, a pretty town of wooden houses with fish-scale tiled roofs. Its happy-sounding name comes, in fact, from a grim event in 1652. The island, at that time, was French, in the sense that Le Sieur Duparquet had bought it from the French Company of the Isles of America, along with Martinique and St Lucia, for 1,600 *livres*. He had also bought Grenada from the Caribs (whose claim to it was surely more valid than that of the French), even more cheaply, for 'some knives and hatchets and a large quantity of beads, besides two bottles of brandy for the chief himself.' Under Duparquet's orders, his men set about a systematic extermination of the Caribs, which they justified by asserting that the Caribs had gone back on the terms of the sale. The warriors retreated to a nearly inaccessible, hidden place in the north. The French found the only way in and attacked the refuge. Rather than be captured, the defeated survivors of the battle leaped to their death from the high cliffs of what is, in consequence, now known as Sauteurs.

After driving through lost rain forest of extraordinary beauty, we were back to the west coast and cries of 'Hey, white boy'.

We were taken for lunch with Paul Slinger, a man of such spontaneous and generous hospitality that we gravitated to his house on almost every occasion when nothing else was happening. The Tower lay up in the hills some twenty minutes away from St George's. It was a most peculiar house, built of grey stone, looking exactly like those mansions put up a hundred years ago in North Staffordshire for successful pottery owners. The interior was as ponderous as the outside. The floors were of greenheart from Guyana, the ceilings of dark mahogany from Honduras. It was as dotty, in its way, as the houses we had seen on the suburban-style peninsula, but it was much more sensibly designed for the climate, with its high rooms and verandah. Paul himself was tall and dark, with a very round head, a man whom I took to be in his early forties. One might have taken him for a Spaniard. He said he was primarily English, but had Carib and Indian antecedents and also some French blood, being descended from a Chevalier. It is agreeable that people in the Caribbean are nowadays proud of their mixed ancestry, whereas, forty years ago, white people would not have been grateful for any mention of Carib or Indian, let alone African, blood.

The first time we went to the house, it was full of extremely energetic young men who, despite having been at a discotheque until five in the morning, were planning to run in an elaborate paperchase. There was Sean from the Canadian High Commission; Brian, a quantity surveyor; Richard Huber, an American forestry expert; Chris, a dentist from Trinidad; Peter, in charge of a car-assembly plant in Trinidad.

These runners called themselves Hash House Harriers, which I at first took to have some connection with marijuana. It turned out, however, that this was a club, which originated in the early thirties in Malaya. It has spread all over the world, so they said. I imagine they meant those parts of the world which were once British, for where else would you find people prepared to give up their Sunday afternoons to running, in tropical heat, through the thick undergrowth of a rain forest?

We went with them to the start, which was from the ruins of the late Lord Brownlow's estate, La Sagesse. The shell of the house stood a few yards back from the beach of a broad bay on the windward side of the island. It was surrounded by coconut groves and a large banana plantation. Behind lay the forest into which the runners were soon to plunge. While they got ready, I went through the house. It can never have been very attractive, the rooms being poorly proportioned, and I wondered why Lord Brownlow had bothered to have a house here, when he already had one of the most beautiful plantations in Jamaica. In any event, some of the People's Revolutionary Government troops were barracked here and they destroyed it.

There were some forty runners, about two-thirds of them white and quite a few of them women. They strengthened their sinews by drinking several bottles of Carib beer and then trotted off into the forest. It was not in any way a race. There were many false trails set in order to mislead those who arrived first so that, by the time they got back and found the right trail, any stragglers would have caught up. When we met them again some hours later, the young men were lacerated, their legs bleeding from a mass of tiny cuts. One of them sat in a corner of Paul's huge drawing-room, in mock disgrace. It was he who had laid part of the trail through country which, the others maintained, was overgrown entirely by some savagely prickled bush.

Richard was an interesting man – one of an unending stream of advisers and consultants provided by America in the hope of averting any resurgence of Marxism on Grenada. One day, when we were drinking on the beach of Grande Anse, he told me that the beach was receding at the rate of half a yard a year. One of the causes was the cutting of trees inland. The erosion which results fills the river with silt, which lands on the coral reef and, with the help of a fair amount of sewage, kills it. There are also natural influences: geologic subsidence and the rise of the sea level. As the reef crumbles, breakers sweep in and eat away the shoreline. This was to be another recurring theme on my journey.

I liked Richard and his colleague Craig MacFarland. They were serious, conscientious young men wholly dedicated to conserving and, if possible, improving the places they come to advise. But how many of these people should there be? They, like tourists, can destroy what they come to conserve. I saw some horrendous blueprints of plans drawn up

35

by the Organisation of American States to promote tourism. There were endless municipal, floral roundabouts, a number of twee, thatched information posts and an abundance of crazy-paved pedestrian precincts. They cannot see that the reality and the fun are the jam and the crowd.

One evening, at Paul's house, there were two American girls. Mary was the head of the Peace Corps. Marilyn, from Idaho, was a consultant on nutrition. Marilyn was funny about some untrained group of sociologists, who visited Guyana and asked all the wrong questions. In their report, they solemnly put down that all Guyanese mothers breastfeed their children and that the whole population goes to church on Sundays. The truth, according to Marilyn, is that they all give their babies Carnation milk, and that unexpectedly few people have any interest in religion. (Others may question Marilyn's truth. I am told that Guyana has no foreign exchange to buy Carnation milk.)

Mary's views on most subjects were very sympathetic. In particular, she had a great dislike of missionaries. At the same time, I could not help wondering whether she does any more good than a missionary. What, for instance, about leaving people alone? I began to question the girls' effectiveness as advisers further when they told me, as admittedly many others had told me, that: 'The Cuban soldiers all fucked the sheep. The women were terrified.' I thought it was the sheep who should have been terrified. Mary saw her job as, 'getting people to express what their problem is, talking the problem over and then finding solutions.'

It will always remain a mystery to me why anybody supposes that sweet-natured young girls from Idaho or Nebraska or anywhere else you care to name are going to find solutions to the intractable 'problems' of an island people of slave descent, with whom they do not share one grain of common heritage. One of Paul's guests, I noticed, found it almost impossible to get on with a young black man who had lived in the house since he was nine. They had furious rows. It was not a question of obstinacy on either side, but rather of neither of them having the remotest notion of the premises from which the other started. The certitudes of old-style missionaries and those of American youth may differ greatly, but both are too strong to permit real understanding of other ways of thought.

*   *   *

The man whom I decided everyone should consult was Alister Hughes, a mixture of historian and journalist. No one knows more about the history of Grenada and he is full of unlooked-for nuggets of information, such as that the little square door, on the side of what is now the Barclays Bank office, was originally the place where the owners of the house put a bucket of night soil, for collection by the cart which went round St George's every night. Mr Hughes was a most cultivated man, with fine patrician features and a gentle, tolerant voice. He is plainly quite fearless, which resulted in his being imprisoned by Bernard Coard, the extremist leader of the New Jewel Movement after the murder of Maurice Bishop.

I was somewhat afraid that the only articulate assessments of Maurice Bishop that I had heard had all been from those who detested him. I knew that I would get a dispassionate view from Mr Hughes. The question, really, was whether Maurice Bishop had been a gentle revolutionary, who wanted merely to better the lot of his people and remove government from the hands of the eccentric Eric Gairy, whose speeches to the United Nations on the subject of UFOs caused merriment but hardly instilled confidence, or whether he was a hard-line communist, who wanted to foster revolution throughout the Caribbean. 'From the documents which have been released,' said Mr Hughes, 'it's quite clear that Bishop was intentionally deceiving us from the start.'

This, in itself, might not have been justification for the American intervention. For a politician to deceive the public is not so exceptional an event. So I asked Mr Hughes how much support there now is for the followers of Bishop.

'Who's to say? You may be sure that when Bishop was in power there were no supporters of Gairy to be seen. But in the general election which followed the American intervention, Gairy got thirty-six per cent of the vote.'

To believe in flying saucers is evidently no greater an impediment to a politician than a belief in ghosts and phantoms is to an artist. But the majority voted for the more down-to-earth Herbert Blaize, the present Prime Minister.

Mr Hughes also talked of Federation and I told him of A. N. R. Robinson in Tobago, who had wanted that.

'Naturally, they all *say* it is the only course, because it is. But they won't do it. Not while they are in power. In their own muddy hole, they are big frogs. They are not going to give up the chance of making a speech in the United Nations or of a trip to India, by submitting themselves to the will of a big group.'

A Canadian Counsellor, Roderick Johnson, who joined our conversation briefly at this moment said: 'There's only one who would and, indeed, did as a young man, and that is Blaize.'

The Canadian wandered on. Mr Hughes preferred to talk of other things. Language is his favourite topic. I had asked him whether, when the schoolgirls had told us to watch a notice, this was a common usage. He said watch is nearly always used in the sense of look at, as we would say to watch a game. Many modern Grenadan phrases, he maintains, were standard English a hundred years ago. For example, a man will say: 'I hurt my foot above the knee.' The foot can mean the whole leg and the hand the whole arm. Some words differently used are easily understood, as when someone asks, 'Can I have a next drink?' Others are confusing. 'I won't come with you again,' means not that the speaker won't repeat a journey, but that he has changed his mind about an arrangement. That is, 'I won't come with you after all.' Some words are wholly original. Someone may ask for 'a grain match' or 'a grain cigarette', which means a single one of whatever it is. The opposite is grap, which means 'a lot of'. This comes from the French word *grappe*, meaning a bunch or cluster. There are, naturally, many words of French origin. I particularly liked demelly, a verb meaning to sort oneself out or to get out of trouble, from *se demêler*.

From language, we moved to the people of Mount Moritz, a dwindling group of poor whites, who live in a village a mile or two north of St George's. These people came originally from Barbados, where they were known as Red Legs. In slave times, there was a law which insisted that a given number of white people should be employed for every so many slaves on a plantation, in a kind of police role. When slavery was abolished, there was no further need of them. They were landless, many of them being the descendants of the remnants of the Duke of Monmouth's army, routed at Sedgemoor and transported by Judge Jeffreys, and of Irishmen similarly deported by Cromwell. There was no question of the Red Legs finding the kind of rough land which similar groups found on other islands, for Barbados is flat and every inch of it belonged to the plantation owners.

The government had some idea of moving them, but it was the Church, Mr Hughes said, which actually took some of these unfortunate people and found a place for them in Grenada. They were good farmers and hard-working, so, to some extent, they prospered. Alas, they were proud of their whiteness and they refused to mix with the black population of Grenada. They married only among themselves, with the inevitable results.

According to Mr Hughes, their babies are born looking beautiful, but quite soon their skin becomes crinkly. They are also very prone to sun cancer. They suffer, too, from mental instability and look unhealthy and enfeebled. As if this were not enough, they have had grave social problems. Elderly blacks say that they were brought up to despise the poor whites, despite the fact that the old ladies of Mount Moritz are people of great dignity. Mr Hughes remembers that he and his schoolfriends used to sing provocative songs in order to torment them. Even he says that his parents would have been horrified had he had a girlfriend from Mount Moritz. After the war, the prejudice abated. His daughter is married to a man one of whose parents was black and the other a poor white.

On our last day, we went up to Mount Moritz. I felt somewhat guilty going to peer at these people, just because they were different. Against that, it seems to me that the point of travel is to look at people, to learn something of them and from them. The Caribbean islands are enchantingly beautiful and, in many ways, I liked most the islands which are least touched by people, for in them the flowers and the trees grew in undisturbed luxury and the birds were plentiful. But to make a journey through thirty uninhabited islands would seem to me quite pointless. Everything – whether nature, or architecture, or even art – takes second place to people.

The village of Mount Moritz straggles up several different slopes. It looks little different from other villages, perhaps a shade more prosperous. We wandered round for a while. The people varied very much in colour; several of the children were almost pure white. But most were clearly mixed and rather beautiful. I cannot say that I noticed in them the crinkly skin of which Mr Hughes had spoken. Nor did any of them look idiotic.

In the graveyard, we could see how few surnames there had been for the number of families – Harris, Winsborough, Lewis and Greaves were endlessly repeated over the decades. Now, there were more. With luck, in a few more decades, there will be no noticeable difference between the people of Mount Moritz and those of any other village.

As we left, one very pale old woman, to whom we had been talking, said, 'Goodbye, and God bless you, my dears.' Gentility is almost as difficult to erase as colour.

We called on Mr Otway, the manager of Liat, the airline which serves all the islands from Trinidad to Puerto Rico. He was kind enough to help me with a cheaper ticket for all the little flights we were to make. His family is an example of the families one finds on each island, who seem to have a finger in every pie. I noticed, next door to Liat, the Otway Travel Service and, next to that, the Otway Funeral parlour. Is hell a good 'destination', would you suppose? The devil, doubtless, pays a high rate of commission.

4

St Lucia

THE ONLY ELEPHANT

Little aeroplanes are both cosier and more frightening than big ones. Every bump feels as if one has plummetted a mile; the wings look as if they are going to snap off at any moment. But I like being able to see the pilot. On this flight we had two pilots: a girl who started up the engines (there were two of those as well) and a man, who was the captain. They both looked happy and confident. I told myself that they would probably mind dying more than I would. That settled, I could look down at the landscape, which had become familiar from our drives. There was Sir William's plantation and Gouyave, then the cliffs of Sauteurs, and now the little islands at which I had gazed from the sinking car. I looked at the turquoise and aquamarine water below, so pale compared with the Mediterranean. Homer could never have called this the wine-dark sea.

We flew over the whole chain of the Grenadines, past Carriacou, Union Island, Bequia, Mustique and St Vincent, to land at Vigie airport on St Lucia. Had I known then what I learned later, about Vigie being one of the most difficult airports to land in, I might have looked with more apprehension at the long graveyard between the airport and the beach. As it was, our spirits were lifted by the first welcoming

41

immigration official we had encountered. He questioned me about what I wrote, what sort of book I would write about the Caribbean, what I would say about St Lucia. When I met him again a few weeks later, we carried on this happy conversation. He really wanted me to like his country. Apart from this charming man, nothing seemed to be quite right. The person with whom I was to have had lunch had left for Miami. The car that was to have met us was not there. The telephone lines to the town where we were going were not working. But while nothing might be quite right, equally, nothing seemed to matter.

In Castries, the capital, we hired a car and had lunch in a pretty, fast-food restaurant, called, most aptly, Rain. We ate in the tiny courtyard of the wood-framed house and the rain poured down, but we could keep half-dry under a vast green umbrella. The waiter leaped, laughing, across the puddles, bringing an enormous pizza. I have seldom seen a man who smiled so much.

Castries, having an unlucky habit of being burnt to the ground, has nothing worth looking at. With its wider streets, laid out in the French colonial manner on a grid pattern, the town had a modern, bustling feel to it, quite different from the crowded languor of the steep streets of St George's which, in any case, has one-seventh the population. There was nothing to detain us.

We were told that the coast road to Soufrière was blocked by a landslide. We would have to go the long way round, crossing the island to the windward side, going right round the southern end and coming back up the leeward side, that is to say about three times the distance. The road climbed steeply out of Castries and then fell again into a valley. We passed a notice saying 'Trespassers will be violated'. We were soon in open country.

Once again, I fretted as to how I could describe the differences in appearance of St Lucia from Grenada. I noted down: 'The differences can't really be so subtle because they feel so strong, but what are they?' We drove through a huge banana plantation, covering at least 200 acres of a wide valley. We had never seen that before. I decided that St Lucia, while still steep, was on a grander scale, more open, with wider vistas. I decided that this was true of the people as well. They were much more open. Those beside the road smiled and waved, and no one shouted 'white bastard'.

Their language was hard to understand, even when they were addressing us directly. Every so often, they would break off and talk among themselves. Then it was impossible. They spoke the Creole patois spoken in the central islands of the chain, a mixture of French, English and Spanish, but with the words of each language often corrupted beyond recognition. The English word 'one', for instance, has become 'yon' in patois. A horse is not *cheval*, but *chonzal*. There are a few purely Carib or Arawak words left – *ananas* for pineapple; *carbet* for house; cacao, *hamac*, the original of hammock, *manioc* for cassava (itself a Taino or Arawak word), from which tapioca is made. The patois varies from island to island but people from Dominica, Guadeloupe, Martinique and St Lucia can all understand each other.

St Lucia is almost exactly twice the size of Grenada. Unlike Grenada, more than one-third of its slightly larger population lives in the capital. The countryside is, therefore, far less built-up and, on the windward coast, much wilder. Windward coasts throughout the islands are usually less inhabited, although it occurred to me that, if you do not mind nearly continuous winds and rougher seas, there is much to be said for living on those coasts. They are cooler and the winds blow away the insects, instead of blowing thcm towards you.

The southern end of St Lucia is flat and dull. It is here that the Americans had an air base and now there is an international airport, bringing jumbo jets from New York and London.

As we started to go up the west coast, I had to revise my view that St Lucia was more open. The hills became sharper and we climbed into a rain forest, far lusher than anything we had seen in Grenada. We took a turning signposted to Soufrière, leaving the reasonable highway we had been on. The road soon narrowed and its surface became like broken fingernails. After a while we came to a village. Was this the right road?

'Yes,' they said, 'but no one uses it since they built the new road.'

It was hardly worth turning back. The road took us through the dripping forest. The land rose and fell. At one point, it was evident that we were travelling along the lip of a long-dead volcano, much of which had crumbled away. Below us, in the crater, the rich vegetation made it look like a giant's salad bowl. Perhaps not so long-dead, because our noses were soon assaulted by the rotten-egg smell of sulphur. Shortly, we came back onto the main road, no distance from what the St Lucians like to call the only drive-in volcano in the world. It is really nothing of the sort, but a series of sulphur springs from which emerge bubbling grey mud and spurts of malodorous steam. From near there, too, we caught our first glimpses of the Pitons, those two strange peaks, which have become almost a national symbol of the island and which should rank as one of the wonders of the world.

The road wound in abrupt curves down to the town of Soufrière, where we were to stay in a house rented by Lord Glenconner, better known, as the 'deads' would say, as Colin Tennant. Soufrière, squeezed into a scallop of flat land under the mountains, is a large fishing village with a population of about seven thousand people. It is the oldest settlement in St Lucia and, in 1746, the French laid out the town on the usual grid pattern. For a long time it was the largest town on the island, but never became the capital, because Castries has a superb natural harbour, which was, and still is, exceptionally safe in the hurricane season. In 1775, Soufrière had a population of 2,000 and was surrounded by about a hundred prosperous sugar and coffee estates. Louis XVI gave a large sum of money for the building of mineral-spring baths, about a mile to the east of the town, so that his troops might bathe in the waters, which were said to have the same properties as the waters at Aix-les-Bains. A devastating hurricane in 1780 razed the town to the ground. What was left of the Diamond Baths was completely destroyed in the Brigands' War, after the French Revolution. Soufrière never really recovered.

Today, Soufrière is rather shabby, but somehow most appealing. The large Catholic church dominates the regular streets of wooden houses, mostly unpainted. Soufrière House, which Colin rented from the De Boulay family (who used to own the whole town), stood on the hillside well above it. It was a fairly new bungalow made of stone and wood. It was ugly, but with large, airy rooms. In the sitting-room, there were pictures of French châteaux – a reminder that, although St Lucia, having changed hands fourteen times, finally became British in 1796 (when Queen Victoria's father, the Duke of Kent, raised the flag over the fort at Morne Fortune), the French influence has remained very strong.

The maid in the house was called Leoni, and was both an indefatigable worker and an ardent Christian. I never managed to work out how many times a day she went to church. Whenever there was a lull in the proceedings, Leoni would appear in sombre clothes and a hat and say, 'I just go to church, I leave some juice for you.' She made delicious grapefruit juice, but she would never put it in the fridge. Indeed, she would never open the fridge door, but always got someone else to do it. Sometimes she would call Hamish for this purpose. Then she would crouch in the furthest part of the kitchen and call instructions to him, as to where things should be put or could be found. When I asked her about this, she explained that there was a great risk from the cold.

'It might not matter if I didn't do the ironing. You can't do both. Not that hot and then that cold. It can kill you.'

It is a view held throughout the Caribbean.

Colin's manager and agent, Lyton Lamontagne, was an exceptionally intelligent and charming man. His family came from Soufrière, where his father is in charge both of the Post Office and of something to do with tax-collecting, a man of considerable prosperity. Lyton and his wife Eroline entertained us for a couple of days before Colin arrived. They made a striking couple. He was tall and powerful, with a deep voice and a habit of emphasising the last syllable of a sentence, which lent a masterful quality to his manner. His wife was elegantly thin, with an Ethiopian-looking face. She wore her hair in tight plaits. Her clothes were chic and adventurous, usually of one colour – all white, all red or all black. She appeared quiet, but her character must have been as forceful as his. Lyton, it was said, had been engaged to three, if not four, girls simultaneously, with perhaps no very lively intention of marrying any of them. It was Eroline who had actually captured him, albeit at a second attempt.

We dined at a restaurant with them and with Leonard Rivière, the Attorney-General and representative for Soufrière, and his lady. He was a very small man, well-remembered, I should imagine, at the Inner Temple for his mental agility. As I had now learned to expect, he was all for a Federation in the Caribbean. What he felt was needed to produce it was an external threat, otherwise each island would naturally be more inclined to look after its own interests.

What the threat could be was a harder question. 'Grenada made us all think and there was unity among a number of the islands in asking the United States to intervene.' But, for the most part, politics was a matter of local problems, and about these Mr Rivière took a pragmatic view. St Lucia wanted to avoid being swallowed up by anyone, but while the United States and Russia were prepared to woo them, why should they worry too much – $10 million goes a long way in a country of this size. Especially in St Lucia where, he maintained, there is no corruption. 'When we did have a corrupt Prime Minister, people of all parties, including his own, told him to go.' And he went.

We agreed that Grenada still had a highly-charged political feeling about it, with anti-white undertones. 'A few years ago, you would have found that here, but not now.'

Wandering around Soufrière, I found that this was so. In so small and compact a town, a stranger soon becomes a familiar figure. The children stopped staring, the local Rasta greeted one as an old friend after three days. On Saturdays, there is a big market, held down by the waterfront. There are no stalls. The women sit on the ground, having spread their produce in a row. The choice was not great: yams, plantains, christophines (a tropical marrow, with a single seed), oranges, soursops, cocoa sticks and not much else. At other times of year there would be mangoes and avocados. It was a poor collection, when one thinks what could be grown in this beneficent climate. At the far end of the market there is a large shed, given over to meat. There is no question of hanging meat in a tropical place, which has no refrigeration. The meat comes from cows slaughtered the previous evening or early that morning. There is always a dreadful smell attached to newly-killed meat. Of course, there is a worse smell to meat which is going off. The gap in time between the two events in tropical climates is short. We did not linger.

At the other end of the bay from the meat shed is a track leading, at a distance of about quarter of a mile, to a cluster of houses at the shore's edge, that form almost a separate hamlet. It is the fishermen's village, known as Coin l'Anse. I was drawn to it because I had seen an early nineteenth-century print of Soufrière, which made this particular part of the town look exactly as it looks today.

The houses turned out to be very poor and run-down. They cannot have kept the rain out. The people's clothing looked ragged. There was, nonetheless, comedy to be found. The public lavatory was a strong-looking, though quite small building on stilts, about thirty feet out to sea, with a gangway leading to it. Not long ago, it blew down in a hurricane. Officials thought to replace it with something more modern and hygienic. There was a furious outcry from the regulars. They wanted what they had always had, and what I like to think I could discern in the old print – a sociable eight-seater, perched over the sea.

I liked the bars and rum shops. Over the door of any bar there was always a notice saying: 'Licensed to sell intoxicating liquor'. There was no pretence about the reason for drinking. It reminded me of a Kingsley Amis hero called Bowen, who used to daydream about owning a brewery. The advertisements for his beer would have none of that nonsense about its being good for you or being made in a traditional manner. They would simply announce: Bowen's Beer Makes You Drunk.

Lyton brought some young men from the town to lunch. Michael worked in a bank and Francis in a small plastics manufactory. It was interesting how much they knew of Britain and British politics, despite Mr Rivière's view that Britain counted for little or nothing in the Caribbean. Michael had been to London, but found it too rough for his taste. He said that he preferred the peace of St Lucia to the higher wages of London. Both young men admired Mrs Thatcher's assault on the trade unions. Michael, surprisingly, even thought her attitude to South Africa was understandable and, at a pinch, forgiveable. 'Britain has such a big investment that she cannot pull out or support a hard line. There is too much to lose.' Their stance on South Africa with regard to cricket was very different. The English team was due to arrive in Trinidad. The inclusion of Graham Gooch in the team offended them. 'Those guys should be banned for life.'

Christmas was coming closer. Lyton and Eroline gave a party. West Indian parties have their hazards, because when one arrives nothing much is ready. The preparations for the party are themselves a part of it. As the Caribbean is nothing if not sexist, this means that the men have little to do but drink while the food is got ready, which may mean several hours.

Among the guests were quite a few people who had come home from England for Christmas. There was a cousin of the young man, Michael. He lived in Lewisham and worked in the City with a firm of Lloyds brokers. And there was Patricia, a person of exuberant build, who turned out to live near Michael's cousin. She was a cook and had recently started her own catering business. She specialises in weddings. It was strange to hear their London voices, and stranger still, when I asked them about life in England, that they answered without any reference to colour. When I pressed them about it, they made light of it, as if they found it irrelevant to their experience. 'St Lucians,' they said, 'never have any trouble and we are all working. It is the Jamaicans who get into all the trouble.'

One of Lyton's cousins, Boswell, told me a long story about Lyton's uncle, who had some row with the local priest. The story involved a young girl, but I rather lost the thread. The power of the Lamontagnes being what it was (another uncle is an archbishop), the priest was moved to another district. On the way home, somebody else said, 'The truth of that story was that Lyton's uncle put a spell on the girl.'

*   *   *

When our host, Lord Glenconner, arrived, everything was at once a festival. Colin Glenconner is in his late fifties, a tall, balding man of studied elegance, who manages to look well-dressed in the shabbiest clothes and the superb model of an Englishman in smart ones. He affects the air of an eighteenth-century plantation owner, with a broad-brimmed hat and a cane. His bright, innocent blue eyes reveal a perpetually bubbling sense of humour, but conceal a shrewd intelligence and a serious purpose, coloured by a tinge of mockery.

Colin had invited a young couple, Chantal d'Orthez and Glen Burke, to come over from Mustique for the day. They were to be married the following week in Colin's house there, which he had lent them. Colin wanted to show us all his plantation, Jalousie, between the Pitons, which he plans to turn into an hotel.

The best way to get there is by boat. Indeed, until Colin scratched out a track which a four-wheel-drive vehicle could manage, it was the only way. I was rather glad to go with him in a Range Rover, because he shed new light on the places we passed. The road went past the eight-seater lavatory and along the coast for a mile or so, towards the Pitons. The road curved to the left and started to climb the high shoulder of land that one must surmount before reaching Jalousie.

On the left was a modest shack where there lived a Miss Webb. She was, according to Colin, a woman of about sixty, the daughter of the owner of the shack and few acres round about. The owner has lived in Guyana and entrusts the running of his 'estate' and the care of his daughter to an overseer, Mr B. This gentleman performs his duties with fine conscientiousness. He allows Miss Webb one dollar a week, an East Caribbean dollar that is (worth about 25p). Mr B. forbids her to smoke. Fortunately, passers-by take pity on Miss Webb and give her an occasional cigarette. But if the overseer catches her, he gives her the lash.

A little further on, much higher up, one can see some houses. This is a small property where two Indian brothers live. One of the brothers, Ramesh, has not left his yard for twenty years. They are both married and have grown-up children. Both have transferred their affections to their daughters. The daughters, far from resenting this arrangement, have welcomed it. They have demeaned their mothers and each has had a child by her father, one of them paralysed. Lyton said, with satisfaction, that nothing like this could ever happen in a black family.

We drove round behind the first Piton and came down into Jalousie.

The plantation lay in two scallops of land, with a Piton rising abruptly at the extreme north and south ends. These Pitons are spires of lava, left after the volcanoes, of which they were the cores, eroded away. They are astonishing in that they shoot up, straight out of the sea on one side, to 2,500 feet and 2,600 feet. Below the surface, they plunge a further 600 feet to the sea bed.

The Pitons do not look as high as I felt they should. It may be an illusion created by their small circumference. If there were a path, one could walk round the base of the Petit Piton in less than half an hour. They have scrub on part of them, but are largely plain rock covered in many coloured mosses and creepers.

The plantation, which they and the green-covered cliffs behind contained, was exquisitely beautiful and peaceful. Cattle, horses and mules, belonging to the workers, have grazed the grass between the tall, tall coconut palms, until it seems almost like a lawn. We sat on the ground at a level place, perhaps 300 yards back from the sea, which here, because of the great depth, looked dark enough for Homer. Colin had put up a Rajasthani tent for our picnic. Below, the workers shouted and played. Pigs grunted. I thought I had never seen a more idyllic place, and quite managed to forget Patrick Leigh Fermor's account of the attempted scaling of the Petit Piton by a party of British sailors in the last century, all of them falling dead at various points on the way to the summit, from the bite of the *Trigonocephalus lanceolatus* or *fer de lance*. On another occasion, I saw some people waving from the top. This terrible snake has here been eradicated by the mongoose, which was introduced for this purpose on many of the islands. A few snakes still survive in valleys further north.

The rest of the party came by sea and we all lay on cushions and ate lobster and drank Chablis. In response to some idle enquiry of mine, Lyton shouted to someone, 'Get on a horse quickly and go to fetch some guavas.' It was not a sentence I ever expect to hear again. Then Colin, to whom everything is an occasion, made little formal speeches about the guests – Chantal and Glen, Lyton's parents, Lyton and Eroline (who was all in scarlet), and myself.

It was time to feel drowsy. Then an elephant came wandering up through the coconut palms and we all woke up. This was the only elephant in the Caribbean. She was nine years old, and was called Bupa. Originally an orphan found in Uganda, she was brought to Dublin where, after a while, the zoo declared her redundant. Colin bought her and shipped her on a Geest banana boat to St Lucia.

Bupa wanders about, seemingly content and well provided for in the matter of food, the tropical hillsides affording more free fodder than Dublin Zoo ever dreamed of. She overcomes loneliness by befriending the pigs. To one she was most particularly attached. Unfortunately, one day, Bupa sat on her friend. Although she is only five feet tall, that was that. It was a little heartless of Colin, I thought, to roast and eat Bupa's friend.

Bupa's arrival caused a big stir. In the first week, ten thousand people came to see her. She is looked after by a young man called Kent, who worked as a docker. The dockers' union has made an unusual arrangement with the port authorities. Each docker works roughly one day a month, but is paid about $130 for that one day. As soon as Kent saw the elephant on the Geest boat, he ran to fetch his father to finish his working day for him. He then jumped on the bus, which was taking Bupa from Castries to Soufrière, and when he got there, told Colin that he must employ him to look after the elephant. Kent's father used to work Kent's day as well as his own, because, Kent told me, it is most important to keep your day. Quite apart from the pay, the company will pay your funeral expenses which, at the very least, amount to $335. I heard later that Kent's father had died and his funeral was duly paid for.

When Bupa wandered off, two young Indians appeared – the sons of Ramesh on the hill. Their names were Anias (short for Ananias) and Eastman. They explained that they were Rastas and we quizzed them about what this meant to them.

'We live a natural life and we are vegetarians, but we eat fish.'

Lyton had little patience with them.

'If the problem is killing things, what about the fish?' he asked.

'That is different,' they said, adding that they worked their father's land.

'One day a year,' Lyton said.

Anias had large, liquid eyes and an epicene beauty. Eastman had a fine face and long locks – so long, he said, that he now has to wash them with a proper shampoo, not just coconut oil. They were very insistent upon their African origins, wholly ignoring the Indian side of their background.

'One is closer to the mother,' they said, 'for she carries you nine months in the womb.'

'The father is the seed,' said Lyton, 'even more original, I would say.'

What was interesting about this conversation, besides the young men's way of looking at things, was the bantering good nature with which it was conducted. Anias had at one time worked for Colin. He had stolen many things, had broken into the house when Colin was away and run up a $1,600 telephone bill, chattering to friends in the States and England. And when sacked, he had gone off with other things Colin valued, including a girl who lived in the house.

Despite all this, there was no rancour, only a measure of teasing and, on Lyton's part, a modicum of contempt. Colin himself has achieved a rare rapport with the people of the islands, living in many ways more freely with them than with his fellow Europeans and being well loved by them.

It is a phenomenon of the Caribbean that grudges are rarely borne. Forgiveness flows easily. I began then to wonder whether vendettas and feuds are not European, Arab and Far Eastern affairs. Tribal animosities may split Africa apart, but, below the Sahara, vengeance is foreign to that continent. Or perhaps it is a matter of religion. Christians, Jews, Moslems and Hindus are all vengeful, Shintoists too I daresay, though not Buddhists. But then the West Indians are Christians. Ah yes, but of what a funny kind. Their religion blithely excludes many aspects which we hold paramount. There is no disapproval of pre-marital sex. Indeed, it is almost a requisite, proving that a girl is not barren. Given that one commandment can be ignored, why not eschew vengeance?

The afternoon wore on, and the beauty of the place increased as the sun shone lower, sending shafts of misty light through the palms and making elaborate shadow patterns on the cropped grass.

So pleasant was it that I felt regret for Colin's plans for Jalousie. He intends to build 200 cottages in one of the two halves of the 500-acre plantation. There was quite an outcry when he first proposed his scheme. The Pitons, said the conservationists, are a national treasure. They should be left in their natural state.

Colin maintains that nothing can destroy the Pitons. They are impressive, I realised that afternoon, not for their height, which one does not perceive, or at any rate believe, but for their sugar-loaf shape, for their abrupt, sheer rock faces and for the fact that there are two of them so close together. A single Piton would be mildly splendid, but it would not be a wonder, stirring to the imagination. The land between them can hardly be described as natural, if it has for centuries been used for agriculture. If it has been changed for that, Colin argues, why should it not be changed again for tourism, particularly if whatever is done is done with taste.

51

Unemployment on St Lucia is, on average, about forty per cent. In Soufrière the figure is probably higher. Colin's scheme would provide at least 300 jobs for the people of Soufrière. Colin believes that Caribbean governments take little real interest in tourism, because they seldom have any direct investment in it.

'Do you know that I have never met the Tourist Minister of St Lucia? He is always too busy. They concern themselves more with the traditional cash crops: bananas, copra, cacao. This attitude means that tourism does not bring anything like what it should to the islands. For example, there is nearly as much spent on importing food for the tourists as the tourists spend while they're here.

'The Government gets a little bit from airport tax and bed tax, that sort of thing. Those huge hotels are useless. A few bell-boys get tips as studs, but money does not really circulate.

'They need quite different things – more up-market places, using local produce which the local farmers could be encouraged to grow.

'The World Bank, of course, does not help. Being bankers, they like to lend money only to projects which will show returns. Such as a hydroelectric scheme producing masses of electricity which people won't be able to afford, but not for tourist infrastructures.

'They worry about repayment, something which did not matter in the old days, when governments lent to other governments. If they didn't pay, the creditor just took over the country.'

One of the madder tourist projects of the islands was the plan to link Pigeon Island with the St Lucia mainland, by a causeway on which would be built a large number of huge hotels. The causeway was built. Pigeon Island was in danger of being ruined. Fortunately – for history and beauty – no hotels came.

It is one of the problems of the islands. Speculators plan some wildly expensive development. The government spends huge amounts on 'infrastructure'. Then there is a strike, or a riot, or someone gets eaten by a shark or gets murdered by a lunatic. The investors vanish, the tourists stay away. The government's money (which would, in any case, have been better spent on schools or health), is wasted. It is perhaps not surprising that the World Bank does not care for tourist infrastructures.

The absence of investors made it possible for St Lucia's National Trust to take over and preserve Pigeon Island. It is a peaceful place now, with a number of ruins scattered among the palms and grassy banks. But it was not always so. The ruins are of the naval barracks and fort which were the headquarters, in the Windward Islands, of Admiral Rodney before the battle of the Saints. The gentle name of this tiny island came, it is believed, from Rodney's carrier pigeons.

The battle of the Saints in 1782 ranks in importance in British naval history with the defeat of the Armada and the victory of Trafalgar. The British, as a result of the War of American Independence, had lost control of the Caribbean sea. They were also having trouble with the Dutch, whom they accused of giving refuge to what they saw as American pirate ships. The French and Spanish, in alliance, were planning to attack Jamaica. The French fleet, under the Comte de Grasse and Admiral Bougainville (after whom the flower is named), had besieged St Kitts and, despite a brilliant series of manoeuvres by Hood, in which he lost only seventy-three men to de Grasse's thousand, Brimstone Hill – the supposedly impregnable fortress of St Kitts – fell to the French troops under the Marquis de Bouillé.

Rodney, sent out from England with Lord Sandwich's admonition sounding in his ears, 'The fate of this Empire is in your hands . . .' arrived too late. De Grasse, triumphant, had retired to Fort Royal in Martinique to repair his ships. His own flagship, the *Ville de Paris*, had been pierced by more than eighty balls from Hood's broadsides.

When he did arrive at St Lucia, in February 1782, Rodney anchored his ships in Gros Islet Bay, behind Pigeon Island. From the island he could see Martinique. He waited until de Grasse should venture out; de Grasse waited for the rains and the storming winds to be over.

In the extraordinary way in which they conducted wars at that time, de Grasse decided to give a ball. It was a glittering affair and, naturally, he invited Rodney and his officers to go to Martinique for the occasion. Rodney had gout at the time and so he did not go, but many of his officers did and they took presents of cheese and ale from their admiral to de Grasse. The French admiral sent back *bonbons* and liqueurs to Rodney.

The British, however, maintained their vigilance. On 8 April, they saw de Grasse sailing from Fort Royal, planning to join the Spanish in Cuba for the attack on Jamaica.

Rodney set off in pursuit. So swift were his lightly-laden leading ships that, the next day, eight of them caught up with the French ships off Dominica, weighed down with troops and supplies. The eight British ships were seriously outnumbered but, after a brief engagement, de Grasse pressed on, anxious to get his fleet through the channel between Dominica and Guadeloupe.

He nearly achieved his objective, but when two of his ships collided and the British bore down on the damaged ships, de Grasse decided to fight. He turned his ships and came to face Rodney. The advantage lay with the French. They had thirty-three ships, two fewer than the British, but they were far bigger and more powerful vessels.

Early in the morning of 12 April the two lines of ships began to sail, in solemn style and in single file, one north, the other south, passing each other, all guns blazing when each vessel drew abreast. Suddenly, when the first British ship had just passed the last French one, the wind changed. The French line wavered. A gap appeared. Rodney, in the *Formidable*, was opposite the gap. His captain of the fleet, Sir Charles Douglas, suggested they sail through the unexpected space.

Naval training had never heard of such a thing. In battle, you went straight. You never changed the order of your ships. Rodney sailed through. He broke the line.

The French were so confused by this that, by the afternoon, their fleet was divided into three groups. Poor de Grasse was cut off from all but five of his ships. Bougainville was belting off in the wrong direction, later to be accused of indiscipline. There was nothing to do but surrender.

The British had regained command of the Caribbean sea. They had, incidentally, developed a new naval manoeuvre, known as 'breaking the line'. Above all, they had established what was to be confirmed at Trafalgar, that Britain was to be top-dog during the nineteenth century.

While in a historical mood, we called on Robert Devaux, the head of the National Trust, in the office of the national archives. These lay beside the airport and not long ago a plane had crashed on them. Mr Devaux's family came to St Lucia from France in the 1740s. He said that his grandfather would have thought of himself as French. He, rather tentatively, supposes he is English. I wondered why he didn't call himself St Lucian. There seems to be a greater reluctance among those whose families were originally French to identify with the island nationalities. On the more British islands, the white people are more easily inclined to think of themselves as West Indian.

Nonetheless, Mr Devaux battles fiercely to preserve the history of St

Lucia, whether Arawak, Carib, French or British. He struggles to prove that the Empress Josephine was born on St Lucia, rather than on Martinique. Her father, Tascher de la Pagerie, was in the French army and was appointed an intendant – or steward – on St Lucia, in charge of the section which includes Soufrière. He had a property near Soufrière, where it is known that Josephine spent childhood holidays. It is now known as Malmaison, but whether this is coincidence or *arrière pensée*, it is impossible to say.

Mr Devaux argued that there is no record of Josephine's birth in Martinique, where records were kept and had been kept for fifty years. Her baptism is recorded in Martinique. Mr Devaux believes she was born on St Lucia, not at Malmaison but somewhere in the north. No records were kept on St Lucia at that time, so it was likely that her father would have taken her back to Martinique to be christened, in order to establish that she was French. We will meet Josephine again and hear more of this when we go to Martinique.

The indefatigable Mr Devaux also believes that he has identified an early site, dating back to 2,500 BC, which is the West Indian equivalent of Stonehenge. We did not have time to go to see it on this visit, but we would be back.

5
Mustique & St Vincent
MILLIONAIRES AND A LOST PLANTATION

'Mustique is an irrelevance,' someone had said.

Nevertheless, we went; flying in a nine-seat Islander, even more cosy and even more alarming than the Twin Otter. Two girls on the same flight, total strangers to one another, held hands during the take-off.

Again, through Colin Glenconner's kindness, we were lent a pretty house, with the engaging name of Serendipity. By Mustique standards, it was fairly simple and small, with two bedrooms and two bathrooms, but the views from it were beautiful. Houses on this island rent for $5,000 a week. For one of them, the charge is $10,000.

The maid in our house was called Venice. Her use of English was intriguing. On the telephone, I would hear her say, 'She out; I tell she.' If somebody rang while we were out, she would say, 'The telephone call you.' And, when we asked Chantal and Glen for lunch, she telephoned a friend. 'We have two more people for lunch, they who get marrying, how I boil the christophine?' Her most disconcerting habit happened if she did not hear what one said. Instead of 'what?' or 'pardon?', she would say 'hullo', with a curiously drawly emphasis on the 'o'. 'Can we have scrambled eggs for breakfast, please.' 'Hullo-o-o?'

The picturesque quality of West Indian speech is hard to recapture if one has not written it down. Colin's groom, whose sister lay dying in St Vincent, said one morning, 'She lingering. She ought to go. She suit an injection.'

Mustique was originally a plantation, belonging always just to one family. Colin bought the island many years ago. It is very small – barely three miles long and half a mile wide. At the same time, it is a physical microcosm of the other islands. On the windward side, big rollers sweep onto wild beaches, where it is dangerous to swim. On the leeward side, all is calm, indeed in some places almost swampy. After half-past three it is impossible to stay on these quiet beaches, for the sandflies devour you.

Colin divided his island into plots, one of which he gave to Princess Margaret as a wedding present. Oliver Messel came to build charming, gingerbread houses for the rich. The style of the place is essentially British, which is to say understated, as opposed to the large American developments, which we shall see later. Very few of the roads are surfaced, which preserves the illusion of wildness and makes the island seem bigger.

There is only one shop, one bar and restaurant, one hotel. There is really nothing to do. There are a couple of tennis courts, a few horses to ride, some houses with a squash court, and there is, of course, the sea.

At the beginning, it must have had the charm of a club in which all the members were friends. Now that Colin has sold the controlling share in the island, its character has changed. At one of the highest points of the island, visible from almost anywhere, Mr Harding Lawrence, the former managing director of Braniff Air, is building a monstrous palace which – rumour has it – will be turned into a casino. Fortunately for us, the season had not started and the people on the island were fewer and more agreeable than might have been the case.

On the first day, Chantal and Glen got married. Colin's house, where they were staying, is something of an oriental fantasy. It is built of pure-white coral, brought from Barbados. Round the lip of the shallow, central dome, and round the eaves of the two wings and the pavilion-verandah, run bands of brilliant, jade-green, Chinese roof-tiles. The windows and the arches are Indian in design. Wonderful glass chandeliers hang in the verandah. The bed is of solid silver from Rajasthan, with a peacock design.

57

Separate from the house is an open dining-room and it was in this that Chantal and Glen's wedding ceremony took place. Looking out from there, over the swimming pool, there is a small Indian temple. It is an early, eighteenth-century Moghul pavilion with the most intricate carving. Colin had it brought from near Agra, the marble having come from the same quarry as the marble for the Taj Mahal. Two Indians travelled with it so that they, who had taken it to pieces, would know how to reassemble it. It took them three months, because they had forgotten to number the pieces.

It was a happy party, with a band from Bequia, who were spurred to wilder and wilder rhythms by the presence of Mick Jagger and David Bowie.

Later in my journey, I was to find myself becoming more and more weary of the incessant reggae beat, which thundered out of every public place. David Bowie was of the opinion that reggae in Jamaica was becoming too commercialised. It was interesting, too, that he had noticed that, while Bob Marley is still as popular as ever all over the rest of the world, he has lately suffered a decline in the West Indies. This coincides, I believe, with the decline of Rastafarianism and with the Jamaican view that, towards the end of his life, Marley betrayed his principles, selling out for success and popularity.

At this stage, however, as Christmas crept closer, we heard endless carols. In particular, there was a calypso version of the *Twelve Days of Christmas*. 'A partridge in a pear tree', a mystifying enough idea of a gift to me, must, I could not help thinking, have been totally bewildering to, say, Venice.

'What do you think about a partridge in a pear tree, Venice?'

'Hullo-o-o?'

It took me some time to decide whether Mustique was 'relevant' or not. By 'an irrelevance', I presumed my acquaintance had meant that Mustique was not really anything to do with the Caribbean, that it was just a rich man's toy. When I considered Venice's life and that of her friends, I came to the conclusion that it was very much a part of the Caribbean and, in some ways, a pointer to part of the future of the islands.

There were times later when, on some islands, I felt that the locals were really little more than cheap, black labour for white neo-colonialists. On Mustique, I did not feel this. When Colin bought the island, there were fewer than a hundred people living there. Now there are 600 St Vincentians, all with jobs, who live in a decent village, in conditions far superior to most of their compatriots on the main island. In fact, the Mustique company is the largest employer of labour, after the government, in St Vincent.

Jocelyn, the girl who looked after the next door house, used to charge round the island in a little Daihatsu, taking her children to swim on one beach or another. It was reasonable to think that her life was a happy one. The girls did seem to be part of a population explosion. Venice had three children, Jocelyn four, and Lina, who lived in a nearby house, six, all born within four years.

There was a certain sophistication about Jocelyn, who spent a fortune on clothes and who asked if I had a Polaroid camera, as she had a fancy to take some pornographic photographs of herself with a champagne bottle. On the whole, though, the traditional morals of the people obtained. These have never included sexual restraint. On no island is there any shame attached to having children out of wedlock, no matter how extravagant the imprecations of the missionaries. Yet there was a girl, serving in the Mustique store, who refused even to handle a bottle of drink, which made the buying of liquor something of a problem.

In the end, I decided that, as a pattern for tourism, Mustique was extremely relevant – provided that Mr Lawrence's grotesque mansion does not become a casino.

There was a pleasant English couple called Fenn, who had rented a house on the island. Colin Fenn was in the garment business. He had done reasonably well in London and had a warehouse in Hong Kong. Then he had realised that, while English shops might order fifty or 500 cashmere sweaters, Saks, in New York, would order 50,000 at a time. The Fenns now live on Long Island and he is, as his wife Anita put it, 'the only gentile on Seventh Avenue.'

Anita Fenn was a most surprising and open person. She was the daughter of a London publican. She said that they did not quite know whether to buy a house on Mustique or not. 'You see, we have only come to riches recently and it is hard to decide.' Her husband had bought a fifty-foot yacht, which she did not much care for, as she was seasick. They planned to charter it when they were not using it, and had engaged a skipper, a New Zealander called Murray Lord, and a girl to cook, a nurse from Bristol called Megan. As the project was new, they had little prospect of getting charters for that season. I proposed my hiring the yacht for two or three months, for a nominal sum to cover their expenses.

59

We had what Mr Fenn termed a 'power breakfast' to discuss the idea. At once, I learned the truth of J. P. Morgan's remark about the cost of running yachts, 'If you have to ask that question, you cannot afford it.' Mr Fenn's suggested figure was, I came to realise, a very generous offer, about a third of the going rate. It just happened to differ from my extreme limit by £5,000. We munched through our grapefruit and bacon and eggs in some disappointment on both sides. I had a nagging feeling that the real and romantic way to see the islands was by yacht.

Instead, we flew off in the tiny Islander. Leaving Mustique, I looked down on the pathetic wreck of the *Antilles*, the French liner which ran onto the reef between Mustique and a deserted island and broke her back. Nostalgically, I remembered sailing in this beautiful ship thirty years ago, from Jamaica to Europe.

The Captain must have been mad to attempt to pass through this channel. For the people of Mustique it was a red-letter day, reminiscent of *Whisky Galore*. Colin nailed a notice to her mast, claiming her as salvage. Two days after the wreck, there was nothing left on board, every neighbouring islander having taken everything that was moveable. For several years she lay, still almost beautiful, her name easily legible above the waves. Now she is settling, lower and lower, a sad rusting hulk – just opposite where Mick Jagger is building a Japanese-style house.

I sat behind the pilot on the Islander. The needle of the exhaust gas temperature gauge was whipping to and fro, like a demented windscreen wiper. Should I draw the pilot's attention to the crazy thing? Of course, I didn't. What if a dial said the port engine was on fire? Would I tell him then?

Our journey through the islands varied in style according to the number of introductions we had. My only one on St Vincent was from a friend in the Hammersmith public library, who had been born in Kingstown. He told me to stay in apartments belonging to his friend, Ricky Hillocks.

We took one of Rick's apartments at $22 a day, which contrasted agreeably with the $290 one could pay for a double room in the grand hotels. We had two bedrooms, with a kitchen and shower. The living-room was bright lemon yellow. There was a plastic yellow sofa and two armchairs to match, a Formica table and six Hille chairs. The lighting came from two naked bulbs. There was also a splendid figure called

Belle, with one crooked eye and few teeth. She said she would clean the place and make our breakfast. Hamish, whose tastes are for the grand life, was not too pleased with this change of fortunes. I found it restful.

When we had been there for about an hour, a girl knocked at the door. She had large, wide-apart eyes and broad lips, and was beautiful. She wore tight jeans and a red shirt. She was living above us and wondered whether we had a telephone. I explained that we had had one, but that, when we plugged it in, it rang without cease, in a long, unbroken ring. We offered her a drink instead. 'A soft one,' she said.

Her name was Ann-Marie. She lived as a rule with her mother and stepfather. Yesterday, when her elder, married sister had come for a visit, there had been a row. Her stepfather had beaten up her sister and had kicked Ann-Marie out of the house.

'My mother used to be kind and loving, but lately she change.' Ann-Marie had four sisters and one brother. Their father had been an inspector. She did not say of what. He had died.

'My stepfather has always hated us. Now he is unkind to my mother too.'

I asked why he stayed with them in that case.

'She has some things,' said Ann-Marie. 'Maybe if she marries him, he gets them. But I must smile. Even when things are bad, I smile.' And tears filled her eyes, which looked larger than ever.

Ann-Marie proposed that we all go to a play at the Agricultural School where, she said, she was a student. In sounded a little dismal and we had booked a table at a restaurant. She decided, too, that that was a better idea. She went to change and reappeared wearing a turquoise-blue trouser suit, with a silver belt. On the way to dinner, we noticed a brilliant flashing light, coming from near the shore, which illumined the whole landscape. Ann-Marie told us that it was a memorial to a planter, who had left money for a huge cross to be put on a rock. On the top was a light, which was to flash till the end of time. I had noticed the cross earlier, so I believed Ann-Marie's story. Later, I learned that the light had nothing to do with the cross, which was a memorial to a Mr de Freitas, who developed Indian Bay. The light was to guide aircraft.

Ann-Marie was, perhaps, a mythomane. In the morning, Belle came to make our breakfast. Her wandering eye rolled, as she flashed one and a half teeth. 'I never like to talk anyone's business,' she said, and proceeded to discuss Ann-Marie. According to Belle, Ann-Marie's mother had kicked her out, because of her relationship with a lawyer. It was the lawyer who had brought Ann-Marie here, which did not much please Mr Hillocks, to whom the lawyer owed money. I asked if Ann-Marie was at an Agricultural School. Belle's eye and tooth looked sceptical.

'I know nothing about any school.'

But I liked Ann-Marie and she brightened up the place, popping in and out, usually in a new outfit.

Kingstown was very run-down. The clapboard houses, some of them with arcades at ground level and sloping Grenadine shutters above, look as if they might fall down, and few of them have a coat of paint. The three main buildings are the churches, all in a group. First is the Anglican Cathedral of St George, a supremely English building, dating from 1820. It is calm and simple, with Palladian windows and a plain, square tower, with castellations at the top. In the nave is the tomb of Alexander Leith:

> His death was occasioned by the great
> Fatigue he endured during the Carib War
> In which as Colonel of the Militia
> He bore a distinguished part
> The Carib Chief Chattawar
> Falling by his hand.

Then there is the Wesleyan Hall. And finally, the preposterous Roman Catholic Cathedral of St Mary's. This is a riot of towers, belfries, spires, turrets, courtyards, balconies, cloisters, crenellations, castellations and machicolations, in the Romanesque, Moorish, Byzantine, Ghibelline, Guelph and Gothic styles. This architecturally ecumenical fantasy was the creation of a Belgian priest, Dom Carlos Verbeke, and was finished in 1935.

The Botanic Gardens in Kingstown were founded in 1765 and cover about twenty acres. A crowd of boys at the entrance, each claiming to be an official guide, offered to take us round. Only one talked more about the plants than about himself, so we chose him. He was called Cordell and was twenty years old. It turned out that he knew next to nothing about the trees, but he did know where the interesting ones were to be found.

There were always such surprises. I had never supposed that the clove had such a pretty white flower. I had never before seen a sealing-wax palm, with the red streaming down its trunk as if it were bleeding. This was also the first *Euphorbia leucocephalus* I had seen – a beautiful feathery relation of the poinsettia with narrow leaves which are white rather than red. There was the Breadfruit, probably grown from a third-generation sucker from one of the original seedlings brought back from Tahiti by Captain Bligh, on HMS *Providence* in 1793. Most intriguing of all for its rarity was the *Spachea perforata*. This, so Cordell said, was the only one of its kind in the world. It grew, according to legend, only on the slopes of Soufrière, a volcano in the north of St Vincent. The eruption of 1902 wiped out every tree on the mountain. The only surviving specimen was this one in the Botanic Gardens. Less romantic accounts say that this tree came from Guyana, where it is not uncommon, in the late eighteenth century. It does not seed, but has been propagated and there is another specimen in these gardens and in the Botanic Gardens in Port of Spain.

Cordell gave us a bud from the tangled, twiglike branches of a Cannonball Tree. He assured us that when the flower opened it would make a noise like a gun going off. It made no such noise, the tree having got its name from the shape of its fruit. Perhaps it was education in the fantastical buildings of St Mary's Catholic school which gave Cordell such fancies, or was it merely the fun of teasing cruiseship passengers? He said he was the only Catholic in his family. 'The rest belong,' he said, 'to other religions.' He had twelve brothers and sisters, so the scope was broad.

The buses on the island were mostly Japanese vans, often gaily painted and all with names in large letters on the front of them: Murmur Not, Heavenly Love, Missing Link, Who to Blame?

St Vincent had much in common with the islands we had already been to, but, as usual, it felt quite different. It had more than the average ration of derelict and abandoned cars. One could not travel a mile without seeing one by the roadside, especially at sharp corners. Often, the vegetation would have grown over them, giving them the surreal look of leguminous transport. I decided that if I were an entrepreneur in the Caribbean, I would be in scrap metal.

One of our first expeditions was with Marilyn Ballantyne, a journalist. She thought we would like to see Montreal Gardens, a sort of nursery, open to the public. It lay up in the hills. To reach it we had to climb up, following a road which looked over Mesopotamia Valley. When we were at about 1,500 feet, we could see far below us the banana and cacao plantations, the fields of root vegetables, eddoes, tannias and dasheen, the coconut and nutmeg groves and, finally, the sea. The hills across the valley were dappled white with the flower of what Marilyn said was a trumpet bush. It was the most beautiful view we had yet seen.

Marilyn drove her own car and we followed. She hooted at every corner and at any object, like a large rock or overhanging tree. She also stopped to ask the way every four or five hundred yards. She had her seven-year-old daughter with her.

About a mile from our destination, her car broke down. 'There now,' said Marilyn, 'Daddy will have to buy us a new car. He would not like to think of us stuck out in the country like this.' She and Melissa got into our car and Marilyn, having quite decided that she was getting a new car, hardly gave the old one another thought. Perhaps it has joined the hundreds of other abandoned hulks.

The gardens proved to be dull, growing mostly those ghastly anthuriums, which look like plastic red or pink arum lilies. They are apparently very popular in the United States, having a horribly long life for such an ugly object. I found Melissa more interesting. She had an opinion about every subject. 'You are just like my daughter,' I said, 'who has an answer for everything.'

'How many daughters have you?' I told her and asked how many brothers and sisters she had.

'Three brothers and three sisters and . . .' There was a long pause. Then, in a rush: 'It's complicated you see. A long way. I can't explain. My Daddy's been married about ten times.' We moved to safer ground, but I did wonder whether Daddy would be so easily forthcoming with a new car, if he had ten wives to provide for.

A correspondent in the local paper complained that St Vincent was becoming racist, that is to say anti-white. There was, as far as I could judge, no overt hostility, but there was a constant colour-awareness. This was something which varied very much from island to island. Trinidad, while probably more doctrinaire on the subject, actually gave me little feeling of active anti-white racism, though racial animosity between the Indians and the blacks was strong. Grenada was racist; St Lucia not at all. On Mustique there was no feeling, except for the occasional white householder who went on about 'these people'.

But everyone goes on about 'these people'. We went for lunch to a restaurant called Emerald Isle. It was on an island in a river, a pretty place, lying under high, red cliffs, draped in greenery. It was an odd establishment, as it became a casino in the evening. Two cross girls from Birmingham were attempting to sunbathe by the empty pool. They were croupiers, who supervised the two roulette wheels and the three blackjack tables.

'There's three locals and uz,' they said. 'We don't like it much. They said it'd be soonny and 'taint.'

Mrs Thomas, the charming black manageress, a Trinidadian, seemed almost as glum as the English girls.

'The trouble is, except for these two, I have only got staff from this island.' She raised her eyes to the peaks.

If one comes to think of it, there is every reason for 'these people' to do as little as possible. The only thoroughgoing tradition of the blacks in the West Indies is the tradition of having been slaves. Under slavery, it is commonsense to do as little as you can get away with, without being punished. This attitude must pass from one generation to the next as readily as any other.

The main topic of interest on St Vincent was the fate of the Orange Hill Estate. This plantation lies in the north of the island, underneath the volcano Soufrière. It covers 3,200 acres, nearly one-tenth of all the arable land on St Vincent. Until recently, it belonged to a family called Barnard. They had bought it in 1907, five years after it had been totally devastated by one of the worst eruptions of Soufrière.

Early in 1985, the Barnards sold the plantation to a group of Danes for $2,100,000. On several counts, there was a tremendous outcry. In the first place, it was a scandal that one-tenth of St Vincent's agricultural land should be owned by foreigners. Secondly, it was illegal for foreigners to buy land, so some skulduggery must have gone on. Rumour had it that thirty of the Danes had married St Vincentian girls in order to be able to stay on the island and buy land. Thirdly, the Danes, who were professedly a philanthropic group, brought out deliquent youths from the slummier boroughs of London, by way of reforming them. Little reforming went on. Instead, the delinquents, it was said, brought their habits with them and taught the locals to rob, take drugs, mug the public and generally disturb the peace.

The Government sequestered the land and kicked out the Danes. Denmark broke off diplomatic relations with St Vincent. The Danish consortium sued. The Caribs, a group of whom live just to the north of

Orange Hill, claimed that the land was rightfully theirs under eighteenth-century treaties with the British. It was a lively dispute.

The coast road which went to Orange Hill ran up the windward side of the island, through prosperous-looking villages. The countryside was wide and open, though steep. At Georgetown, the atmosphere changed. The clapboard houses looked dowdy and neglected. Other new houses stood unfinished and bleak. We tried to buy a sandwich, but there was nothing to be had of any sort. It was a poor, sad place.

After Georgetown, the road became a track, wandering through dunes until we came to Dry River. On the other side of the river was the Orange Hill Estate, possibly the largest coconut plantation in the world. Behind it, Soufrière rose, higher than 3,000 feet, looking rather sinister. The volcano has had two serious eruptions during this century. The first was the eruption of 1902, which killed 2,000 people, two days before Mont Pelée erupted on Martinique, wiping out 30,000. The second eruption was on Good Friday, 13 April 1979. Twenty thousand people were safely evacuated. No one was killed, but there was much damage to farmland and the pretty crater lake disappeared in a cloud of steam.

We crossed the dry river-bed and drove gently through the vast groves of coconut trees. These groves looked astonishingly beautiful in the haze, with the sunlight shafting through the palm leaf crowns, down past the randomly angled, grey trunks, and onto the carpet of green.

The track wound up and down, never far from the sea. We passed the plantation house, an uninteresting building, but pleasant enough as a home, I daresay. We passed, too, the trim village of Overland, with its own little chapel and school, where the estate workers lived. The estate used to employ about 450 people.

In its heyday, the estate was a large producer of bananas, citrus fruits, spices, cola nuts and aubergines. There was also a herd of 500 head of cattle. Little manufactories used to produce lime juice and marmalades and buttons made from coconut shells. As we went through, there did not seem to be much activity on the estate. Two bulls that were being led along the track took fright at the approach of our car and plunged off into the undergrowth, dragging their owners with them. Otherwise, we saw no signs of husbandry.

We came out of the estate just before the village of Sandy Bay. The houses were just wooden shacks. The poverty was intense. The children crowded round us when we got out of the car. They had the swollen stomachs of kwashiorkor and noses which streamed in two crusty lines

66

down their upper lips. Several of them had cleft palates and one had a strange, metallic, discoloured ear.

These are the 'Black' Caribs, descendants of the Caribs who accepted and intermarried with shipwrecked slaves from the *Palmira*, which foundered in 1675, between St Vincent and Bequia. The Caribs, who fought fiercely against Europeans, always accepted black people with friendliness. For many years neither the French nor the British were able to subdue the Caribs on Dominica or St Vincent and they were declared neutral islands in 1748. The Carib wars went on until 1797, when Chattawar was killed. Most of the 'Black' Caribs were transported to British Honduras, but a few remained here at Sandy Bay and further north at Owia and Fancy. These last two villages can only be reached in a four-wheel-drive car, so we could not see them.

Despite their being called 'Black' Caribs, the people had the paler skins, straight black hair and the broad flat features of Amerindians. They were fine looking, but plainly very inbred. Sandy Bay was very quiet compared with most West Indian villages. There were no transistors blaring and we could hear the sea below us as we sat drinking beer, which some boys had run to fetch from the other end of the village, scrupulously bringing back the few cents change. It felt remote and it was noticeable that the children took at least half an hour to get used to us. It was a sharp contrast to the fishing village we had visited on the leeward coast, where the clapboard houses were painted and there was much life and chatter and shouting; and where the people were rich by comparison.

I talked mostly to Keith Baptiste, one of the twenty teachers at Sandy Bay. (This was not so great a number, as there were at least 650 children of school age in the area. Often, there were ninety pupils in a class.) Keith was darker than many of the other villagers, bearded and with curlier hair than many, but very certain of his status.

'On the other side of Georgetown, if we go to work anywhere, they do not trouble to learn our names. They just call us Carib – with a superior feeling. I don't mind. I am proud to be Carib.'

He defended the Caribs, in a rather confused argument, against any suggestion of their being a warlike people. It would have been a great insult even to hint at the question of cannibalism, although the word itself derives, via a Spanish corruption, from Carib.

'The Caribs are neglected,' said Keith. 'We were promised a road, but the British who were to build it refused. They said it would only benefit one family. The Barnards.

67

'In Belize, the Caribs are all lawyers and professional people. In Dominica they have a reservation. Here we are repressed. We have no electricity. There is only one telephone – for the police. To go to Kingstown costs $3. If we work on the estate, we get $3.85 a day.'

The people would be lucky to find work in Kingstown, where unemployment is very high. Anyhow, they did not want to leave Sandy Bay.

'I think it is the most beautiful part of the island. On a clear day, when you can see the mountain tops, it is so beautiful and the shore is beautiful. But our land is steep and hard to work.'

Keith's political stance was a little obscure.

'I believe always there are two lots of people: the conservatives, who are going along gently, and the liberals, who like to change one or two things.'

He did not appear to entertain any more extreme views, although he said, 'We have the highest paid politicians and the lowest paid workers. Why do you laugh? I am telling you facts.'

On the subject of the Barnard family, his views became very firm. He reminisced about picking up limes on the estate when he was a boy, for $4.50 a week. He wanted to think ill of the Barnards, but produced little evidence, apart from the fact that they alone had had electricity. (They had had a generator.)

He was rather vague about the Carib claim to Orange Hill, which led me to believe that it was one of those ideas bred in fancy. We talked then about overpopulation. Keith was inclined to dismiss this on the grounds that it was the same on other islands.

'Barbados has 160 square miles, we have 130 square miles, but they have 250,000 people while we only have 120,000.'

I pointed out that Barbados was flat and fertile, while St Vincent had little more than sixty square miles of arable land. Keith pondered this and said: 'It is the duty of governments, the schoolteachers and the church leaders to educate the people in contraception. Although I have to say, there is a problem. I mean, how should I say, a condom, the pill, they aren't good. I know about the side effects.'

I thought it too difficult to get into what the side effects of a condom were. Psychological, perhaps? Or merely a diminution of pleasure, which Keith found unacceptable?

'Anyway,' he said, 'I wouldn't ever recommend my girlfriend to use the pill.'

'How many children have you got?'

Keith laughed a lot, bending double. 'Well, I am still single.'

More laughter from both of us.

'Does that give you the answer?'

As we parted, Keith said it was good to meet a writer. 'I love books. All those Shakespeare books. Wasn't he a great writer?'

I asked if he read a lot.

'In my job, you often have to read when you don't want to. Just now, I like what I'm reading. James Hadley Chase.'

Martin Barnard and his wife now live in a hill-top house, not far out of Kingstown. It had the look of a ship, being completely surrounded by glass. Their furniture and their collection of china is in execrable taste, but as a family they and their children are astonishingly beautiful. They are also warm and welcoming.

It was Martin's grandfather who had bought Orange Hill, and the family had lived there for nearly eighty years. Recently, one disaster after another had overtaken them. When Soufrière erupted in 1979, the falling ash killed all their bananas.

'We went to the bank. In 1980, a hurricane uprooted hundreds of coconuts. We went to the bank. Then we had a plague of insects which destroy coconuts. Our production fell from 1,200 tons to 560. We could not go to the bank again.'

The history of all plantations is always a litany of this sort. In former times, planters could lie low and, with luck, recover. With huge interest rates, that is impossible.

'Either we could sell 2,000 acres and concentrate on building up the rest, or we could get out. My father was in favour of getting out. A reduced Orange Hill did not appeal to him.

'We found a buyer, but then Grenada happened and the deal collapsed. Then the Danes appeared. They kept on changing their minds, but finally they did buy it, using an ingenious but perfectly legal scheme to overcome the restrictions on foreign buyers.'

The Danes formed four separate companies. The directors of each were three Danes and four St Vincentian women. Thus the companies were St Vincentian, not alien. There were eleven different Danes, but the same four St Vincentian women were in each company. The women were employees of the Danes' lawyer. Then all four companies formed a fifth, called Windward Properties Ltd, pooling their resources.

Windward Properties, it was said, intended to do exactly what the Barnards had contemplated, that is, sell off two-thirds of the estate to local people on easy terms and then make a model farm on the rest.

The Barnards thought the Danes had been maligned. They believed that they were genuine philanthropists.

'Naturally, we feel a bit guilty, having got their money. How will they get anything back? How can St Vincent pay compensation? They haven't got any money.'

The Barnards are wholly honourable people, with a style which I had almost forgotten about. They genuinely believed that no one could understand the people on the Orange Hill Estate better than they did. They talked, like English landowners eighty years ago, of how everyone came to them with their troubles. Mary was the midwife and the nurse, Martin used to drive serious cases to the hospital in Georgetown.

'Everything worked round us,' they said. Probably that was true, but perhaps, also, it was the complaint. Keith had said with a wry, twinkling look: 'Slavery didn't end in 1838. It ended a little bit about 1958. That's when people began to see it was over.'

The Barnards agreed that it was a paternal relationship. It was, they believed, the only way a large plantation could work. And they can point to the muddle now. Little gets done. Pay is lower. Fewer people are working.

Christmas was coming. The Barnards were wrapping up sixty-five presents to take to the children in Overland. It is all over now, but they cannot forget their seigneurial role.

It was, no doubt, a pretty thing. For an hour or so, everyone would be able to pretend that everything was as it used to be.

6

Barbados

QUESTIONS OF COLOUR

It was our eighth flight. Airports, I reflected, have as strong personalities as railway stations. Mustique had been whimsical. A bamboo affair, or so it seems in memory. St Vincent's Arnos Vale must be the most casual airport. The duty-free shops are in a place well before the customs, so that anyone can wander in and out – not that there seemed to be much difference in price.

Ann-Marie came to see us off. Even her exotic appearance was dimmed by that of the other passengers. There was a girl in black trousers, with broad silver stripes down the inside leg. A man wore lilac trousers, a white jacket with lilac cuffs and four white buttons on the cuffs, a lilac shirt and lilac belt, and white shoes.

There was a middle-aged English trio of a man and two women, all in straw hats. One of the women looked quite sensible. The other wore floppy, white shorts and looked like Miss Joan Hunter-Dunn, with a great slash of orange lipstick. The man wore grey flannels and carried a cane. They spoke in loud voices with carefully adjusted vowels, talking of a 'dinner-dance' they planned to go to. The man's voice was even shriller than the women's and he had an aggravating habit of breaking

71

into indifferent French, still spoken with his refined English vowels. As he got on board, he wished the air hostess, in his affected tones, a Happy Christmas and 'an especially prosperous New Year.' They filled me with a dread of Barbados.

Oddest of all was a St Vincentian woman with her grandson. She was very black, but with Carib features. She wore a very thin, orange, flowery print dress, with a scalloped hem. On her head, she had a bright orange demolition hat, which she never took off during the journey. Did she know something that we didn't?

Landing in Barbados, we were in another world. Moreover, we were, to Hamish's delight, back in the *grande luxe*, owing to the hospitality of an old school acquaintance of mine, who owns the extremely comfortable Cobbler's Cove Hotel. So there was a car to meet us and we were whirled away, leaving the woman with the demolition hat standing, presumably awaiting her fate.

The surprise in Barbados was its flatness. After weeks of sharp hills and confined views, it felt peculiar that one's eyes could roam over so much space. Much of our journey, however, lay on narrow roads, with high walls of sugar cane on either side. The road rose and fell, as we crossed the island from one side to the other. Every so often, we would come across what looked like an English parish church, surrounded by dark mahogany trees leaning at awkward angles over the graveyard.

Then we came to the main road, running up the coast on the leeward side – miles and miles of touristic horror. Nearly the whole of the west coast, north of Bridgetown, is one long holiday resort.

Barbados seemed to have three separate existences. There was the serious business world, exporting sugar, rum and electrical components, the last representing more than half the island's total exports. Then there was tourism. Around 375,000 tourists come to Barbados every year and a further 125,000 look in on cruise ships. Finally, there was the interior. There is a certain absurdity in talking of the interior of an island twenty-one miles long and fourteen miles across, but within five minutes of the coast, the whole feeling of the place changed and another way of life took over. These three worlds obviously impinged on one another to a certain extent, but not as much as one might suppose. This may have been because so much of Barbadian life is a question of colour. I gained the impression that the politicians and the businessmen have a tacit agreement not to trespass too far on to each other's territory. The politicians are black, while the businessmen are predominantly white.

Père Labat, writing in 1700, noted the prosperity of Barbadian business: 'The shops and merchants' warehouses are filled with all one could wish from all parts of the world. One sees numerous goldsmiths, jewellers, clockmakers and other artificers . . . One notices the opulence and good taste of the inhabitants in their magnificent furniture and silver . . .'

There has been a long tradition of trade. At the time of the Inquisition, Jewish refugees from Spain, Portugal and the Spanish colonies fled to the British and Dutch islands. Some three hundred came to Barbados, and their descendants are still in commerce.

I met few businessmen, but I did go to the house of a former Colonial Service architect, Jimmy Walker who, with his wife Jill, had started a chain of shops called The Best of Barbados. He had balding hair, some of which, especially long, he scooped up from just above his left ear and carried over the top of his head. His two front teeth crossed each other in a worrying way. Jimmy was a Scot, not dour, but certainly hard-headed. He spoke without any pause in a gentle Scottish burr. Before they started their own business, he had designed hotels all over the Caribbean. In their shops, they sold the products of Barbados, many of them designed by Jill, who was an artist. They catered mostly for tourists, though they have recently started another shop for locals. The business is very successful, with a turnover of $750,000.

Jimmy was an enthusiastic gardener. He showed us his collection of orchids and his yellow poui, a bignonia climbing up the remains of the old sugar mill in his garden. The leaves of this tree fall off in about March. Then it sprouts a cloud of brilliant yellow flowers, like powder puffs, which last only a matter of a few days. In the garden as well, Jimmy had restored an old chattel house – the kind which slaves put up after emancipation. The clapboard houses, which if one did not have to live in them were charming, were designed to be easily dismantled, so that if their owners were kicked off the estate, they could be taken away as chattels.

The Walkers' house was an old plantation house. It was dark terracotta in colour and had a wide verandah. From the outside it looked sparsely beautiful. Inside it had that feeling which modern architects so often describe, and then overdo, of joining the indoors to the outdoors.

Jimmy made the most delicious rum punch, according to a recipe which he gave me, printed on a tea-towel:

73

Put 2 tablespoons of brown sugar syrup in a jug. Add 3 bottles of tonic water, the juice of 3 good limes and 12 ounces of Barbados Rum. Stir and chill. Later, add ice and 1 more tonic water. Sprinkle with grated nutmeg and add sliced cucumber to remove sweetness.

As we drank these nectareous punches, Jimmy expounded his fury at the OAS, which had asked him to instruct a woman from the Dominican Republic in how he had built up his chain of shops.

'They were going to give her a subsidy and put her up in the Hilton here for three months. I told them to get lost. All this help stops people getting off their backsides and thinking.'

The Walkers were newcomers, completely lacking in colour prejudice. The old plantocracy, they told me, was still racist. 'On the other hand, there is now a Black Businessman's Association.' They did not seem to have worked out the implications of this odious notion. In no other island would such an institution have been either necessary or thinkable.

The tourist side of Barbados is manifestly a success. On this island their contribution to the economy is very valuable, for far more of the money they bring remains in the island than is often the case elsewhere.

The hordes arrive. They lie on the beach, often not leaving the confines of the hotel. I hated them. I tried to work out why I disliked them so much. The pleasures of the beach, with the serious exception of sunbathing, are no sillier than many of the things that I enjoy. Hamish would reproach me for my intolerance. These people, he pointed out, had worked hard all year, why shouldn't they relax? Why not, indeed?

It is that awful word 'relax', I think. How can anyone actually desire the mindless state that 'relax' implies? How can anyone fly 4,000 miles to a country and never even look at it? How can people have so little curiosity about how other people live? The fault may very well be mine, but it doesn't help. I cannot bear to do nothing – though I can do it very adequately when pretending to write.

Even so, and even though our hotel was probably the most civilised on the island, when I looked at those people just lying there, empty red husks of people, I was filled with despair. I remembered Bernard Berenson once saying, 'I often wish I could go down into Florence and say to each of those men who stand there all day, "Won't you give me just five minutes of your lifetime? You have so much and I have so little."'

*　　　*　　　*

74

I thanked God for the third side of Barbados, for the 'interior'. I would drag Hamish from his windsurfer or his water-skis to go to look at things. We had hired a Mini-Moke, not a very suitable thing, as the rains were still with us, a fact which people variously attributed to Halley's Comet, the volcanoes or the Americans.

There are more than nine hundred miles of asphalt road on Barbados – little roads which twist and turn in a most confusing way. Although, as a coral island, it is pretty flat, its highest point being scarcely more than 1,100 feet, the land rises in a series of tablelands, so that, often, one cannot see very far. Almost unbelieveably, it is very easy to get lost.

One of our earlier expeditions took us first to Farley Hall, a huge mansion of a magnificence quite uncharacteristic of the island. It was gutted by fire not long after being used in the film of Alec Waugh's *Island in the Sun*. It is surrounded by a spectacular stand of mahogany trees.

Not far from it is one of two Jacobean Great Houses on Barbados – St Nicholas Abbey (There is only one other English house of that date in the Americas, in Virginia.) The house was never an abbey. It looks like a small manor-house in England, with Dutch gables, and was built in the mid-seventeenth century. The owner is Lieutenant-Colonel Stephen Cave, a descendant of the family who bought the property in 1810.

We were with some friends. The Colonel greeted us, sat us down in his drawing-room, gave us each a sheet of paper about the house, and started to tell us its history. His account varied somewhat from the story on the sheet of paper, but it seemed immaterial.

The house was very handsome, with wonderfully high doorways and tall, elegant windows. Oddly, there were fireplaces in the bedrooms, in a country when no one ever needs a fire. Some of the furniture was elegant enough, but was much later than the house.

The house was open to the public. There was a shop selling film, prints and bottles of Barbados Hot Sauce, on which there were bikinis in embarrassingly awful taste.

Colonel Cave very much belongs to the old plantocracy. He showed us old photographs of the estate. One of these included a picture of a man who had been a slave in 1838. This man had stayed on with the family after emancipation and had lived into the twentieth century.

'He was contemptuous of anyone who had not been a slave,' said the

Colonel. 'He told my grandfather he would rather have been a slave. That's not what anyone says nowadays, is it? Ha-ha!'

No, I thought, wondering once more at the human capacity for believing absolutely anything.

We went on that day and swam on a glorious beach on the windward shore. Huge rollers humped their way onto the sand, sending long fingers of foam up to where we were eating our picnic. There were a few other people swimming, who greeted us with great friendliness and some surprise. It turned out that although this was a public beach, as a rule it was used only by black people. They were far more welcoming than I felt people would have been to black visitors on a beach used mostly by white people.

On another day, we went to Andromeda Gardens. This astounding botanic garden was the creation of Iris Bannochie. Mrs Bannochie started the garden in 1954 and it is now world-famous. She was an impressive woman with an attractive spirit. She had hazel eyes and dyed chestnut brown hair. Merely to be with her was to be inspired with her enthusiasm.

The garden lies on a steep hillside, not far above the sea. It is long and narrow, following the line of an ancient river-bed filled with huge, dramatic boulders. The river used to be big, but now there is only a little stream, although twenty years ago, in one of those excesses so frequent in the Caribbean, the stream became a raging torrent, after twenty-two and a half inches of rain fell in eighteen hours.

Andromeda is one of the most intelligent gardens I have ever seen, because it is satisfying in every way. There is nothing pretentious about it, but it contains plants and trees from South America, Malaysia, Natal, Taiwan, Madagascar, Tahiti, Zaire, Burma, India, Java, Kenya, South China, Thailand, New Guinea, Australia, Japan, Polynesia and probably a score of other countries. Many of them are great rarities.

Even if one had never heard the name of any plant, the place would still be a delight, because Mrs Bannochie does not eschew prettiness. One wanders from one place to another and at each turn one finds some new pleasure: a burst of flowers, a tree of unbelievable shape, a secret garden, a lily pool. The paving-stones are made of concrete, impressed with the leaves of the trees in the garden.

We sat by a pool and her husband brought us drinks. Dr Bannochie is a tiny, grey-bearded man with vivid blue eyes. He was a medical officer in the Colonial Service. He has a very cultivated voice, while hers is exuberantly Barbadian. The drink he brought was called sorrel, for no reason that I could think of. It is bright pink and has an unusually pleasant taste. It is an infusion of the pod of *Hibiscus sabdariffa* and is very much a Christmas drink in the Caribbean. The only other places I have ever had it are in the Sudan and Egypt, where it is called *karkadeh*.

Sitting with the Bannochies in the garden she created was a civilised experience. We talked of the egrets which flew over us on their way home to roost. They said there was certainly none thirty years ago. Barbados is small enough for them all to nest in one place.

They told me, too, about the whistling frog which produces a formidably loud noise. It is a tiny creature, no bigger than a little-finger nail. The female lay eggs which look like glass balls, the size of a bicycle ball-bearing. The eggs are absolutely transparent, so that one can see the minute frogs inside. They have no tadpole stage. Moreover, their feet are not webbed, so they cannot swim.

Another morning we drove north, the land rising almost to downland, where cattle grazed. Then there were sudden valleys of great charm. It seemed hardly possible that this was the same island as Tourist Row, with its golf courses and supermarkets. In the north, on the windward shore, the green closely-grazed land has been swept bare of all other growth. The Atlantic beats in and a spray haze hangs over the hills. On the shore road there are many warnings about the dangers of swimming. It is the prettiest part of the island.

In a remote place, some way inland, we found George Money, a retired bank administrator. He was a thin man, browned and wrinkled like a nut, with blue eyes hidden behind dark glasses. He had a brisk, down-to-earth charm, which I found particularly sympathetic. He had built his own house, which was finished in 1972. It was interesting that, in the same way that St Nicholas Abbey was, in its time, built in a European style about fifty years out of date, so Mr Money's house had about it a feeling of the thirties.

As was almost anybody of interest in Barbados, he was an enthusiastic gardener and claimed to have introduced Snow on the Mountain to the island. This was the feathery, white *Euphorbia leucocephalus* which I had first seen in the botanic gardens in St Vincent. As with so many of the plants, it had a different local name on almost every island.

Mr Money's collection of hibiscus was sumptuous, and he was proud that he was called upon to provide blooms to decorate the dining table of the yacht *Britannia* during the Queen's visit – a relief to her, who is said to loathe the ever-present, plastic-looking anthurium. He grows figs and grapefruit, not for sale but as a hobby.

He chose to build in this remote place to be away from the expatriates.

'If I wanted to live among English people, I would live in England.'

He was not surprised at my dismay at finding prejudice and a colour bar.

'When I came here in the early fifties, the colour bar was intense. The bank employed only whites. In three weeks I changed that. Now, of course, there are only blacks and they run it extremely well.

'In those days, if I asked even so well-known a person as Sir Grantley Adams to dinner, there were white planters who would arrive, take one look and walk out.'

He did not say whether he ever asked the planters again, but I assumed not.

'Now, the bar still exists among the stupider people, but I see some of the young whites doing almost the reverse. They try to grow their hair in an Afro style and affect Bajun accents and manners.'

I asked whether the black population actively resented the racial prejudice.

'No, they do not seem to bear a grudge. I think, in one sense, Barbados was lucky. The planters here were not ostentatious, flashing their wealth about. Plantation houses were modest, compared with the palaces built in Jamaica.

'In Jamaica, the planters were ostentatious and extravagant. The result was that when Independence came, the blacks took their cue from their former owners. Jamaicans are very different from Barbadians. People in England imagine that all West Indians are alike, because they are black. They are as different from each other as Poles and Portuguese. And often as far apart from each other.'

Mr Money was optimistic about the future. In general, he was very sanguine about the stability of the region and, in particular, encouraging about his own island.

'After all, it costs nothing to bale out a country of 100,000 people. Ten million dollars goes a long way, compared with, say, Turkey, where ten billion would be needed to make a start.

'Barbados is well-governed. The Prime Minister, Bernard St John, is highly talented. He could have been a leader in any country. It is an example of better education on this island and also of the advantages of a larger population.

'The difference between the political parties is not great. Their policies are so alike that, when the last switch of government took place, *The Times* said it was a slight swing to the left and the *Financial Times* said it was a slight swing to the right.'

Mr Money's concern was mostly for the poorer people of Barbados. In many ways, they were not doing so badly. While the large sugar enterprises with managers and overseers were losing money because of the prices, the smallholder could grow cane profitably. This was because he took no account of his time, working his land mostly during the weekend, while doing a job during the week – rather as Mr Money grew grapefruit.

It is true that unemployment is about twenty per cent, but there is no reason why it should get worse and a few why it could get better. They do not have the population problems of the smaller, less educated, often Catholic islands. The Barbadians are good, also, at getting round the immigration laws of the United States, Canada and Great Britain. The population growth has been halved in recent years and many Barbadians have emigrated, so the actual population is roughly the same as it was when Mr Money arrived, some thirty years ago.

There is an irony in the fact that many Barbadians in Barbados are better off than their cousins who emigrated to Birmingham, where the unemployment among black people is probably higher than it is in Bridgetown and the education almost certainly worse.

By now the radio was playing carols all day long. Our hotel was filling up with Christmas clients. It was time for us to move on. Or rather, to move back, as we were going to St Lucia, to Colin's house at Soufrière.

I was not sorry to go. This island was the most English we had seen and although the people, for the most part, were far better off than those on the other islands, it distressed me that so many of our worst traits had survived so vigorously. The colour bar, the pomposity of asking people to wear dinner jackets for Christmas and what they call Old Year's Night, the general philistinism.

It is a smug and snobbish island. As we drove to the airport, through

Bridgetown, could I really have seen what I thought I saw, from the corner of my eye, on Millers Brothers Building – two highly-developed, naked male figures, the equivalent of caryatids? On so pi an island? I do hope so.

7

St Lucia

CHRISTMAS STORIES

Returning anywhere when one is on a long journey is always a delight. All *angst* is removed and for once there is some familiarity. Kent and another boy met us at Castries in a minibus. We tried everywhere to hire a car, driving all over town and going out to the marina. Suddenly, the boys gave up the search without any explanation and without telling us. We had driven halfway out of town before we realised that they were heading home, but they showed no resentment when I insisted that we go back to do some shopping, though it was plain that Kent was anxious to get back. We learned later that he and a friend had bought a bull together for $600. They were to slaughter it that night. Everyone was slaughtering, for all must have meat for Christmas.

It struck me, as we did our shopping and on the drive home, that the people in St Lucia were infinitely better-looking than the Barbadians. The road to Soufrière was the one that we had been told was impassable on our first visit. The first part of the journey took us through sadly deforested land. The lack of trees exposed the rocks and boulders, which had a burnt look. St Lucia, most of all the islands, feels volcanic. We passed through villages, most of which looked more prosperous than

81

Soufrière. In two of them there were lovely clanking iron bridges of sheet metal. A man in Anse Le Raye, with no hand, waved a greeting to us. Somehow his wrist looked much too small. The forest, when we reached it, drenched by rain and sun, had a special bright quality. In one short stretch, there were fern trees, looking like grown-up bracken. They seemed to grow only in this one place.

Soufrière looked festive. They had put up Christmas decorations while we were away – rather touching and fluffy. In Grenada, the decorations had been loud and garish, too big and somehow faintly familiar. For good reason; they were old Regent Street ones. Apparently, they ship them out every year.

Soufrière House, when I came to look at it again, was, I decided, practical, comfortable, decorated in a sort of non-taste. There were no real horrors, except the rubber grapes on the table. Equally, there was nothing pleasing, except the wonderful wooden floors. The wooden cupboards were of just the wrong orange-coloured wood. Perhaps it was colonial taste. George Money's house, on Barbados, though newer, had been practical and comfortable but lacking any real charm.

In St Lucia for Christmas, I felt far happier than I would have done in Barbados. There I would have known people, but that would have made it too like home with children and family.

I came across this in Theroux:

> I saw a young couple picking out a vacuum cleaner, and I felt guilty and homesick. Nothing was more unconsoling to me in all of Central America than the sight of this couple proudly carrying their new vacuum cleaner out of the San Jose store. I think I began to understand then why I was always happier in a backwater, why the strangeness of Santa Ana had charmed me, and why I had sought the outlandish parts of Guatemala or the wastes of Mexico. Perhaps this explained my need to seek out the inscrutable magnetisms of the exotic: in the wildest place everyone looked so marginal, so temporary, so uncomfortable, so hungry and tired, it was possible as a traveller to be anonymous or even, paradoxically, to fit in, in the same temporary way.

The last bit I only half agreed with. In Barbados poor Hamish would have been so much happier, because, at bottom, he wanted to be at home, to sleep with white girls not black ones, and to do homelike things. For me those would have immediately become responsibilities. In England or France, I feel that I stand, as it were, in relation to other

82

people. In an unfamiliar village like Soufrière or in the desert, one has no position – one is oneself (or anybody one chooses to be) – a *tabula rasa*, unmarked by all one's past. White, of course, and people have attitudes to that. In my case in a wheelchair, which prompts responses of one sort or another (not very much in the West Indies, where they accept things) but apart from that, you are simply you. I like that.

All travellers feel something of this sort. There is great loneliness in travel, but a purity of contact. Not to be forgotten is that the locals think you are rich.

Dinner was the first event of our Christmas Eve, as we had no car. Kent had disappeared – it was said that his partner in the bull enterprise had cheated him, of all profit anyhow; also that he was probably trying to organise a cock-fight. He had great plans always to buy cocks but Lyton said he knew nothing about 'fowls' and was forever being sold duds. We had dinner at the Humming Bird, a pleasant enough restaurant as a rule, but suddenly crowded with German tourists. Lyton had arranged for us to dine with Sir John Plumb, the historian. He turned out to be a peppery but very entertaining figure. He was accompanied by a Dr Joe Whalley. I noticed that Sir John was very polite to black people and genuinely concerned for them. On the other hand, he was extremely rude to a German who tried to sit at our reserved table. 'This man is being a bore,' he said when I turned up in the middle of the argument.

On our way home, we could see the people of Soufrière at Mass through the church windows. From the house we could hear the sound of hymns. When the devout had gone home, quite a different music took over, booming away all night with the pulsing rhythm of reggae. It was hard to sleep but I rather liked the way sound wafted up from the village – it was mostly voices, certainly no traffic noise. It reminded me of camping on the dunes above desert oases. It is a pretty noise, somehow as old as man and very comforting.

On Christmas Day, Lyton asked us to lunch. He sent Robert, the National Insurance Inspector, to pick us up. Robert told me he wanted to do a course in administration and labour relations. Lyton had also asked the couple who ran the hotel where Eroline worked. I found these people's attitude perfectly extraordinary. They had worked in Mauritius, South Africa, in Zimbabwe, which they still called Rhodesia, and had now moved here to St Lucia. Which, I asked, was their favourite? Without hesitation, they said South Africa. It was so beautiful. And apartheid? 'You know, when in Rome, do as the Romans do.' I said I didn't know. I couldn't have a row in Lyton's house. I remembered Randolph Churchill's complaining, 'I can't insult people in other people's houses, I can't insult them in their houses, I can't insult them in my house – where can I insult them?'

After lunch, a much more sympathetic man called Dick arrived. He was scrawny, dressed in a T-shirt and shorts. He was a vet in West Sudan and told us hideous tales of the slaughter of whole villages.

I liked Dick, largely for his lack of self-importance and a measure of wry self-mockery. He said an expert was anyone 3,000 miles away from home. He recognised, in a modest manner, that his job was to find out and understand what it was people wanted – not to tell them what they wanted. He reckoned that it usually took about three years to find that out.

Dick's conversation on all subjects was lively and informative. He maintained that sixty-two per cent of Jamaica's foreign currency came from cannabis. When we talked of population control, he said that the only way of achieving anything was by making people understand the cost of a child. For the most part, this was borne by people other than the parents, so it was hard to get the message across.

Dick owned a house overlooking Soufrière. He said that when he first saw it, he thought that if he could not be satisfied living there, he had better give up. 'There may be places as beautiful, but there can't be anywhere more beautiful.'

He was attractive because he was vital and doing something. He hoped in a few years to have formed a consultancy group with an agriculturalist and another expert – then he would spend six months a year in St Lucia. Would he then, I wondered, take on that apologetic, self-justifying quality of expatriates? How much more interesting, I reflected, had been the genuine white locals as compared with the refugees: the Pringles, Charles Turpin on Tobago, the Barnards, and Mrs Bannochie.

Kent, apparently, was supposed to have laid on girls for us to sleep with. He had failed in this enterprise as in most others. Fortunately, I suspect.

Lyton came that night at nine o'clock to take us to the dance in the Town Hall. *Le tout Soufrière* would be there, he said. The Town Hall was a rather dismal building, a little inland from the sea. When we arrived, there was a fight going on outside, not a very serious affair. The dance, organised by the Lions at 75 cents a head, was upstairs. The huge room, about eighty feet long and fifty feet wide, was totally dark except for one short strip-light, mostly covered in cardboard, over the bar, and a few faint glimmers for the band. The noise was prodigious but there were curiously few people, perhaps twenty couples. The boys were dressed, with a few exceptions, much as they usually are, in subfusc colours. They wore dark trousers, often with flared bottoms, and drab T-shirts, or singlets. The exceptions, like Lyton, seemed to prefer white clothes; he wore white trousers and a bright Hawaiian shirt, decorated with palm trees and lagoons. Eroline wore tight, tight white trousers and a loose white shirt and looked, as always, wonderfully dressed.

The dancing, to familiar hits of Stevie Wonder, was largely erotic. Both boys and girls would press their loins fiercely together and dance with a gyrating motion. One boy, all in white, his shirt with two slashes over each shoulder, thrust himself for a long dance against a girl in yellow trousers. As they gyrated, their bodies moving in lecherous revolvings, the girl caressed his buttocks with searching fingers in a way I could not have stood. When the music stopped, they parted without a word or a glance. This was perfectly usual. Another boy in red, shiny shorts danced with a girl in baggy trousers. Their feet never moved, only their bottoms rotated and pushed and pulled. They moved like Siamese twins, rooted to one spot. When the music stopped it was plain that he had an erection. Yet he left her.

Among them were older people, both men and women, more drunk than the young ones. One man in floppy trousers, an old shirt and a hat, swayed for a long while near the bar, making little quick movements to reassure himself that he was sober; he would take two firm steps in one direction then stop and smile, then he would snatch his hat off and replace it with a thump. Again, a smile of triumph. There was a large woman, made larger by her too-short dress of broad black and white stripes. She, too, wore a small floppy beach hat. At length these two got together and danced. At first, it was hard to say which was supporting the other. Their combined swaying was like ruffled bathwater, threatening, when two stirrings coincide, to overflow or, when they conflict, somehow stopping menacingly dead. The couple sometimes hung poised for two or three beats. At others they swept halfway across the room in the same time. His hat fell off; in the end, it was she who retrieved it, he not daring to bend so far.

The Attorney-General bounced happily round, introducing me to bemused ladies, no one able to hear what anyone said. The place gradually filled with more people. We left at 1.30 am. Kent and Lyton explained that there had been another disco up in the hills. Everyone had gone there first but would now come to the Town Hall. I could still hear the music at 7 am.

Boxing Day was a *non-dies* because Lyton never turned up and we still had no car. Kent came at six, saying he'd be back in a minute with two girls. He never came.

The following day, we had lunch with Sir John Plumb. 'Happy is the St Lucian who knows his father,' he said. Afterwards, we went to Belfond, the place where Robert Devaux had told us that there was an Arawak equivalent of Stonehenge. Sir John was very caustic about the likelihood of there being any such thing, particularly after he had read the article about it in the local historical magazine. He didn't bother to come with us.

The road climbed steeply. To one side was a deep, broad valley. Like all Caribbean valleys, it was made up of patterns of green. Indeed, all landscapes are like that, the predominant species of tree providing the variation. Pale yellow palms, darker bananas, through still darker breadfruit to mahogany.

Belfond belongs to a Mr Rickards and his wife, who came to St Lucia from Surbiton ten years ago. They are veterinary surgeons. Their land, which amounts to only sixteen acres, is 1,600 feet up, with a fine view over the Pitons. The house itself is pretty tumbledown. Mrs Rickards was a nice woman, with gold tips to her teeth. She is lame in some way. Their enormous Alsatians kept on nearly knocking her over. They say that the terracing below their house is different from agricultural terracing. They believe the site lies at a point of astronomical importance in relation to the Pitons. Mr Rickards told me that he had meant to photograph the sunset on 21 December, but he could not see ten yards for the mist.

The land was too steep and rough for me to reach in my chair. The Rickards say that there are large numbers of beautifully cut stones, which they think were originally erect. On one of them, a bird's wing is carved. He believes that the people who made the site worshipped sun and water. The evidence for water worship, Mr Rickards maintains, lies in the conduit system on the terraces. He thinks that they were cascades. Although he believes this, he says, 'I am a trained scientist, I know the evidence is insufficient.'

The Rickards claimed that there is also an Arawak site which, they say, is the highest in the Caribbean and the most inland. This is certainly not true, as I was later to see in Puerto Rico. Once again, I thought it wonderful what people will believe. Mr Rickards pointed to a step shape near the crest of a mountain behind, which he said lined up with a 'pimple' on a skyline hill. This was due north. He claims the step was cut away by man. Fiddlesticks.

On our last night, we went to a public meeting at the Town Hall. The purpose of it was for the people of Soufrière to see and discuss a project for the development of their town. Mr Nick Trobitscoff had prepared elaborate drawings and plans, entitled 'Magnificent Soufrière'.

The leader of the Soufrière planning committee was Colonel Pelham-Reid. He looked just like his name. He started the proceedings by introducing a man from the Organization of American States. This rather self-satisfied figure made a speech in which he managed to imply that the OAS had conceived it all. Actually, as I discovered, they had done volumes of jargonistic reports and hideous designs.

For no pay, the modest, spectacled, and least vainglorious Mr Trobitscoff, doubtless horrified by the OAS plans, had done this new design which we had come to see. It was sensible and practical and was so arranged that it could be implemented gradually.

Very few people attended the meeting, but there were two who asked intelligent questions. The government planning officer said that he had never been in favour of developing Jalousie. 'One must look at the greatest benefit for *all* the people of the island, now and in the long-term. To employ the people of Soufrière, of course it's good. But the people of Castries, are they benefitting? And the place, will future people think it was the right use?'

He wanted it to be a park. Of course it's nonsense to talk of natural. There is nothing natural about it now. Coconuts, bananas, nutmeg, guava – none of these would have been growing there naturally, indeed none is indigenous. The banana, for instance, was not introduced into St Lucia until 1856. As for its being a public park, I pointed out that Pigeon Point was hardly popular.

At about this moment I became aware that a short, grey-haired, rather red-faced man was suddenly the centre of attention: '. . . kindly donated . . . great gesture . . .'

It turned out to be Mr Rheinhardt, supposedly negotiating with Colin. He owned the Dasheene Hotel, on the cliff above Jalousie (anyhow, the major share, he later told me). It seemed an odd moment to make rather dubious donations; he had promised to back the waterfront project, but no sum was mentioned. This was meant to be a consultative exhibition. What, I wondered, if no one liked the waterfront project?

By no choice of ours, we found ourselves dining with Mr Rheinhardt. He asked where I was staying. When I told him that we were at Soufrière House, he said, 'I rent half that with Colin. I own half Jalousie.' 'Then I'm staying with you,' I said to his wife, who gazed past me with stony lack of interest.

Rheinhardt went on to tell me more of what he owned. 'The most expensive clinic in the world,' he said, as if this were a recommendation. The clinic was that questionable place where the old are injected with monkey glands, a form of treatment supposed to rejuvenate the cells of the body. He claimed that Pope Pius XII, Somerset Maugham and Sir Winston had all been patients. I asked if he had tried it? He said it was too early.

His twelve-year-old daughter was having dinner with us. He treated her with a disagreeable contempt. She asked what the difference was between red wine and white wine. Was one stronger than the other?

'Red is made from red grapes, white from white grapes. If you want to know the difference taste them.'

He became cross when I told her the facts. She wanted to tell a story: 'too long,' he said. She was actually a better conversationalist than he was. His wife spoke of Vermont and the extreme seasons, but had never read *Ethan Frome* or *Summer*. Indeed, neither of them had heard of Edith Wharton.

Then he produced his sketch plan for the development of Jalousie – a 300-room hotel, on the beach. A monorail from the Dasheene. It would have been hard to imagine a more philistine approach.

After dinner, I escaped and sat looking at the Pitons. The one to the right was in darkness, the other and the shoulder of land before it, caught the full brilliance of the moon. At sea, a ship was passing. Above, the clouds scudded, as they used to in the movies.

8
Martinique
AN EMPRESS AND A VOLCANO

The shock of arriving in Martinique had nothing to do with a new arrangement of coconuts or bananas or breadfruit trees. It was the equivalent of crossing that most sudden of borders, the one between Mexico and the United States. A leap from the Third World to the developed world. The telephone worked. There were new cars, familiar advertising, big highways, parking meters.

Hamish had left behind the hotel guide from which we had chosen a hotel. He had no memory of the name. (He always left something in each place.) There was a tourist booth in the airport and an efficient girl who found a room for us and a taxi. All the self-drive cars were booked.

Martinique is a *département* of France, not a colony or a dependency, but actually a part of France, with a *préfet* appointed by Paris and with representation in the French National Assembly. They have their own local Assembly as well. In this way, Martinique and the other French West Indies are very much cut off from the other islands of the Caribbean. By their connection with the EEC, their trade is largely with Europe. They find it more practical to do business with Germany or Spain than with their own neighbours. While most Caribbean countries look west to the USA and Canada, Martinique looks east to the old world.

The result is a tension and a great political consciousness, which is common to all the French islands, but quite different in mood on each island. The taxidriver was much amused by our astonishment and at once translated it into political terms.

'Absolutely, you see, one does not want independence from France. In Martinique, we have no resources. The market for sugar is gone. That for bananas is limited. There is only tourism.

'After all, it is decentralised now. We direct our own affairs, but we have all of France's wealth behind us.'

He was the first of many on this island to tell me that they preferred comfort to independence.

The country we drove through was broad and rolling, with not very tropical vegetation. I had not seen so many cows for a long time but there were no egrets. They couldn't shoot them could they? There were lots of signs saying *Chasse Interdite*. The thought of shooting had simply not crossed my mind on any other island.

The girl at the airport had chosen a hotel at Anse Mitan, which lies across the bay from the capital, Fort-de-France. It is a small, bourgeois holiday resort, reminding me of somewhere like Cavalaire in my childhood. The hotel was almost comically French. The telephone was locked up. The bar opened only when it suited the owners. The water was cold. There was no room cleaning on Thursdays, the *femme de chambre*'s day off.

There was always a smile, but never anything which might cost a franc. They looked surprised when Hamish and I said we did not want to share a bed. They brought another single bed, for which they charged fifty francs.

The illusion of being in Europe continued at breakfast. There was an Italian group in one corner who were abominably rude to the waitress. Next to me was a much-travelled French girl, who went every year to Asia. Apart from correcting someone's notion that the beaches on Réunion were black, she talked only of the price of everything.

We took the ferry across the bay to Fort-de-France. Wind-surfers scudded across the choppy water at a speed which impressed even Hamish. It was a pretty way to go to the town, because one landed in the very centre, by the large open space called the Savane. The old town is crowded onto the short space of flat land, before the hills rise sharply behind. The streets are straight, as usual on a grid pattern, and narrow, with tiny pavements hardly wide enough for two people to pass.

Everywhere was jammed with cars and there was a feeling of energy which I had not sensed for a long time. There were no groups of young men hanging about with nothing to do. The shops were filled with all the goods you would expect in a large French town. The telephone boxes were all vandalised. The houses were not particularly interesting, though the buildings round the Savane, with its marble statue of the Empress Josephine, were grandiose.

The exception was the cathedral in the centre of the old town. It was built in 1895, on the site of a church which had been finished only thirty years earlier. Father Janin wrote a florid account of its destruction in the great fire of 1890, which destroyed three-quarters of the town. 'The bell-ringers rang the tocsin with a farouche energy until the very last minute. They did not leave until the fire drove them out. At that moment, heavy silence fell on the whole town. Everybody gazed at the bell-tower, which began to burn. Suddenly, the bells began to ring in a wild and violent manner. The twisting irons and the burning wood had set the bells ringing in one final clamour – a sound so sad that everyone's eyes filled with tears. Then everything fell with a horrible clanging, the bells, before they died, sounding one last sob over the blazing city.'

As we passed, we heard boys' voices, singing. It made me stop and look at the building, which I suddenly realised was made of metal. After the disaster, it was intended, despite its 180-foot spire, to be not only fireproof but also invulnerable to earthquakes. The architect, Henry Pick, who also built another metal building on the Savane, the Bibliothèque Schoelcher, must have been inspired by the same spirit which moved Eiffel to build his tower in 1889. Inside the cathedral, everything was metal. There were cast-iron pillars and pew ends. Only the pulpit was wooden. Everything was painted white and picked out in browns and yellows.

In the modern part of the city, there are huge new buildings. Some of the apartment blocks, painted in a variety of pastel shades, might have been transported from the suburbs of Toulon.

More attractive than anything were the people. The Martiniquais are tall. The men are reasonably handsome and they move with a striking elegance. The women are quite startling in their beauty. Wandering through the streets of Fort-de-France, we would stop, awestruck, at least once every ten minutes, for the pleasure of watching some wholly entrancing girl go by.

It was a puzzle that, amid all the Frenchness, there were so few cafés, and none where you could sit and watch people go by. Perhaps it is just as well, with all those girls.

Not wanting to spend another night without hot water, we found a hotel in the outskirts of the city. It was an old Creole house, high above the town with a beautiful view over the harbour. We asked the young man behind the desk to telephone to our hotel to say we were giving up the room. He did so, putting on an absurd voice. When I looked surprised, he laughed and explained that the receptionist at our hotel was his girlfriend. He was afraid she would accuse him of poaching her clients.

This hotel, too, was marvellously French. There was a gate to the breakfast room, which the proprietor locked on the dot of nine o'clock. When Hamish was smoking in the television room, M. Victoire snatched the cigarette out of his mouth. My room had French wallpaper, stripy with medallions.

Jacline Labbé, to whom I had an introduction, came at once when I telephoned. I was waiting on the verandah of the hotel. As she got out of the car, I knew it must be her. She was a wonderfully elegant figure, moving a little like a dancer, her long clothes swaying as she walked. As she came closer, I could see that she was beautiful. Her face was deeply marked, with lines not wrinkles, so pronounced that they divided her face like a geometric design. Her skin was an exquisite colour – honey and spice-coloured. I have rarely met a woman so dignified and yet so spontaneous in her warmth.

She had brought with her her son David, a friendly young man of about twenty-two. At once we were plunged into a serious conversation about the social distinctions in Martinique.

'The island is divided into cliques of class and of colour,' she said.

How odd it sounded to hear her talk of '*colons*' and to hear that word again, pronounced with its full pejorative sneer.

'The old *colons* never mix – oh, they are polite and gracious, with their *noblesse oblige*, but for them it is still the same as it always was. They never intermarry or make *alliances*.'

I wondered how that could be when real negro colouring and features are rare. The people, in general, were the palest we had yet seen, ranging over the widest spectrum of browns.

Jacline also spoke furiously about poverty. I wondered then how many islands she had seen. At that meeting I had not got a measure of the intensity of feeling which informed much of her conversation.

It was New Year's Eve, or Old Year's Night. Jacline asked us to her house for the evening. She wore a white dress, lacy, but well restrained. Her hair, which in the morning had been hidden under a foulard, now sprang up in two high bursts, with a deep central parting between them.

The house was very small, in what I took to be a lower-middle-class district. But it had some land and Jacline hoped to build on a studio workshop. Jacline originally had a hairdressing shop, but now that has a manager. She spends a lot of time making marionettes and puts on shows for schoolchildren.

We drank champagne and rum punch. Jacline kept on saying it was all so simple, whereas it was fun and lively. She had twin daughters, Barbara and Nicolette, younger than David. They were not as pretty as their mother, but they were immensely vivacious and wanted to take Hamish off to dance. Jacline and I continued our conversation of the morning.

The poverty she had spoken of, she said, was really a poverty of spirit and artistic energy. She believed that Martinique should have independence and not depend on aid. She did not mind about the comforts. She wanted her country to have a more modest standard of living and a more dignified life.

In some ways Jacline was like a good American liberal, with left-wing views and an admiration for ethnic craft. There were important differences. In the first place, she was not rich. Secondly, she had a dry sense of humour and considerable sophistication. Having expounded her theory of the sacrifices of material things bringing greater rewards in the form of self-respect, she added with a wry smile: 'Anyhow, France would never let us go under.'

Once we had got a car, we made many expeditions. We started by setting off on the huge highway running south past the industrial town of Lamentin. We were still unused to so much traffic and speedy driving. A hearse carrying an ornate coffin flashed past us at an alarming rate. When it was just ahead, the huge silver cross on its roof fell off. There was much swerving and hooting, but at least we felt we were really in the Caribbean and not in Europe.

Later in the day, in Marin, we saw the hearse again. The cross was back in place, albeit a little bent. The funeral was gathering. The women were all in white and the men in dark suits. The deceased must have been a person of importance. Some twenty youths, all in clean white shirts, each carrying a single stem of white flowers, walked in procession before the coffin. It was a touching sight.

The south of the island, which was less rugged, was also dull, everything being dedicated to tourism. There was what the guide map described as a petrified wood savannah at the southernmost tip, but we found only people turned to stone as they lay worshipping the sun and the great god Tan.

St Anne had a very pretty church with a classical facade, dated 1824. It had a fish-scale roof, as did the houses of the little fishing village of Anse d'Arlets. They made me nostalgic for Grenada.

Another day we headed north, searching for the poverty Jacline had spoken of and for some trees. I had grumbled to her that there were so few compared with other islands. She had said that on the Route de la Trace there were so many of such a size that it felt as if they were going to eat you up.

Not long after leaving Fort-de-France, we came upon a huge church in a tiny forest village. Somehow, it looked familiar. Then I realised that it was a copy of the Sacré Coeur in Paris and was hideous, with raised pointing between irregularly-shaped stones. It made me puzzled as to how one could ever have had any affection for the original.

As the road climbed, we got into real tropical forest – with vast, nodding clumps of bamboo, like the ostrich plumes of Victorian débutantes' mothers, beautiful mahoganies and tall silk cotton trees. Here there were masses of fern trees, which had been such a rarity on St Lucia.

The road ran twisting through the forest in the centre of the island. Towards the northern end, we could see the clouds and mist shrouding Mont Pelée, the 4,500-foot volcano of savage reputation. Then we dropped down, through lush plantations and enormous fields of pineapple, towards the windward coast.

At Basse Pointe, we went to the Leyritz Plantation, which claims to be the most important in the Caribbean, on account of the number of its old buildings and their state of preservation. It was founded in about

1700, by a Bordelais of Croatian origins. Over the centuries, following economic fashion and beset by all the disasters to which the Caribbean is prone, the plantation has grown spices, manioc, tobacco, citrus, sugar cane, avocados, bananas and pineapples, has bred cattle and has produced sugar and rum.

It now belongs to a couple called Charles and Yvelines de Lucy de Fossarieu. In the steady evolution of things, by which the latest crop to cultivate is tourists, they have turned the old buildings into a hotel and restaurant, with *'piscine, tennis, discothèque'*. They have just about managed to maintain some of the romance of the place, with its aqueduct, water wheel, rum distillery and bachelors' quarters, the buildings all of dark volcanic stone. The plantation house itself was rather dreary and small. I could not associate it with the glamorous dances in chandeliered ballrooms, which were part of my imagined picture of old, aristocratic Martinique.

We followed the coast, gloriously pretty and rough, until the road climbed over a promontory and then plunged into a ravine with high cliffs, draped in greenery, from which we emerged to find ourselves in Grande Rivière, a fishing village where the road ended. On the front, boys were playing boule. From there, we could see Dominica looming, high, dark and mysterious. On the way back, on a lonely stretch of road, we turned a corner to find eight or nine young men dancing down the road to the music of one of those big double-speaker radios that they all carry. They were all perfectly in step and looked like a well-drilled chorus line.

On yet another day, we went up the leeward coast to see St Pierre, the original capital. We lunched at Carbet (the name means house in Carib), the place where Columbus landed in 1502, and recorded in his diary that it was 'indeed a most beautiful sight'. The restaurant was on the beach, a simple, happy place. There was a long table with a lovely, jumbled party of sixteen people of all ages, having a tremendous lunch. It was easy to see that the party was to welcome two American grandparents on a visit to their son, who was married to a very dark Martiniquaise. This was in marked contrast to the restaurant at Leyritz, where I had thought the rest of the clientele suspiciously white.

Shortly before St Pierre, we saw a sign saying Musée de Gauguin. The painter stayed here for about four months in 1887 and wrote home: 'We are now housed in a Negro hut, and this is paradise . . . Below lies the seashore lined with coconut trees, above grow all kinds of fruit trees, twenty-five minutes from town . . .' The museum was not very interesting, but I could not help speculating as to what sort of paradise he would have thought it fifteen years later.

St Pierre lies directly under Mont Pelée. In 1902, it was considered one of the most prosperous cities in the Caribbean. There were fine buildings of four storeys, a cathedral and six churches. There was a theatre modelled on the one in Bordeaux and famous performers came from France to act there, and great orchestras to play.

No writer can ever resist relating the fate of St Pierre. No matter how often it is told, the story is somehow archetypal – revealing the vanity of man in the face of nature's capricious power.

On 24 April 1902, Mont Pelée sent up a great column of smoke. Ash floated in the air. No one thought much of this. Everyone knew Vieux Père Pelée grumbled away from time to time. Just turning in his sleep, they said. On 5 May, it was more serious. The mountain threw out a molten mass. The river boiled. Mud, lava and rocks engulfed the Guérin sugar factory, burying twenty-five people alive. People began to wonder. Was there worse to come? Several families packed and left for Fort-de-France. That night the sky was bright with flames and sparks. The lip of the crater caved in.

The authorities moved quickly. Monsieur Fouché, the mayor of St Pierre, issued a governessy statement: '. . . entitled to reassure you . . . no immediate danger . . . lava will not reach down into the town . . . Do not surrender to panic . . . stay where you are . . . set an example of courage . . .'

The Government appointed a committee of experts to examine the situation. They must report quickly. They did. The Governor and his wife drove out to St Pierre on 7 May. Elections were due on 11 May and no one wanted any panic before that. And 8 May was Ascension Day, traditionally a day of great festivity in St Pierre. The presence of the Governor would allay all fears.

He and his wife must have passed an unpleasant night. There was an appalling thunderstorm. Rain lashed the town. Never mind, it would wash the streets clean of dust and ash. They would be spruce for tomorrow's parade. Indeed, 8 May dawned bright and clear. In Fort-de-France, the report of the committee of experts was published. People read it with comfort. The committee made six points.

The phenomena observed had no abnormal characteristics. The craters were wide and would release fumes and lava but not throw out rocks or cause earthquakes. The loud explosions were merely gases blowing up, the mountain was not collapsing. The lava flow was confined to the valley of one river. The relation of the crater to the valleys meant that the lava would flow to the sea; St Pierre was absolutely safe. Three other rivers were flowing at their normal temperature; they were black only because they were full of ash.

The people of St Pierre did not take such comfort from these words. For the people of St Pierre were dead. At ten to eight on the morning of 8 May, Mont Pelée burst apart. It looked, according to the survivors on the one ship which escaped from the harbour, as though one side of the mountain had broken away and rolled down upon the town.

Twenty-eight thousand people died, including the Governor and his wife, including the committee who had undertaken to maintain their careful investigation, including the twenty-one-year-old fiancée of a man whom Alec Waugh met in 1929. They were to have been married the next day and he had come to Fort-de-France just for the night. He was fifty when Waugh met him, and, although happily married and with children, he said: 'I don't know that since that day I've felt that anything mattered in particular.'

Only one man survived in St Pierre – a drunkard called Siparis, imprisoned in a vault where neither the lava nor the incandescent ash nor the fumes could reach him. He spent the rest of his life as an exhibit in Barnum and Bailey's circus in America, supposedly as an example of the fickle nature of providence.

Today, no one can remember what was one of the world's greatest natural disasters, yet there is still a haunted feeling about the place. The rebuilding of the town has been haphazard. There are gaps in the main street, the rue Victor Hugo. Some of the new houses use one existing wall of whatever was there before. For some reason, the houses on the sea front have never been rebuilt, despite their pleasant situation. The crumbled bases of the old stone buildings sit there like empty eye-sockets.

There is a museum, a little reminiscent of the museum at Hiroshima. There are twisted bottles, a great pile of scissors fused together – from a barber's shop, I wondered? There are lumps of coins, even scorched coffee. And there is part of a tombstone, with an inscription in English, a relic of one of the British occupations of the island.

St Pierre is a forlorn place, appealing to our taste for the ghoulish, but also to the romantic side of our natures, as witness Patrick Leigh

Fermor's enchanting novel, *The Violins of Saint-Jacques*, inspired by this terrible eruption.

The people there are particularly friendly. Our car broke down and a passer-by went to find a mechanic, who fixed it. The charge was F.150 (£15). When I had only two one-hundred franc notes, the mechanic said: 'Oh no, if you've no change, let's call it one hundred.'

They seemed unaware or insouciant of any danger. The tourist brochures, written by the idiot inheritors of Mayor Fouché and the committee of experts, say that Mont Pelée is now quite safe.

How do they know? It could go up tomorrow.

Béké is the Creole name, originally for a white man, but now reserved for the old planter families. These families have, or had, romantic-sounding names: de Lucy de Fossarieu, de Jaham de Vertpré, Cacqueray de Valmenière, Villaret de Joyeuse. For the most part, they stick very much together, preserve their whiteness by avoiding marriage with anyone with even a hint of coloured blood and generally think – privately – in the style of the last century.

Guy de la Haussaye, whose family came to Martinique from Britanny in 1635, is a rather exceptional *Béké*, with more modern ideas than most. He is a large man with greying hair. He has a grand, impassive face and a distracted manner, which seem to contradict one another.

He is the chairman of an extremely luxurious hotel at Trois Ilets and also of the only hotel on Mustique. We sat on the terrace of his hotel and he discoursed upon the differences between Martinique and Guadeloupe.

'During the French Revolution, the old settlers in Guadeloupe were made shorter [by the guillotine], while they survived in Martinique and, as a result, we have a great mixture of white and black. Nobody knows how much of which anyone is. In Guadeloupe, the only whites are Europeans.' (Even Jacline accepts that Guy de la Haussaye is in no way racist.)

M. de la Haussaye dismissed any suggestion of Martinique's ever choosing independence. 'Point nought five per cent, perhaps, would vote for it – young people taught by Ghadaffi, the same as everywhere else.'

He believes that a French presence in the Caribbean is really valuable to France, 'particularly with all the talk of undersea riches.

98

'France behaved quite differently from Britain with her colonies. She began, in 1947, to invest in the islands, later making them a part of France itself. The result has been a guaranteed price for sugar. This, unfortunately, does not mean that the old plantations can survive. Even at Leyritz, where they have diversified, they are in difficulties. Banana protection has been quite insufficient for several years. The products simply do not fetch enough.

'Most of the old plantations have been sold off. Under law, any agricultural land must first be offered to a government organisation, who buy it at lowish prices, which they fix, and then sell it again at a subsidised rate to a potential smallholder.'

Land is worth about F.20,000 (£2,000) a hectare. As George Money had said on Barbados, only smallholders can really succeed.

'It must be a little family business. As in France, for every franc paid in wages, the employer must pay another sixty centimes in various taxes and insurances etcetera. Even little airlines can only work if they are family-run businesses.'

Monsieur Edmond, the President of the Bureau de Tourisme, was a perfect example of Guy de la Haussaye's point as to who knows what colour anyone is. He was a humorous man of seventy-eight, but I found his French very hard to understand, as his accent was very marked.

He talked first about the beauty of the girls. He maintained that the girls are so pretty because Martinique was the centre of the slave trade and so was able to keep the best-looking slaves, sending the rest to other islands.

'A thick-lipped person used to be known as a *noir Anglais*,' he said.

As with all officials, he was quite clear that Martinique was better off under France. He approved of the moves towards decentralisation, which gave the Martiniquais more control over their own affairs, but they needed the money. 'As Falstaff said, money is the leading soldier,' observed Monsieur Edmond.

'At the end of the Second World War, the Americans said that they must possess Fort-de-France by the end of the century, because it is the most important base in the Antilles. But they will not.

'There are problems here, but they are not too bad. The population is now static at 328,000. We have 36,000 unemployed, but it is not so terrible here as in France. It is warm, so you don't need so many clothes.

There is less need to eat and, in any event, food is easily available. One can catch fish. If one catches a lobster, one can sell it for a good price to a hotel. Very often it is a question of not wanting to work on the land. It is the usual thing. They say it is slaves' work, but that is just a pretext.

'We do have too many people. We have one million square kilometres, but only half those are cultivable. I think 200,000 would be about right. Do you know that more than one third of the population is in some form of scholastic establishment?'

I said that Martinique did not seem so crowded to me.

'What? With all these cars? There are about 200,000 cars. Every girl in the Tourist Bureau has a car. As an Arab loves his horse, so a Martiniquais loves his car. They go without anything in order to have a car. Please don't have an accident. Very often people are uninsured, because they can't afford the premium.'

On his particular subject, Monsieur Edmond was informative. Martinique had originally based its tourism on the higher end of the market.

'We went for four-star hotels. This was the wrong approach. This is a middle-class resort, so now we are encouraging two-star hotels. Most of our tourists are French but we get, say, three thousand Italians, two thousand Germans and two thousand English. Then three or four hundred cruise ships call in every year. They bring in $10,000,000.

Henri Theuvenin is another *Béké*, his family having come to Martinique in 1680. 'Before the British came to St Kitts,' he said proudly and erroneously. (Sir Thomas Warner arrived in St Kitts in 1623 and died there in 1648.) While we talked on his verandah, Hamish went to swim in the bay below his house. M. Theuvenin advised him to be careful.

'Two or three people are drowned there every year. They either swim out too far or are drunk.'

M. Theuvenin is a scholarly man, who marshals his facts in a most orderly fashion. He explained to me that there are four classes in Martinique – the *Békés*, who number about three thousand including children, the bourgeoisie, 'the lesser people and . . .' (he hesitated a moment, perhaps rejecting the word blacks), 'the agricultural people.'

He reiterated what Guy de la Haussaye and Monsieur Edmond had said about the difference between Martinique and Guadeloupe.

'Guadeloupe had second choice of everything that arrived. You can look at the blacks there and see how much darker they are. In addition, Victor Hugues slaughtered 1,200 militiamen who had served under the British.'

Victor Hugues was one of the most disagreeable figures of Caribbean history. Originally a baker in Marseilles, he became a trader in what is now Haiti. At the time of the Revolution he returned to France and was appointed public prosecutor in Brest. So vicious was he in this role that he was dispatched to Guadeloupe as Governor. He took with him a guillotine.

The British had taken advantage of the confusion which reigned on the French islands to seize them all. In most islands, there was little resistance. Guadeloupe had surrendered after a token fight in which the British lost only seventeen men.

When Hugues arrived to recapture the island, half the British troops were suffering from fever. Nonetheless, Hugues was outnumbered. He waited till the fever spread among the sickly troops. The British surrendered. Hugues guillotined all French royalists. He also butchered many British wounded and dug up the body of their commander, General Dundas, and flung it in the river.

'All the élite were wiped out. Those that were not executed left for Trinidad or other islands. There were only the lower class left. Even after the Revolution was over and slavery restored, few of the élite returned. The people had no capital, so it was people from Martinique who created the sugar factories, which made the people of Guadeloupe feel they were being colonised.'

Jacline and her friends had so impressed upon me their need to break away from France that I asked M. Theuvenin whether he thought that there was a separate Martiniquais culture.

'The Caribs left nothing. The slaves came from at least fifty different tribes. So we are a mixture of African and French, melted together; but it is a process that is still continuing.

'What you must never forget is that the black people were slaves, suppressed, with no rights of any sort. Now they have rights and they have education. So there is always anger, not hatred, in the background. They want to prove that they can do everything themselves.

'For example, they say, "We must find a way to transcribe Creole in such a way as to be as un-French as possible." This is absurd, because the base of Creole is nearly all French.

101

'The change in Martinique in the last twenty-five years is tremendous. Education, health, food – instead of a ninety per cent rural population, we have a new generation who need to understand things. In the thirties, there was no elegance among the people. Now the whole population is nicely dressed and they speak good French.'

M. Theuvenin is optimistic about the future.

'Probably we will have more autonomy in time, but we will not have revolution. Our situation is unlike those other examples. In New Caledonia, there is an indigenous people who were there before us. Here there is no indigenous population. In Algeria, there was a question of religion. Here there is no religion but Christianity.

'I tell pessimists that history shows that the settlers over the centuries have faced far worse difficulties than today. There were the attacks from the British. They assaulted Martinique nine times and occupied her four times. There were slave revolts. Sometimes they would poison whole families.

'I say that we are the same as the settlers who faced those challenges. We are not soft.'

This firm speech made me wonder whether he really thought that things were less cosy than he had suggested. It was not I who had mentioned revolution.

Hamish survived the undertow. Soon after leaving M. Theuvenin's house, which was on the south coast, we came level with Diamond Rock. This barren rock lies about a mile and a half off-shore. Like the Pitons, it is deceptive, looking quite small. Yet it is 600 feet tall and about a mile in circumference and is easily visible from St Lucia.

In 1803, the British admiral, Sir Samuel Hood, came to realise that French ships often evaded his cruisers by slipping behind this rock, heading for the harbour of Fort Royal (as Fort-de-France was then known). He stationed 120 sailors on the rock, which is accessible from only one, easily defended point on the lee-shore. He equipped them with five guns, which they hauled up onto the rock, the sailors 'hanging like clusters' and looking 'like mice hauling a little sausage.' The Admiralty christened this unlikely outpost HMS *Diamond Rock*. Naval records say that, under Lieutenant James Wilkie Maurice, 'they defied and harassed the French navy and merchant ships for seventeen consecutive months. Only when the powder kegs were empty did they surrender and then to a French squadron of two 75s, a frigate, a corvette, a schooner and eleven gunboats, which they had severely mauled before surrendering; wounding seventy men and sinking three gunboats. Their own total losses were two men killed and one wounded.'

French accounts of the end of this affair are rather different. Hearing that the provisions on the rock lacked the usual naval ration, the French set adrift, on a judicious current, a boat laden with large quantities of rum. This washed up against the Diamond Rock. When the British sailors had drunk their fill, Admiral Villaret de Joyeuse attacked, and won a resounding victory.

Much further round the coast, not far from where we had spent our first night, we turned down a road opposite a golf-course, went past the botanic garden, which was always shut, and came to La Pagerie, where the house in which the Empress Josephine was brought up, once stood. How different this approach was from that of Patrick Leigh Fermor forty years before: 'The rustic track from the village passed through acres of sugar cane that narrowed into a valley, and then rose and sank into the windless green hollow of La Pagerie.'

The wilderness that he records has been cleared away. Nothing remains of Josephine's house, nor did it then. But the rectangle of foundation stones, surrounding two beautiful Flame of the Forest trees, is neatly kept. Where the old sugar mill stood, there is a little gallery of prints. The ruins of the old refinery are tidy and clean. The old kitchen, which stands apart from the house, as they always stood for fear of fire, has been built up to house a museum.

It is well done, with portraits and letters and clothes. I noticed one pair of shoes, described as *Directoire* period. They were very pointed, with a pretty, rather modern design embroidered on the toes. The label inside them read Kelly and Company, manufacturers, No. 45 Fleet Street.

As I was ruminating upon these things, a sudden American voice pierced the calm, asking the guide, 'Did Josephine have syphilis as well as Napoleon?' Everyone laughed or stared in amazement. It was a bespectacled, buck-toothed girl, a 'College kid'.

'Well, it's important,' she said, in response to the stares. We all wondered why.

Having gone round the museum, we went to call on Dr Robert Rose-Rosette. Four days before, he had sold the museum and the site of three and a half hectares to the Conseil Regional. His first question to me was whether I had heard of Patrick Leigh Fermor, and he produced a copy of

The Traveller's Tree. Mysteriously, half the book had been torn out, but he showed me the passages which referred to himself.

'Rose-Rosette is in his early forties, tall and fine-looking, with a rich coffee complexion, and features notable for their regularity and strength.'

Those words, with the substitution of eighties for forties, apply perfectly today. One would never, in fact, guess that Dr Rose-Rosette was more than in his sixties, so spry and lively is he. His wife, all in white, looked to be in her forties.

I explained that I was an acquaintance of Patrick Leigh Fermor.

'In that case, you will want a *p'tit ponch*. I have never known anyone so fond of our national drink. When we made expeditions together, he would always spot a rum-shop and say, "What about a *p'tit ponch*?". We had great fun.'

While his wife made the drink, which is quite different from the British planters' punch, he explained the derivation of the word punch.

'It comes from the Indian word *panch*, meaning five – for the five ingredients.' His *ponch* seemed to have only three ingredients: rum, cane syrup and lime juice. I am not sure what the other two would have been, water perhaps, and nutmeg.

Dr Rose-Rosette bought about eighty acres of the La Pagerie estate in 1944. He was not rich, but he could not bear to see the place neglected, and so much history being devoured by the tropical forest. The original estate was nearly a thousand acres, much of it now being the golf-course with its black sand bunkers. It is hard to recapture what Leigh Fermor described as: 'the atmosphere that must have dominated the childhood of Josephine. For a kind of lovesick sloth, a heavy languishing drowsiness, prevails among the palms and the hibiscus and the mango trees.' The tourists have woken up all the ghosts. Against that, the doctor has preserved, single-handed, a large slice of the heritage of both France and Martinique, and has now handed it over to the nation.

We discussed the question of Josephine's birthplace, which had come up in St Lucia. He was not adamant on the point, but he thought it more likely that she had been born in Martinique, on the simple grounds that women prefer to have babies at home and near their own mothers. He attached little importance to the accuracy of the records kept in Martinique at the time.

'The Curé recorded Josephine's death in one entry when, in fact, it was one of her two younger sisters who had died at the age of thirteen.'

Josephine's father, Tascher de la Pagerie, was very fond of women and liked to escape to St Lucia where he could carry on affairs. The doctor thought that most of the stories of Josephine on St Lucia were doubtful, because she married her first husband, Beauharnais, when she was sixteen.

'Everybody wants her because she is so good for tourism. A man came from Guadeloupe, claiming she had been born there. Of course, he had no evidence. I found a Guadeloupian hero for him to promote and he went away satisfied.'

Dr Rose-Rosette demolished even more positively the old story of Josephine's going, as a child, with her cousin, Aimée du Bucq de Rivery, to consult an old negress fortune-teller, Euphimie David. To Josephine, she said, 'You will one day be an Empress.' To Aimée, she said, 'You will be more than an Empress.' When Aimée was about sixteen, she was returning to Martinique from France. The ship was driven by a storm into the Mediterranean. Corsairs seized the ship and delivered Aimée to the Bey of Tunis for his harem. He thought her so beautiful that he sent her, unharmed, to his overlord, the Sultan of Turkey. She was put into the Sultan's seraglio. Evidently, Aimée became his favourite and, after his death, she was known as the Sultana Valideh, the title given to the mothers of sultans. She was the mother of Sultan Mahmoud II. Lesley Blanch, the author of *The Wilder Shores of Love*, likes to believe that Aimée, behind the scenes, may have influenced Turkish foreign policy in Europe, especially in France, where her cousin was Empress.

The doctor pointed out that Aimée was thirteen years younger than Josephine and could not, therefore, have gone with her to the soothsayer.

This does not mean that Dr Rose-Rosette was without his fancies.

'I took a female writer to the site of Aimée's home on the other side of the island. She was insistent that we went there first, rather than to La Pagerie. She was stung by three bees. Napoleonic ones, of course. Josephine was offended by her going to Aimée's house first.'

The doctor bubbled with information and opinions and stories. The place-names round Mont Pelée – Megève, Chamonix and so on – were chosen by a Savoyard who bought 10,000 hectares for one franc a hectare after the second eruption of Mont Pelée. The egrets (which he said were not true egrets) arrived in Martinique forty years ago. At about the time of Leigh Fermor's visit, the doctor had told the government that they should concentrate on tourism. They had a meeting in Paris about it. They did nothing. Twenty years later they said, 'You remember that meeting in Paris? We only had it just to please you. We are sorry now – you were right.' That called for another *p'tit ponch*. Dr Rose-Rosette was probably the most civilised man that I met in all the islands.

We drove happily back through dramatic weather. The rainbows in Martinique were unlike any I had ever seen, sometimes flat and straight, like the side of a box. The clouds whirled in strange rushing formations. The sea glowed like burnished gunmetal under the grey of the sky.

My dialogue with Jacline continued at different times. Sometimes I would laugh at her when I thought she was overstating her case. I asked her about there being, according to Monsieur Edmond, so many cars.

'He didn't say it was because public transport is so bad; there is none at all on Sundays.'

One day, in the course of discussion, she said, 'I am a black woman.'

'But you're not, you have just as much white blood. And your culture is far more French than African.'

'That is true, but even in Paris, with friends, I can discuss things up to a certain point; then there is a shutter.'

'Surely with L.,' – I named the white friend we had in common, who had introduced us – 'you cannot feel a barrier.'

'No, not with her.' She added politely, 'Not with you either, but with Monsieur de la Houssaye I do feel it.'

'So what is it?'

'It is the oppression blacks suffer, I must identify with that.'

Jacline sent me to see Joby Bernabé, a poet, who is extremely popular in Martinique and now is becoming known in France. She thought he might help me to understand.

He was a striking figure, not very tall, quite fuzzy-haired with a narrow, spade beard like an ancient Egyptian. His power lay in his deep, gravelly voice and his flashing eyes.

His house was wooden. The room where we sat was painted mauve, blue and white. There was no conventional furniture. On the floor was a long mattress, covered with spangly cushions, like a gypsy caravan. In one corner was an old sewing machine, surrounded by large pebbles.

There was a mobile of a dove, with an olive branch in its beak. Also hanging on threads were some sausages, painted in different colours, one of them in gold. There was a Haitian-looking, naïve print and one perfectly traditional watercolour.

I liked him at once for his intensity and conviction. In his eagerness to explain, he was often difficult for me to understand, his accent being very strong.

'We are desperate for independence, which must come, to give us the opportunity to express what we are. It is not a question of being either more French or more African. It is that we are stifled because we are in a French context.

'Who can say what is Martiniquais? Traditionally this room would be full of heavy furniture. But look at it, this is in Martinique. I am Martiniquais.'

He felt frustrated by the social structure, it inhibited creativity, he said. Moreover, there were no art schools, no music schools. 'Under independence we would have the opportunity. Look at Jamaica,' he said. There is an art school there.

What he was saying, I thought, was what Monsieur Theuvenin had spoken of – a need to say we can do it ourselves. As he waxed more and more vigorous, almost ferocious, I thought to myself that M. Theuvenin doesn't know the half of it.

Joby resented deeply the provincial atmosphere in which he lives. 'Anybody who goes to France and it does not matter for how little time, when he comes back, he is labelled "International". It is pathetic.'

The problem for all of these islands is that they think of themselves as countries, when they have really the population of what we think of as joke countries – like Andorra, San Marino or Lichtenstein. That does not make the emotional predicament any less real.

Talking again for a last time with Jacline, I felt a mixture of respect and sorrow. She looked wonderful in a great billowing dress of Batique print, her hair in tight plaits round her head – both things, she said, unacceptable in smart society until very recently.

Perhaps because it was our last conversation and she wanted me to understand her as well as her beliefs, Jacline was mellower in her expression. Much as she longed for independence, she quite accepted that it might not come in her lifetime. Meanwhile, her choice lay between joining in the embourgeoisification of the island, as she had done with her hairdressing salon, and going mad with frustration, or dropping out. Her nature was too gentle for the third alternative – the violent protest of Guadeloupe. So she pursues her simpler life. She does not vote. She tries to teach her children values which have nothing to do with materialism.

When I left Martinique, I felt it had been a disappointment. Now, when I have just finished writing about it, I think I was wrong to be disappointed. I had been looking for something which was not there, something which, perhaps, was never there. Instead, I had, without realising it, learned much more than I had supposed. I had stretched my understanding. I had found real friends. Sometimes I play one of Joby's somewhat gloomy records. His gravel voice, speaking his incomprehensible patois, reminds me of them.

> Madanm lan pa te le fi-ya
> maye epi jenn gason-an
> pas i trouve jenn gason-an
> te ni an ti lapo two nwe
> tak two konngo ba jenn fill-ya

> (La dame ne voulait pas marier sa fille
> à un jeune homme du village.
> Elle lui trouvait la peau trop sombre
> bien trop congo pour sa donzelle.)

9

Dominica

THE PARADISE OF WATER

Everyone said that we must not, on any account, fly to Melville Hall, the old airport on the north-east coast of Dominica. The road from there to Roseau, the capital, on the south-west coast, was appalling. It would take five hours to cover the twenty or twenty-five miles across the island. For some reason or other, we took the flight to Melville Hall.

We flew up the windward coast of Martinique. Although we had driven over almost every square mile, I was surprised to see how much sugar-cane was growing. Then how many acres of pineapples. These seemed to me somehow inappropriate. Mont Pelée lay to our left – asleep, but with one eye half open, according to an expert, biding its time.

Dominica loomed ahead, dark and hung with grey cloud. As we came close, the island appeared to rise straight out of the sea. There were steep valleys with clustered settlements running down to the coast. With the dense vegetation, it was hard to see how anyone could get from one valley to the next. The roads, I supposed, were concealed by the trees. There were no beaches to be seen. The island was surrounded by a ring of white foam. We flew along this inimical coast until, coming to a wide river, we swept into a valley and landed.

Almost at once I fell in love with this island. The airport building was a scrubby little affair. A child's drawing said: 'No Smoking'. The immigration officer and the woman customs officer were polite and welcoming and smartly dressed in crisp white shirts. Hamish had to buy a driving licence for $11.10, but there was no car to hire on this side of the island. The taxi proved to be a red pick-up van, with few overt springs. I looked forward to five bumpy hours with some apprehension.

We set off on a road of exceptional smoothness, as good as anything we had found anywhere. We crossed the wide river we had seen from the air and came soon to Marigot. There is a Marigot on almost every island. The word is rather obscure, meaning quite simply a place where the stream flows into the sea.

There are many words of this sort which have greater importance in the Caribbean than in their country of origin. Every bay from Grenada to St Martin is called *anse*, which in France mostly refers to the handle of a cup or basket. The common word for a mountain is *morne*, but this derives from a Spanish word *moro* and is unknown in France (except as an adjective, of quite different derivation, meaning dejected or gloomy).

This Marigot, though we did not know it at the time, uses a rather different English from the rest of the island, the people having been brought at some point from Antigua. They do not even understand patois. The town looked sleepy. A few people hung about. They waved and smiled as we passed.

After the town, the road climbed abruptly and we were immediately in some of the most dramatic scenery we had so far encountered. Below us, to the left, was the wave-battered shore. Above us, steep hillsides curtained in green. The road threaded its way through dense vegetation. Even the coconut groves, which we had hardly seen since St Vincent, were thickly undergrown. The fern trees stood out and the pale undersides of what I thought was a kind of breadfruit tree, but was actually *cecropia*, a tree which grows often where another one has fallen. From a distance the pale underside to its leaves often look like huge white flowers. The day was warm and humid. Every so often, there would be a brief shower, and there was a lethargic sweetness in the air.

A few miles further on, I was aware first of a subtle change in the construction of the huts, then of the land round the huts. The houses were on higher stilts and there were attempts at gardens with cultivated flowers. Then I saw a complete change in the people. We were driving through the Carib territory, the Reserve of which Keith Baptiste on St

Vincent had spoken with such envy. These Caribs are supposed to be of purer stock than the 'black' Caribs of St Vincent, but they looked much the same with their broad, high-cheeked faces and long, black hair. Twenty minutes later we were back among African faces.

We left the coast and started to climb up through real rain forest. I peered about to see if I could see one or other of the two parrots peculiar to the island – the sisserou, which is used as the supports for the coat of arms of the Commonwealth of Dominica and appears on the flag, and the Dominican parrot. As we climbed we could see little, the rain dripping from the tall forest trees.

Some schoolboys waved us down. The driver slowed a bit and pumped furiously on the brakes, which did not work well. The boys hopped on the back. Two or three miles later they whistled. The driver stopped. The boys came round to the front and said in precise tones, which might have belonged to English public-schoolboys, 'Thank you very much.'

The other passenger in the pick-up was a businessman. He was returning from Cuba, where he had a married sister.

'I love Cuba – especially the shops for foreigners. They are cheaper than Panama even.'

When we started to go down to the coast, the rain poured in earnest. Dominica has anything up to two hundred inches of rain per annum. It is a damp island, gratefully off-putting to tourist hordes. Already these people had told me that Dominica has 365 rivers, 'one for each day of the year'. We came down into a ravine where a river flowed, wide enough to be on a continent. All this way the road was perfect. It had recently been rebuilt by the Canadians. Other stretches had been done by Britain, still others by the United States, so that Dominica has some of the best roads in the West Indies. Such is the eternal misinformation of travel.

I was much struck by the generosity of Canada to the islands and was surprised to see a Bank of Nova Scotia on every single island. Apparently, during the Second World War, when traffic across the Atlantic was impossible, many West Indians, unable to reach European universities, went to Canada to study. The connection and resulting friendship has survived.

The whole journey to Roseau took barely an hour and a half. After Fort-de-France, it looked tiny. It was not just that the population was small – everything seemed to be on a miniature scale. The only large building housed the Government Offices. All the others were very small, an effect emphasised by the fact that hardly any building was connected to the next. The buildings were mostly wooden, many of them pretty.

The taxidriver took us to a car-hire place where a wonderfully dapper 'Syrian', called Albert Astaphan, said he could let us have a car in the morning. He recommended us to stay in a hotel called Reigate Hall. Its name didn't sound promising, I thought. The taxidriver had not heard of it. So we went to look at several others. They were dismal. Then we got a puncture. The taxidriver, reasonably enough, grew fed up with my dithering. So I decided to go to Reigate Hall. There never was so twisty a road. The driver sighed at each hairpin bend. Eventually we reached it. An untidy-looking man with a shock of curly hair was wandering vaguely about. He turned out to be the owner, a Welshman. He said he had a room. Rather than enrage the taxidriver further, I took it. (The taxidriver asked for an outrageous sum and beamed happily when I gave him far less.) It was a happy decision, because the hotel was to become very much part of our lives.

Gordon Harris, the owner, was a most unexpected character. He had made a lot of money out of property dealing in Britain and had come to Dominica for a holiday. He decided to stay. He bought this property, way up on the hillside, and turned it into a hotel. It was hard to make out what the original house consisted of, for he had built on so much. The dining-room was a lofty Scandinavian-looking affair with a vast waterwheel in it. The bar had a penny-farthing theme to it for no logical reason that I could see. The bedrooms were luxurious, lacking only some feminine touch to make them pretty. Mine hung over a ravine filled with lush plants and trees. The views over the valley to the sea were superb.

Usually, it rained in the morning. Sometimes one could see a perfect circle of a rainbow, hovering like a saint's halo over Roseau. One could watch little storms move like grey, gossamer tubes over the otherwise sunlit sea beyond, or gaze at the rusty, hollowed hull of an old freighter, now filled to the brim with water from the 365 rivers, being towed by a tug to Guadeloupe, or even Antigua, to supply those less rainy islands with water, an inexpensive product, bringing in a decent revenue.

In the evening, when it was usually clear, one could sit by the pool and watch the sunset, hoping to see the green flash made famous by Herman Wouk in his novel about the Caribbean, *Don't Stop the Carnival*. The green flash is supposed to be a phenomenon visible occasionally at the last second as the sun sinks over the horizon. It is caused, according to one theory, by the sun, as a result of the curvature of the earth, shining through the water for that brief moment when a line from your eye to it would pass through the surface of the sea. Another view has it that it is occasioned by the refraction of beams of light as the sun disappears, so that the green band is isolated in the last flash (or some such). I never saw it. Hamish claimed to have done so on another island, but by then he was in love.

The hotel staff were all local boys, who must have been drilled by Gordon with regimental precision. Every one of them was meticulous in his work. Stephen, the headwaiter, always carried a green napkin over his arm. If it slipped, even for a moment, he was mortified. The wine waiter used to go through a ritual, when he brought a bottle, which would have dazzled a *sommelier* in a three-star restaurant in France. On arriving at one's table, there was an array of cutlery, perhaps eight implements on either side of the plate. When one had ordered, the waiter took away anything not needed from the serried ranks. When I asked Gordon where the waiters had learned this peculiar system, he looked at me with some pity and told me that it was customary in really smart restaurants.

Our room was always neat beyond the dreams of an anal obsessive, every piece of clothing folded with scrupulous care, every toothbrush and bottle of aftershave laid out in lines.

The reverse side of this fanatical attention to detail was a delightful informality. The staff, after dinner, would mingle with the guests. They became our friends and would join us on expeditions, filling our minds with reams of unlikely information. I remember the first night, Peter, one of the waiters, told me that the Caribs build their houses on high stilts because they believe it keeps ghosts away. What about termites, I suggested? Termites can climb stilts, he said. This was true, but they can be detected and discouraged. Anyhow, Peter seemed not to have noticed that most Dominican houses are on stilts or at least stone blocks. That night was the last for Gordon's mother, who was going home to England. It was also Geoffrey, the barman's, birthday. The party went on till four in the morning.

Reigate Hall, although it had been open only a short time, had become the centre of social life in Dominica. We would see the President entertaining his guests there. Often, the serious-looking Taiwanese ambassador would dine there and almost every evening, a

113

particularly vulgar and rather drunken South American ambassador would swill away at the bar with his latest scrubber.

In the morning, Albert Astaphan brought us a car, a terrible thing with sticky seats which were disagreeable in the humid climate. (Later on, he obligingly changed it for a better model.) He wanted to test Hamish's driving and asked us to take him back into Roseau. When he got out, he said to Hamish, 'Please be using a little more first and second gear. And when you see someone on the road, give a friendly toot. Then people can step aside and turn round to smile.'

Roseau felt like a country village. Even the bank could not find any East Caribbean $100 notes, but gave me the rather large sum I needed all in $20 notes, the sign of a wretchedly poor country. Everyone was, without exception, friendly. There were two bookshops in town, which was a comfort as we had run out of things to read. The better of the two gave a bizarre picture of the reading tastes and needs of the Dominicans. There were lots of books of advice: *How to Write Letters*, *How to Win Friends and Influence People*, *How to be a Best Man*; this last was amazingly thick for so slender a role. There were many guides to spelling, many copies of *Roget's Thesaurus* in paperback, and shelf after shelf of medical textbooks. Do all Dominicans want to be doctors or are they a nation of hypochondriacs? Neither explanation seemed probable.

Apart from those, the greater part were torrid romances. Nonetheless, after a long search, I left with books by Alan Sillitoe, Michael Foot, Erskine Caldwell, Truman Capote and, most unexpectedly, Pär Lagerqvist's *Barabbas*.

No expedition was likely to take very long, so we were soon able to know the island quite well. There is a Caribbean joke that, if Columbus were to come back to Dominica, he would find that it hadn't changed since his day. It is true that this island was far wilder, and in its wildness more beautiful, than any of the other islands. Nevertheless, its history was evident in all manner of ways.

The earliest known occupiers of Dominica were the Arawaks – according to tradition, a gentle people, although recent research suggests that they were more warlike than was previously supposed. They were destroyed by the Caribs, whose custom it was to kill the men among their enemies and eat them, and to enslave the women and children.

George, the security guard in the hotel, offered to take us to meet the Carib Chief. George was an interesting man of great charm and helpfulness. He was tall, not very dark and with a pleasant, round face and a cast of features quite common in Dominica. Often I would see someone and think for a moment it was George. He had started life as a meat-cutter (how this differed from a butcher, I never managed to establish), but had gone to Antigua on a course to learn about fishery. He learned about marine ecology and what was called 'sea survival'. 'I was the only one to get a distinction in sea survival.' His ambition now was to work on a yacht.

George had a great capacity for enjoyment and a vivid turn of phrase. When he arrived to take us to the Caribs, we were still having breakfast.

'No hurry, no problem. It is good to eat a large breakfast. You make a little museum of energy inside you for the day.'

As we drove, George kept up a steady flow of information and opinion. He told us that Dominicans still dance the quadrille. There are four variations – 'sharp', 'French', 'Irish' and 'slow'. He expounded his views on homosexuals.

'There are lots of them in Dominica. Some look like me, but others walk and talk like women. It is an odd world. I think the Creator will do something about it. Maybe He even has already.'

I asked if he were religious.

'No . . . Yes. I believe in God and so on.'

Then the conversation turned to Hurricane David, which swept across the southern end of Dominica on 29 August 1979. It was an experience no one can ever forget and I listened to so many accounts of that day that I came to realise – what one could not really have imagined – that an event of that magnitude leaves a scar on the psyche of a whole population.

'It was the most frightening thing of my whole life,' said George. 'The whole house trembled for hours and hours. It was dangerous, crazy to look out of the window, but when it never stopped, I looked and saw sheets of iron, big, big sheets, flying like paper. It went on so long. A woman was praying. She said, "I have been praying for such a time, but God can't be fucking listening".'

We drove along the same road on which we had come from the airport. Now it was sunny and beautifully sharp with that special light that rain gives to the forest air. We stopped at the Emerald Pool, where a waterfall tumbled through a tangle of lianas into brilliant, clear, deep water. Hamish and George swam.

The Carib Reserve was set up in 1903 by an enlightened administrator, Hesketh Bell. It covered 3,700 acres on the windward shore. At the time, there were said to be 400 or 500 pure-bred Caribs. Now it is impossible to say who is pure-bred and who is not, because

115

there has been much mixing of races over the centuries and even more recently. There are about 2,300 people living on the Reserve, which the Caribs prefer to call their 'territory'.

It was in some ways a curious decision to put the Caribs on the windward shore, because they were originally more concerned with fishing than with agriculture. However, they had been allotted a small patch of little more than 200 acres in the eighteenth century, when the British divided the island into lots for sale. (According to dubious legend, this was done to make up to George III for having been brought no dowry by Queen Charlotte. The value of all the lots was put at £313,666 19s. 2¼d.) So it was logical to extend what they already had. The Carib Chief was given a mace and an embroidered sash and £6 a year. His was an hereditary office. In the thirties there was trouble, because the Chief was involved in a smuggling racket. The Governor took away his mace and sash, forbade him to call himself 'king' and deposed him from any official standing. The position of Chief was not restored until 1952, when the post was made part of the local government system, with an elected council whose chairman was styled 'Chief'. Since 1978, it has been an elective post, with elections every three years.

Once more, I was struck by the neatly tended gardens and a tidier air to the Reserve than prevails elsewhere. It is a peaceful place. The houses are built on higher stilts, (*pace* Peter) because the Caribs like to hang produce under them to dry. They are rectangular in shape, whereas the Arawaks built circular houses. Near the beginning of the Reserve, there is a handicraft shop, selling mostly things woven from reeds and bamboo.

I met first Hilary Frederick, who was elected Chief from 1979 till 1984. He is a young man in his late twenties. There is a tendency to elect quite young Chiefs, possibly because the young men have been better educated than their elders. Now no longer Chief, he is one of only two opposition MPs in the House of Assembly, 'left-wing but not at all extreme,' he said. Hilary is handsome, with short, straight hair. He suffers from a serious stammer. I talked to him in his parents' house. His father and mother looked to be very pure Carib. The father was very proud of Hilary and encouraged us to talk while he listened. 'My senses have gone,' he said, and so they had a bit.

It was at once apparent that Hilary was much aggrieved at the treatment that he felt the Caribs receive from the Government. As is the way with minorities, he believed that their problems were the result of a conspiracy. When we talked of the hereditary principle, he said he thought that the

116

deposition of the Chief in the thirties was just a trick to reduce his power. That Chief's sons had just faded away. He felt that a hereditary ruler must be more powerful than an elected one. He would not or could not understand that it was impossible to have hereditary officials, with real powers rather than a merely ceremonial function, within a democratic system.

His complaints, however, did have some substance. There is no electricity in the Reserve, although many really remote villages did have power. There was a public telephone, but it had a vandalised look. There is no Carib teacher, nor any Carib doctor, though there are now sixty children in high school. Hilary maintained that the Caribs were not allowed to raise funds independently abroad. He wanted to create a fairly modest complex to attract tourists – a hotel with perhaps eight or a dozen rooms, a restaurant, a craft centre and a place where his people could put on displays of dancing. The hotel, he thought, could be very simple, perhaps having hammocks (the word was originally Arawak) instead of beds. They do have a new meeting hall paid for by the American Save the Children Fund. Hilary thought he could easily raise the money for his complex in America, perhaps from richer fellow Amerindians, or in France.

He talked a great deal about identity and was very eager to learn anything I could tell him about the Caribs on St Vincent. Moreover, he was keen to preserve the purity of his own people. 'For instance, we must teach girls not to be seduced by outsiders, who have the comforts that we don't have, like refrigerators.'

It is an unwritten custom that a Carib man may bring a black girl to live with him in the Reserve, but a Carib girl who marries a black man must leave.

Hilary did not get re-elected after his five-year term. There was some muddle about the Carib funds. The new Chief, who is also in his early twenties, is a serious young man, called Irvince Aguiste. He, too, felt that the Caribs were underprivileged in many ways and again felt it was a conspiracy on the part of the government. Above all, he was convinced that the Reserve was originally bigger than it is now.

'I have asked to see the original document, but all they will show us is a copy. How do we know if it is genuine? Our old people remember that the boundaries were set much further north and much further south.' I promised to look into the question with the Public Records Office in England.

117

I asked him whether he thought of himself first as a Carib or a Dominican. 'A Carib-Dominican,' he said with some ambiguity. 'We were here first, but we are all here to stay. All we are asking for is a little more respect.' It was interesting, I thought, that he had chosen precisely the same word that Joby Bernabé had so often emphasised to me in Martinique.

It is the everlasting story of separate cultures sharing the same place. Each side torments the other. The Caribs jeer at the blacks, calling them niggers, saying, 'We were never slaves.' The blacks mock the Caribs, calling them *Kwaib Malsauva* (evil savage), saying, 'You were cannibals.'

There is no doubt that the Caribs have a great appeal to the British – rather like the Masai or the Zulus or the Pathans or the Tuareg. They are people of courage and independence and style. In Dominica, they have a reputation for unreliability which is really another manifestation of their independence. They are easily hurt, but in modern times they cannot give expression to their warrior inclinations. They do not protest or argue or fight, they just go away. If they are working for someone who offends them they will often abandon several days' pay rather than submit. I felt much sorrier for them than I had for the intellectuals of Martinique.

When I got back to England, I consulted with the Public Records Office to see whether I could find out the area of land given to the Caribs in 1903. They gave me a photostat of the original plan which accompanied Hesketh Bell's report of 29 July 1902. Alas for Irvince Aguiste, it appears to correspond exactly to the lands they hold today.

On many of our trips, we would have to drive through Massacre, a rather gloomy village on the leeward coast, where a man once shouted 'Good riddance,' as we passed. The name of the village derives from a sad story.

Father du Tertre, one of the early French missionaries who travelled the islands, wrote that Sir Thomas Warner, the Governor of St Kitts, 'had a son by a Carib slave woman of Dominica. He recognised him as his own, he saw to it that he carried his name and saw to his education in his own house together with his other children . . . [the boy's] hair was jet black . . . his height was below average but there was a fine proportion among all his limbs. He had an oval face and a large forehead with an aquiline nose and his eyes were shining and bright – not slit. There was a gravity on his face that bespoke the temper of his daring character . . .'

One likes the boy at once. He was known as Indian Warner, but his happy homelife did not continue after he was eighteen. Sir Thomas died in 1648 and, without his protection, the boy was treated harshly by Lady Warner, though his brother Philip was said to be fond of him. His own mother, whom Père Labat met in 1700 as an old woman called Madame Ouvernard (a corruption, presumably, of Warner), had returned to Dominica. He joined her there and was readily accepted by her people. They made him their Chief. At the same time, Lord Francis Willoughby, the 'Governor of British Possessions in the Caribbee', anxious to placate the largely hostile Caribs, made him Deputy Governor of Dominica.

Indian Warner was undoubtedly loyal to the British. In 1664, he joined with them in an attack on the French in St Lucia, taking with him 600 Carib warriors in seventeen grand war canoes. Later, he was captured by the French, was imprisoned for two years in wretched conditions, and released after a peace treaty between Britain and France.

Not all Governors were as sagacious and diplomatic as Lord Francis. The more usual approach to the Caribs was to kill them. Sir William Stapleton, who became Governor of the Leeward Islands in 1672, belonged to this school of thought. Without apparently consulting his superior in Barbados – a man of more temperate ways – Stapleton despatched six small companies of foot to Dominica to avenge an attack on Antigua by Caribs from the windward coast, who were half allied to the French. The troops were to 'put down the Caribs and be revenged on those heathens for their bloody and perfidious villanies.' In command he put Colonel Philip Warner, Indian Warner's half-brother.

What happened next depends on whose account you choose to believe. A rather garbled British version says that Indian Warner joined his half-brother in a victorious battle with the pro-French Caribs of the windward coast. After the battle, they returned to anchor at the mouth of the Layou River. There they celebrated. The party ended in a drunken brawl. In the fight, someone killed Indian Warner. The Caribs tried to avenge his death by attacking the English. Certainly, the English sailed down to the Carib settlement and there butchered the Indians. Stapleton admitted that eighty Caribs were killed and others made prisoner. Their stores were destroyed and their canoes taken.

The French account, taken from the Captain of one of the British ships, was rougher. Philip Warner and his men went to his brother's settlement. They provided quantities of brandy for a feast. When the Caribs were thoroughly drunk, the British murdered them all. The signal for the start of the massacre was simple and clear. Philip Warner stabbed his own half-brother.

The authorities took the more severe view. Philip was held in the Tower of London for two years and then tried in Barbados, but acquitted. He was nonetheless sacked as Deputy Governor of Antigua and barred from any 'employment of trust in His Majesty's Service.'

In true colonial style, the Antiguans promptly elected him Speaker of the House of Assembly.

The names on gravestones, or less romantically in the telephone book, were like poems: Mary Prosper, Cleopatra Pemberton, Euraline Tele-macque, Baptiste Hamlet, Cletus Jeremiah, Dullabella Laraine, Molande Hypolite, Eustace Hyancinth, Vyleen Jno-Charles.

When I went to find the uncle of a friend in England, I told him my name and he said promptly, 'Jones Bernard, Roseau, Dominica.' Perhaps it was his Carib grandmother who gave him his independent spirit, for he chose to live on the very crest of a hill at the furthest end of a long, steep track, the last part quite inaccessible to any vehicle. The crest was actually the next one to Reigate Hall, across the deep, wide valley in which Roseau lay.

'I like to be alone with my family. And diseases don't come up here.' Jones, better known as Jack, as 'the deads' would say, farmed about a hundred acres of this precipitous but fertile land, growing bananas and mangoes, some citrus and other incidental crops. He had his own water, which he collected in three cisterns and, he said, he had paid for the electricity to come four years ago, but it must have been longer ago, because he had had a television set before Hurricane David.

'I don't trust the new TV. I liked my old one, black and white. After Hurricane David, I washed it and it worked. Those old TVs were tough.'

They must indeed have been tough. Hurricane David had taken away half of Jack's house. Where we sat talking had once been his living room. Now it was just a concrete slab with only three round pillars standing. With Caribbean practicality, his daughter Jocelyn had strung a washing line between the pillars. Gaily-coloured sheets and clothes flapped beside us in the trade winds.

Jocelyn was in her twenties, about the same age as her cousin in London, who was a successful television actress. Jack did not seem particularly interested in his niece and I had to explain more than once which of his brothers was her father. Jocelyn, on the other hand, was intrigued and wanted to know all about her cousin's life. They had a look of each other, the cousins, or so I liked to imagine. But the contrast in their lives was hard to encompass. Jocelyn had four children and worked some of the time in a hotel which never had any guests. She was both dignified and humorous, but her life was very circumscribed, though I thought I would choose it in preference to her cousin's.

Jack, in his reserved way, gave a most vivid account of the horror of Hurricane David. There was no warning of its coming. At nine o'clock in the morning, it hit Dominica. The winds roared in at 150 miles an hour. Jack's house, being on the crest, was exposed to the full blast.

'I lay lower down the hill in another place, near the donkey. We lay together, flat as we could.'

The hurricane blew for six hours. Jack's son lost his hand. In all, thirty-seven people died and 5,000 were injured. Three-quarters of the population were made homeless. There was no electric power, no mains water. The only link with the outside world was the radio of a ham called Fred White, which worked on batteries.

Jack, along with everyone else, lost all his crops and most of his trees. Gradually, he built them up again. But not everyone was so philosophical. 'Many saw the work of their lifetime knocked out in a few hours. They had worked twenty-five years to make a fine thing. It was gone. They think, they can't start all over again. Many just give up and die.'

We sat on as the sun sank lower over the sea, spreading a lambent glow over the valleys below us. The sea was still and smooth. The sky was speckled pink with a few half-formed clouds. The frogs were beginning to call. The humming-birds, as they always did just before sunset, trembled from bloom to bloom of the red bellflower growing over the concrete slab, determined to have one last sip of nectar. A grey bird, which the locals call Pipiris, sat on a wire, darting down to snap up an evening insect, then returning to its perch. It was hard to imagine how this peace could ever be shattered.

Another day, we drove over the mountains to Grand Bay on the windward coast in the south. On the way, we passed high cliffs. Almost to the base of them, the farmers had clawed out banana groves. Everywhere were scattered the hideous, blue plastic bags, which are put round the clusters of bananas – the Caribbean equivalent of those

121

hideous, blue fertiliser bags which litter the English landscape. Below the bananas were coconuts. They, too, often clung to steep banks, growing first outwards, then turning upwards, so they look like the necks of camels. In the villages we went through, the people spread Kush-kush grass on the road to dry. This grass is known locally as Verti-vert and is used for weaving mats. The heat of the tarmac and the weight of car wheels, which crush the hard stems at the base, makes the grass easier to weave. Until I learned this, I used to abuse Hamish for lack of consideration if he drove over the grass. Roads all over the Caribbean are used for drying grains, beans and other produce.

Grand Bay is a long, straggly village that goes down to what would be a pretty beach, if anyone kept it clean. Near the water is a huge church, with five gabled chapels on either side, each with a vast gargoyle. Most of these have, unfortunately, lost their heads. The apse has a shingle roof, which shows one how much more distinguished so many of the buildings of the Caribbean would be if they had shingles instead of the more practical and economical corrugated iron. The church looked Victorian, but I was told that it was eighteenth century. Above it is a high, square tower with five windows, one above the other and, in the top window, a figure of Christ. I took this to be the tower of an earlier church, but learned that it was built as a *campanile*, so that the bells could be heard beyond the hill which divides the village from two important plantations – Geneva and Stowe.

The church was, presumably, built by the wicked Jesuit, Father Antoine La Valette, who first came to Dominica to bless the huge ten-foot stone cross which stands in the cemetery. The *Belle Croix* had been put up by Jeannot Rolle, a coloured planter from Martinique, who was later buried at its foot. La Valette saw the potential of Dominica and acquired the estate now known as Geneva.

La Valette was an ingenious rascal, going to any lengths to acquire a fortune. To stock his estate with slaves (a thing which never troubled the Church), he travelled to Barbados, disguised as a buccaneer, and there bought 200 at the cheaper rate prevailing in Bridgetown. He planted coffee, cacao, indigo and tea, and was soon on his way to making a fortune. He was also running estates in Martinique. By 1753, he had become Superior General of the Mission in Martinique, and Apostolic Prefect.

The crafty Father's spiritual successes were matched, for a while, by his temporal ones. However, he over-reached himself, and after one inquiry by the French Minister of the Marine, which he wriggled out of, his luck changed. Hurricanes flattened his crops; pirates captured his

122

goods; disease killed his slaves. His debts piled up. Once again, he was summoned to France. The Jesuits in Rome refused to pay La Valette's debts. France ordered all Jesuit property in the West Indies and Canada to be sold and they banned the order in France.

The Geneva estate was sold and survived until this century as one of only four plantations of more than 1,000 acres on the island. The plantations on Dominica were broken up earlier than on other islands. We wandered through the coconut groves, past the burnt-out ruins of the old house and the copra factory and worksheds. A river ran through the estate, down to the sea which, in the bay, was calmer than usual on a windward coast. I could think of few pleasanter places in the world. How could such sad decay have come about?

It seems that forty years ago the owners had taken little interest in the management of the estate. The villagers of Grand Bay had come to regard it as their right to use the land. Then Mr Elias Nassief, who belonged to one of the two most powerful 'Syrian' families (the others were the Astaphans), bought the property and kicked off the squatters. Resentment smouldered for twenty-five years. Then, when Dominica was suffering from riots and violence, a gang, led by a ringleader with the unlikely name of Unicef, burnt Geneva House, the factory and Nassief's store in Roseau.

Now the Government owns the land, which has mostly been divided into smallholdings.

Geoffrey, the barman at Reigate Hall, was a perky fellow, not yet thirty, with a great sense of humour and a wonderfully high opinion of his charms – by no means altogether misplaced. Most of all, he thought he was a success with girls. When chatting up a girl in the street, he would call to a passing friend, 'I'll see you in the office in the morning,' adding, after a pause for that to sink in, 'Tell them I'll be late, I have that New York business to deal with.'

Again, Geoffrey's estimation of himself as a lover may not have been too exaggerated, for he claimed to have three or four children, scattered around the place. One day he took us to see one of them, an enchanting little girl called Marika who greeted Geoffrey with great excitement. It was interesting that Geoffrey had difficulty understanding her. She had been away in Martinique for some time and her patois had been much affected. He took us, also, to see the enormous bed he and his brother,

Paquette, who was a carpenter, were making for their mother. She had been in Canada for five years. George regarded this bed rather cynically, in the same way that he looked very doubtful at Geoffrey's story of how his father died of pneumonia while being trained as a gallant commando in the bush.

'They are only making the bed to please her in case she turns them out of the house,' said George.

Geoffrey had filled us with stories of how he knew some Dreads, who lived naked in the bush. We would have to be very careful and discreet, and he would take us to visit them in their lair.

In fact the Dreads would have been no laughing matter, had they existed. At the time of the Black Power movement, there was a strong anti-tourist campaign by young people, there being very few local whites to attack. From this there developed lawless gangs who took to the hills. Because they affected the dreadlocks of the Rastafarians, they became known as Dreads. They took to murder, under their leader Leroy Ettiene, who was known as Pokosion. Their depredations and killings rumbled on through the seventies. Pokosion was eventually caught but, while he was awaiting trial, Hurricane David ripped open the prison and he escaped again to the hills.

In 1981, after a clash with the police in which two Dreads were killed, Pokosion, with seven other Dreads, raided the house of Mr Ted Honychurch, the president of a co-operative which ran a shop they had ransacked. Mr Honychurch's son Lennox was the Government Press Secretary at the time. The Dreads believed that Honychurch was somehow responsible for the death of their colleagues.

They behaved with manic brutality. First, they killed his dog and his parrot. Next, they set fire to his house. They then marched him, his wife and their cook and gardener through the forest to their hideout in a lost valley. Later, they sent his wife, the cook and the gardener with a letter to the authorities demanding the release of two murderers and an inquiry into the deaths of their colleagues that morning. That night, Mr Honychurch tried to escape and killed one of his captors. In return, they shot him and burned his body.

All this involved, as we shall see later, an attempt to overthrow the elected Government.

We did not believe that Geoffrey had any contact with any surviving Dreads, but we thought we would call his bluff. He prevaricated for a day or two, but eventually fixed a day to meet them. Of course, we did not go up into the mountains, but drove straight to Grand Bay. At least Geoffrey could explain to us why there were so many pairs of old shoes hanging from the telephone wires. Evidently, while Grand Bay is very old-fashioned in its ways of cookery, mat-making and other traditional crafts, in politics it is profoundly radical. Shoes over the wires were a symbol of the Labour Party.

We crossed the deep storm gutters at the side of the main street and went a few yards down an alleyway. George had said, caustically, that any Dread Geoffrey knew would be just what he called a society Dread; which was to say someone who liked to be thought of as wicked, but who never did anything wrong except puff a little marijuana.

In the end, the man turned out to be a perfectly harmless Rastafarian. He called himself Ras Jomu, although his real name was Joel Lapierre. He led us to his 'office'. This was a small, bare room with a few shelves on which there were bottles and jars. The labels that I could see read: 'Combination Oil', 'Arthritis', 'Pimples'. There was also a book called *Here is the Healer*.

Ras Jomu did not wait for any preliminaries, for which I was grateful. He would have been much offended, it turned out, if I had thought he was a Dread. He wandered round the room, gesticulating and pontificating. Hamish sat on the floor on a cushion, with a rather enfeebled-looking man, who would every so often put one foot behind his head for no particular reason.

Jomu said, 'It's nature's medicine, man, herbal remedies.' He grabbed my hand and rubbed some coconut oil into the back of it.

'There, you see,' he said, as if some point had been proved. He started to tell us of a show he was going to put on, partly to celebrate his birthday. It was not clear what sort of show it was to be but, he said, it was sure to astonish us, for we were all invited. As he spoke, his head whipped from side to side and some dreadlocks fell from beneath his cap. His beard, too, had curls in it like incipient dreadlocks. Apart from his large cap, he wore a T-shirt and baggy, woollen trousers.

His show, he said, was also a kind of protest about how nothing was done for culture on the island. 'The government doesn't care.' He quite dismissed any idea about shortage of money. 'Of course there is money, man.' When I mentioned the Canefield art centre which has a gallery, he put on a glazed look, as if he did not know what a gallery was.

Eventually, I asked whether the Rastafarians had any connection with the Dreads.

125

'Dread means dread – what you fear. Maybe Reagan is a Dread. You don't need dreadlocks. Dreads were just people. People are good or evil. You could be a Dread, man. Frightening people, killing people, those are Dreads. You don't have to take off all your clothes and live in the bush to be a Dread. Then they think everyone is a Dread and give us a hard time.'

When Jomu got excited, which was a lot of the time, his voice rose with the chant of oratory. He was a born speaker, with the unstoppable quality of a rabble-rouser. I asked if he were interested in politics.

'I am not that, man. I am not aligned. I have to be on no man's side, man. Just be for justice, equality and love. I must go straight down the middle, for if I am on one side, I am against the other side.'

His friend on the floor put his foot behind his head.

Jomu calmed down and we talked about tourism, because he said he did not want the island ruined, as he believed in 'natural' things. I tried to tell him about cultural life in Martinique and he grew fierce, saying how lucky they were; but when I pointed out that they, too, complained of the lack of culture, he waxed even more furious at their being oppressed. Logical discussion was difficult, but gradually, in weird circles, we wandered closer to his Rastafarian ideals.

'I must go back to where I came from. I must have repatriation to Ethiopia.'

'But the one place you did not come from was Ethiopia,' I said.

'Yes, and you know why? Because it was never a colony.'

To discuss slavery and its relevance today, to ask who sold the slaves, to speak of its ancient history as a trade, would have been useless. We were not, I realised, talking about that. We were talking of a search for identity.

'There is a secret place in Ethiopia. I must go there. It is where I come from. Where do English people come from? They go back to King James and stop. Kings with crowns, they don't overstand Jesus Christ. He had no crown, no power like kings, but his kingdom was heaven.'

'Haile Selassie, or Ras Tafari if you like, was a king,' I said. 'He was not a god.'

'He said in Jamaica, man, that any black man could come to Ethiopia. Anyway, Ethiopia is the name for the whole of Africa.'

I asked if he knew what Haile Selassie's religion was. He did not answer, confused for the first time. When I said he was a Coptic Christian and that the religion had come to Ethiopia through Egypt,

Jomu suddenly started dancing in front of me, chanting. His friend's foot went behind his head.

> I am a Christian, I shall have my portion,
> Urgh, Urgh, Eeyow.
> I am a Moslem, yum no problem,
> Urgh, Urgh, Eeyow.
> I am a Baptist, I get my piece,
> Urgh, Urgh, Eeyow.
> I am a Rasta, I shall have my share.

He never got cross, just more and more wild-eyed and ever more rhetorical. When I talked of his Dominican heritage, which might include any ancestry (I did not know then that he was half-French), he declaimed: 'Man, my people were enslaved here, their blood was spilled. All those people cry out to me. I must answer. They had no home, I must go to their home. I am without a land.'

'Where did you learn your history?' I asked.

'One day, they will find in Egypt the lost book . . .'

At this point he lost me. But as I was leaving, he said: 'You may talk to others anywhere. In Jamaica, maybe. They may say Rastas are different, believe something different. Man, each one is himself. I will never die. I am the spirit of me, I cannot die.'

It was Sunday. As I went out into the street, there was a man on the porch of a chapel. He had a microphone. Endlessly he asked, chanting, 'Are you washed in the blood of the Lamb? Are you washed in the blood of the Lamb?'

I went down once more to La Valette's church, in the hope that it might be open. It wasn't. As we drove back past the chapel with the porch, the speaker had changed. Now it was Jomu, 'Each one is himself. I will never die. I am the spirit of me . . .'

Perhaps Jomu is right. Perhaps there is, so far, no Dominican culture. Each person has to make his own.

At the Cultural Centre in the old sugar mill, near the new airport at Canefield, Aylwin Bully, the director, made the point that the people had been taught for so long that they and everything they did was inferior, that they have no confidence or faith in their culture.

They were told that their music was jungle stuff. Their dances were tom-tom nonsense and war dances. Their painting and sculpture, the little there was, was called 'primitive'. When they copied the whites, dancing their quadrilles and the polka, they were laughed at. The Italian artist, Agostino Brunias, who lived in Dominica during the 1770s and the 1780s, left a marvellous record of the life of the blacks at that time. (There were, in 1813, more than twice as many free 'people of colour' as there were white people on the island.) I feel that – however good they are – there is an element of mockery in his paintings, which so often depict black people aping white manners.

Aylwin Bully, who is himself a dramatist, artist and writer, has created something really simple and worthwhile in his centre. He concentrates much of his energy on drama.

'In a country where there is between forty and fifty per cent illiteracy, oral tradition is very important. We go to villages and discuss their problems. Then, quite impromptu, we act them out, and in acting come up with a solution. We ask the people whether that solution would work for them. It is a lively way of having serious discussions.'

Only two artists on the island had had any formal training. They went to the school in Jamaica. It seemed to me that the carving was not as good nor as spontaneous as it had been in Grenada, but the painting was better, in particular, one artist called Royer – though there was a sad general tendency to false sentiment.

Our life in the hotel continued to be happy and funny. Geoffrey and his brother bought a cow for $225. They hoped, after killing and butchering it, to sell the meat for twice as much. Geoffrey asked if we would like to see it killed. I declined, but Hamish went and said that they killed the poor creature by hitting it on the head with a very large hammer. There was no bit of the cow which they did not eat. The skin they cut up into small strips and toasted it for breakfast.

Staying in the hotel for a few nights was a scientist whose surname I forget. She came from Ruislip and I knew her merely as Sandra. She worked at the University of Illinois – a part of the brain drain – and was involved in a grand study of the 'greenhouse' theory that carbon dioxide is building up in the outer atmosphere and acting as a trap to keep in all the warmth of the world. Temperatures will soon rise alarmingly and dreadful consequences ensue. Fallen timber gives off carbon dioxide, but it is difficult to know when exactly a tree fell. Here on Dominica, because of Hurricane David, the fallen trees can be dated with precision.

Sandra had brought with her a young graduate from Illinois to help. He was called Mark and was a nice enough guy. Together they trudged through the dank forests, measuring away. It was tiring work. I decided that Sandra was not just part of the brain drain but of the fortitude drain as well. As soon as dinner was over, Mark had to go to bed exhausted. Sandra would sit up chatting.

I found her conversation not only informative but extremely comforting. She said that the level of carbon dioxide in the atmosphere had often been higher than it is now. I think she said in glacial periods. So did carbon dioxide warm things up so that the glacial period ended? Or did it cause it? Because, of course, there are those who believe quite the opposite of the greenhouse theory. The shield of carbon dioxide keeps the sun's warmth out. That is what I find reassuring. Firstly, that it's not so bad after all. Secondly, that they don't know anything in the first place.

'The world is wonderfully adaptable,' said Sandra. That is what I like to hear, late at night in a distant clime.

We made other friends, too. There was Sister Alicia de Tremerie, a Belgian nun who had been on the island for thirty-six years. Had she not felt a vocation early in life, she would have made a remarkable businesswoman. When she first arrived, she and her fellow nuns, Sister Borgia and Sister Bertine, devoted themselves to getting better conditions for women on the island. They started a social centre, Sister Borgia concentrating on education, Sister Bertine on handicraft and vocational skills, while Sister Alicia ventured into a Credit Union League. Her league grew to be one of the largest financial agencies on the island, providing loans to individuals for house-building and all kinds of development. The league now runs itself.

Sister Alicia's latest project is trying to help farmers. She is living in what was the manager's house of a former Geest banana plantation, in the north-east of the island. Sister Borgia and Sister Bertine have long ago retired, but Sister Alicia still has Sister Maria (who looks like someone out of a Dutch painting, rosy-faced and benign) to help her. They made us a most delicious lunch of vegetable soup and beef with some home-grown Caribbean vegetables, and a fruit pudding.

We then went round Sister Alicia's latest enterprise – a saw mill. This lively and courageous nun has managed to acquire the huge equipment needed to cut up the vast gum-trees from the forest which surrounds the plantation. It is not a dangerous rape of the rare rain forest, for in two years she has only cleared 200 acres to make land for farmers. Next to the saw mill, she has a small furniture factory, giving employment to a dozen young men. The furniture is simple and plain, although in time it may become grander, because gum-trees can provide a beautiful golden veneer.

Another most delightful and helpful friend was Lennox Honychurch, the son of the man murdered by the Dreads. Lennox is a good-looking man of thirty-five, with an endearing smile, dark hair and a large moustache. He has a lilting voice which sounds a little French in its accent, a usual thing among the islanders who speak patois, but who may know no French at all.

Lennox's father came from a Barbadian family, but his mother (the first wife of the Dreads' victim) was English in origin. Her mother was a romantic figure, the daughter of Sir William Gordon-Cumming, the man accused of cheating at baccarat when Edward VII, then Prince of Wales, and he were both staying at Tranby Croft. Having been brought up in the shadow of a great scandal, she was not above creating a little one of her own. When she had been married for some years to the nephew of a not very interesting peer, she ran off with a Mr Napier, whom she first met on a ship in the South Seas. Napier had been a schoolfriend of Rupert Brooke, who had urged him to visit the Pacific islands and he was spending his war gratuity on the journey. He left the ship in Samoa but later pursued her to Australia. She left her husband and later married him in Rangoon.

Early in their marriage Napier suffered from tuberculosis, so they decided to come to the Caribbean which was thought, with the sea breezes, to be healthy. Once there, they became involved in local politics and Mrs Napier was the first woman to serve on the Legislative Council and thus the first women to be a member of any Caribbean parliament.

The young Lennox Honychurch has inherited many of his grand-parents' characteristics. He became a member of the House of Assembly when he was only twenty-three. But his interests are more historical. He is now working on the restoration of the Cabrits, an eighteenth-century fort with room for 500 soldiers and 1,250 barrels of gunpowder, guarding Portsmouth and Prince Rupert's Bay.

Lennox's conversation is a delight, for without showing off, he imparts a mass of information on almost any aspect of Dominican life.

From no one else would I have learned that the old Carib sauce *tomali* was made with the green sperm of the male *ciwik*, which I took to be a kind of crayfish.

Through Lennox I followed the stormy history of Dominica since Independence. The first president fled the country in disgrace. The original Prime Minister, Patrick John, was first connected with a plot to invade Barbados. Next, he signed an agreement with some Americans, leasing them forty-five square miles of Dominica's northern coast, including Portsmouth. The lease was for ninety-nine years at an annual rent of $37.

The area included forty per cent of the cultivated land of Dominica and one-third of the population. The Americans were to have exclusive rights to control all business operations in the so-called Free Port Zone. They were to be responsible for security and would have the right to veto any Government immigration arrangements in the area. At the same time, John's cabinet colleague, Leo Austin, was setting up a deal with South Africa for projects to do with trading in oil.

Such was the outcry that John had to abandon all these schemes. He then tried to pass bills to limit the right to strike and to make newspapers divulge their sources. The protest against these bills led to a youth being shot dead and ten young people being injured by the Defence Force. John had to go. A temporary government survived shakily until Hurricane David almost literally blew them away.

In 1980, Miss Eugenia Charles's party, the Dominican Freedom Party, won all but four of the twenty-one seats in the House of Assembly. Miss Charles became the first Caribbean woman Prime Minister. It was by no means the last that was heard of Patrick John.

John, in 1975, had said of Miss Charles that, if the Dominicans ever made the mistake of electing her to power, 'every time she take one step forward, I will make sure she have to make two steps back.'

It was at this point that John formed links with the Dreads, with the help of sympathetic members of the Defence Force. They planned to overthrow the Government by force at carnival time in March 1981. The plot was delayed. Nonetheless, it involved mercenaries from the United States and Canada, some of them members of the Ku Klux Klan. Money came from a drugs racketeer. In April, the American police arrested two Canadians and eight Americans near New Orleans. They were about to sail for Dominica with arms and ammunition.

Miss Eugenia Charles survived all that Patrick John and others could devise and, in 1985, was re-elected with a similar majority.

One morning, I went to leave a note for Miss Charles in the Ministry Building. Hamish took the note to her secretary, who read it and asked Hamish to wait. She took it in to Miss Charles and reappeared to suggest that I come up right away to see the Prime Minister.

Her office was on the third floor. There appeared to be little in the way of security, except for a languid character who sat somewhere near her office. He had no gun. He did suggest that Hamish, if he proposed to take me in to see the Prime Minister, might at least wear some shoes.

Miss Charles reminded me of an aunt of mine, of whom I was particularly fond, but by whom I was also quite alarmed. She has a handsome, strong face of a lightish brown complexion. Her hair is much greyed. She has a no-nonsense look, but that day she wore a gay, floral print. There is nothing masculine about her; she is just a powerful woman, whom you trust at once. While her personality may be formidable, she has a dry, sharp sense of humour and is well capable of laughing at herself.

She wasted no time on trivialities, but pitched in at once to the problems of Dominica, which are, to a greater or lesser extent, mostly greater, the problems common to all the islands.

'All the things we produce are subject to big price fluctuations. If limes are in demand and making money, then everyone else plants them and the price drops. This sets a limit to what we can produce of anything in the way of fruit or vegetables.'

The history of limes on Dominica is typical. They were introduced in the 1860s. Early this century, Dominica was the largest producer of limes in the world. Rose's Lime Juice Cordial made its name with Dominican limes. There were hurricanes; there were blights and diseases. When Cadbury-Schweppes took over Messrs Rose in the sixties, they rapidly pulled out altogether, finding cheaper sources for their gooey cordial.

I suggested to Miss Charles that copra was a safer crop.

'It is one of our successes, because we make soap and oils. We need to produce some things as well as grow things. That is why I was so put out by the Caribbean Basin Initiative ruling about exporting whole garments to America. It would hardly have been a big shock to Seventh Avenue if we had been allowed to sell a few garments in the United

States. It would have cost them less than aid. We don't want to be living on aid forever.'

As Lennox Honychurch has said, relations with the United States: 'should be tempered with caution, for experience elsewhere in Latin America has shown that US goodwill tends, even inadvertently, to gradually overflow into domination whenever it finds a friend, particularly a very tiny friend . . . Miss Charles has indicated her awareness that a careful balance will have to be maintained to ensure that friendship is not mistaken for open licence by Washington to take arbitrary decisions affecting Dominica's affairs.'

On domestic issues, Miss Charles's views were compounded of brisk commonsense and practicality, untinged by any of that electioneering hypocrisy which colours the conversation of politicians all over the world.

On education, she said: 'It is all very well saying we have abolished school fees. They are the smallest part of it. It is books which cost money.'

On housing: 'I believe the way to stability is for people to own their houses, then they have something they do not want to lose.'

On tourism: 'I would like to see the kind of tourism which attracts people who love nature. The island is so beautiful that I notice it with pleasure each time I come back to it. It is quite unsuitable for package tourism. I am glad of that as, in any case, I am not convinced that it brings in much money, as so much has to go out to support it.

'I think the best for us would be people who build houses which they come to for some weeks every year. They can lend them or rent them to like-minded people whom they tell about Dominica. Word of mouth is very useful and saves our having to advertise, which we can't afford. I like the kind of visitors who get to know the people. That is impossible with package tours.'

On television: 'It is most annoying that the hurricane knocked down the booster which brought us Barbados TV, with a lot of Caribbean news and good British documentaries. We haven't got the money to replace it. All we can get is US stations. That means lots of violence. People say I ought to stop US television coming in. In the first place, how could I? You cannot do that sort of thing.

'In many ways, I have no objection to American TV. At least the people of Dominica can see the conditions in Ethiopia and work out how much better it is to be in Dominica. No one is ever hungry here. What malnutrition we have comes from eating the wrong things.

133

'They can see also that the US has been hit by three hurricanes this year. They can see that they are not alone. Further, though I haven't the statistics, the crime rate, anyhow among smaller children, has dropped since TV came. I can only suppose they are peering through the jalousies to see what is on. For what entertainment is there for people in the evening?

'We will never be rich. This is not a place of riches, but we should all have enough to have a proper house with running water and a reasonable way of life.'

Miss Charles is agreeably pro-British. She says that Britain has given a lot to Dominica and done so not blindly but thoughtfully, going into what would really help the Dominicans most.

'Some people say, so they should. Think what they owe us. What about slavery? Well, that was all hundreds of years ago and it is nonsense. Of course, I always want more, I cannot get enough. But when I ask for help with, say, the banana business, the British could very well say "We buy the damned bananas; isn't that enough?" But they don't. They give money or help to the growing of them.'

Miss Charles is decidedly brisk, without thinking that she is the only person who is right.

'If they don't like the way I do things, they can kick me out. God knows, there is nothing in it for me. I make much less money. It is not as if I had children to work and make a fine place for. I could just enjoy myself.'

Everyone agrees that Eugenia Charles is incorruptible. She is comparatively rich. She was the largest shareholder in the Fort Young Hotel, created out of the old fort which stands above the town of Roseau. It was wrecked by Hurricane David. The same group owned another hotel which has not prospered. They cannot rebuild the Fort Young because the bank took all the insurance money to pay off the building costs of the other hotel. Other Prime Ministers might well have found ways round this problem. The people regard her rather as I regarded my aunt.

On the Caribbean as a whole, Miss Charles is rather less optimistic than she is on domestic affairs. She completely dismisses any idea of Federation.

'I was a great federalist, but it cannot work. Look at the trouble you have getting together in Europe. I admit we don't have the language problems, but we can't get together. We should try to share more. We tried joint representation, that is sharing embassies, but even that didn't work.'

Miss Charles's great fear is communism. It was she who led the Caribbean states in asking America to intervene in Grenada.

'I have gone on saying, and will go on saying, that people do not realise what has happened here. They see democratic elections and think everything is all right, but it isn't.

'In every island there are little nests of well-trained people, coached not in Cuba but in Russia, who are there to destabilise society. People think I am a reactionary when I say this. I am not. It is true. I have seen directives – one saying they must have one man in every ministry. That is why I move people around in the ministries every few months, so that they won't have time to disrupt the work. People say I interfere too much, but it's not that. Our Civil Service is like yours, you can't get rid of anybody. So you keep moving them.'

After the Grenada affair, so Lennox Honychurch told me, a letter came to light describing the arrangements made for a number of Dominicans, who were to go to Grenada on a course. On arrival in Grenada, they would surrender their passports and be given special travel documents. Then they would be flown to Libya for three months' training in guerrilla warfare. On getting back, they would be given their passports, stamped so that it would appear that they had spent the whole time in Grenada.

'Often,' said Miss Charles, 'it is the non-government organisations who support these people. Oxfam gets furious when I say this, but it is true. Oxfam and Save the Children Fund, not yours, the American one.'

How difficult it is to know whether someone just has a bee in their bonnet. And the shrewdest of people can have veritable swarms – my dear aunt, for one. But Miss Charles's words stayed with me, most usefully, in the weeks to come.

Talking to Miss Charles made me look at the island again with new eyes. Dominica has all the problems the islands are heir to – with the notable exception of any colour problem. The hurricanes, the blights, the economic turns of fate, the exploitation, the corrupt politicians, the riots. All those and the byways of history had distressed or intrigued me. But what the island held for me above all was a bewitching beauty.

I went back to the Layou River and watched its waters rushing over huge boulders and, in calmer patches, caressing the pebbles into neat lines. Dark pools, glittering clear water, furious foam. Behind, cliffs draped in green, rising to the mountains with their clinging trees, all so much darker than other islands, but all so green.

The trees never ceased to amaze me. Great gums (*Hedwigia balsamifera*), from which the Caribs hollow out canoes, soar up to hundreds of feet. Silk cotton trees, cedar, mahoe, rise beside them, together with trees with names like *zyeux-crabe* and *bois-cote* which I could not identify, all to make the canopy of the rain forest. Below them, mahoganies, palms, autograph trees with their trailing lianas, and lower still, fern-trees, breadfruits, bananas and a thousand shrubs forming an impenetrable wall of tropical vegetation.

Climbing high up the precipitous valleys, each one of which seems lost and unconnected with any other, gives one a feeling of stepping back to the world which Columbus discovered. Standing high, looking down over the sea, which seems to wash the very feet of the rain forest, it is as if nothing but the weather, with its rainbows, its neat columns of rain, its fanned shafts of sunlight, had ever disturbed this private land.

10
Guadeloupe
REVOLUTIONS AND RUM

Disenchantment with Guadeloupe started at the moment of landing at the airport. Hamish asked the baggage handlers to help him get me out of the plane. They refused. It was hard to decide whether the refusal stemmed from bloody-mindedness or stupidity. A senior official asked them to help. They stood with wooden faces, unmoved. Eventually, the official helped, while they watched. It was an unpleasant jolt – the first time in two months that we had met anyone really disagreeable.

Pointe-à-Pitre was a different kind of shock. It was the most modern town we had yet seen, with high-rise buildings, pedestrian precincts, modern statuary. The shops were even more lavish than those in Fort-de-France. There were a few pretty buildings in the old quarter, but not many.

Everything worked. We got a car in minutes. At the bronze-glass bank, we got money in minutes. In Fort-de-France, and in nearly every island, a visit to the bank took anything up to an hour.

It was the people that I found difficult. They were, as we had been told in Martinique, coarser-featured and less good-looking than the Martiniquais, quite ugly really. Against that, they were livelier. The bustle of the town was attractive and a reminder of what education does to invigorate people. But they were not lovable.

It was raining when we went to the bank, great tropical ropes of rain. We asked a security guard if there were any way to avoid a long flight of stairs. No. We asked a senior-looking, white official. No. But there was. On the way out we found, by chance, a perfectly good ramp designed for wheelchairs. How could two people who worked for the bank not know of the ramp?

The hotel was horribly French, in a way that the French themselves have quite given up. The light-switches on each landing did not give one enough time to reach one's room. The beds were gruesome. The bathroom had that thin, scatchy loo-paper. The advertised roof-top restaurant had been turned into bedrooms. (If the food was as bad up there as it was in their ground floor restaurant, it was a sound commercial decision.)

Already rather despairing, I went to see Melina Ogilie, a friend of Jacline Labbé. She had recently opened a flower shop not far from my hotel. She was tall and beautiful, much darker than Jacline. We got angry with each other almost at once. We had talked of independence – the usual thing. She then insisted on bewailing the great poverty of Guadeloupe. I tried to convince her that, compared with Dominica, no one in Guadeloupe is poor.

'A shop like this,' I said, waving my arms at the orchids in their special feeder-bottles, the azaleas imported from France, 'just would not exist in Dominica.'

'It is just my idea this shop, an idea.'

'No one in Dominica could conceivably have such an idea.'

Mademoiselle Ogilie, although inspired by a kind of radical chic, was intelligent and lucid. When we spoke of the choice between comforts and dignity, she said: 'It is not dignity, it is identity. Before, one drop of black blood made you a slave; now being black here makes you feel incomplete.'

She maintained that blacks and whites never meet together in restaurants or places of entertainment. They might go to one another's houses, but very rarely. Only the French temporary residents that is, never the *colons*. She was not militant and disliked politics.

'Soon, I know, it will change. Independence is inevitable.'

We parted quite amicably in the end. She promised to telephone with the address of an agreeable country hotel, but never did. She was not in her shop by midday the next morning, so we left.

Guadeloupe

It was not a good day. Guadeloupe is, in fact, two islands, divided by an easily-spanned channel. The effect is of one island, shaped like a butterfly, with Pointe-à-Pitre in its narrow body. We had flown over the half called Grande-Terre. It looked flat and dull. We headed, instead, for Basse-Terre which, perversely named, is the mountainous half, its highest point, the volcano, La Soufrière, being 4,800 feet. After Dominica, the mountains seemed tame and lacking in magic.

A sign announcing a rum distillery lured us off the road. We bumped down a lane and found a pleasantly ramshackled farm at the end of it. The cane-cutting season, which lasts for six months, had just started. Most rum is distilled from molasses left over after sugar production. In the French islands, there is still a fair amount made directly from cane juice. This is called *rhum agricole*, as opposed to *rhum industriel*, and is what Monsieur Reimonenq, the proprietor of this estate, was making.

The practice of an old craft is always pleasing and restful. The cane came in from the fields on rickety old carts. A rather hopeless, mechanical grab plucked the long stalks out of the carts and dropped them, like spillikins, on a conveyor belt, which bore them away under a rusty iron roof to a crusher. All the machinery was old. The juice was fermented for between forty and forty-eight hours. A rich, heady smell of the natural fermentation hung over the whole place. The juice bubbled in the tall tubes of the distillery, like a mad professor's experiment. Monsieur Reimonenq sat in an eyrie of an office, watching his dials and checking everybody's every move.

Agricultural rum is, in distilling terms, less pure than the more commercial industrial rum, but as we drank some of Monsieur Reimonenq's fiery *Grand Corsaire*, I preferred to think it was more genuine. It is always *rhum agricole* that the islanders put in a *p'tit ponch*. Industrial rum is more appropriate for cocktails.

It was the only satisfying part of the day. There were pretty parts of the island, but I yearned for Dominica. At a police checkpoint, they were offensive. Then a driver drove at us, trying to push us off the road, in revenge for our having delayed him a trifle. The hotel that we chose was advertised as a 'waterfront' hotel. It was hard to justify this claim, as it was half a mile from the sea. The advertisement also said that they took credit cards. The smile of the owner's wife had all the sincerity of a three-card-trick man on a pavement. She refused my credit card and demanded cash in advance.

139

I suddenly realised, to my astonishment, that there was no law to say that I had to see the whole of Guadeloupe. I was not obliged to stay on this odious island, where no one smiled and no glimmer of good taste enlivened anything. I thought with a shudder of Mademoiselle Ogilie's anthuriums and gladioli.

My plan had been to take a ferry to Les Saintes the following morning. They were not going to be geographically or botanically any different. There were tourist hotels and even a nudist beach, but they were not what I had come to the Caribbean to see. The only interest lay in the people, who were poor whites, the descendants of Breton farmers. There were about three thousand of them. They were said to be snobbish about their colour and therefore inbred, even to the point of stupidity. I convinced myself that my interest in the islands was prurient. I decided that it was ill-mannered, if not worse, to go just to stare at these bigoted, unfortunate people.

In the morning we took the plane to Antigua.

11
Antigua
SAFE HARBOUR

At least there were jokes when we arrived. There were two rival car-hire firms and their representatives shared a desk. Each completely ignored the other, while they both gave us a terrific sales pitch, jostling and pushing. There was Musak playing big band music of forty years ago — all of it flat, as the tape was running too slowly.

St John's, the capital, had a certain charm with its parallel streets of clapboard houses, but it lacked a seafront, the harbour being set off to one side. It also appeared to be fast asleep. The rest of the island I thought bleak, dry and uninteresting, with hardly a tree to be seen. The beaches were white and the seawater especially clear, being unmuddied by any rivers, so that it is ideal for the sunbathing tourist. Indeed, tourism is Antigua's principal source of income.

The wonderful exception to the rather mournful, neglected aspect of the landscape is English Harbour. This is one of the prettiest natural harbours in the whole Caribbean. It was the great eighteenth-century naval base of the West Indies. Here came Rodney, Nelson and my hero, Cochrane. When Leigh Fermor came here, he wrote of decay and

141

disintegration, decrepitude and desolation, mouldering nautical gear and anchors eaten by rust.

In a world where so much change is for the worse rather than the better, how happy to be able to say, for once, that Ozymandias is rebuked. English Harbour has been restored quite beautifully, in excellent taste and to very good purpose. At about the time when Leigh Fermor visited Antigua, Earl Baldwin was Governor. It happened that he saw a schooner arrive at the harbour and then sail away without stopping. This because there were no facilities of any sort. A visiting yachtsman at that time had to hire a taxi to fetch the harbour master from St John's to come to perform the customs and immigration formalities. Lord Baldwin thought that port facilities should be available. Alas, the percipient Governor was soon recalled to England in disgrace. He had had the good nature to enjoy frolicsome parties with black people. The stuffy whites of Antigua complained to the Colonial Office about him and he went home.

But the seed had been sown. Sir Kenneth Blackburne, Baldwin's successor, founded the Society of Friends of English Harbour. A major part of the inspiration for this idea was the arrival of Commander V. E. B. Nicholson. In 1949, weary of the restrictions of England after the war, this retired naval officer had sailed away with no particular destination in mind, unless, perhaps, Australia. He took with him his wife, his two sons and his brother. They put in at English Harbour, abandoned by the navy in 1899, and fell in love with it. The Commander rented what had been the officers quarters, which Leigh Fermor had described as having 'relapsed into a state of barn-like desolation'. There the family started a yacht-charter business, which still flourishes today.

The whole harbour has been turned into the most attractive yachting centre in the world. Two of the old buildings – the pitch and tar storehouse and the copper and lumber store – have been turned into pleasant hotels. Another has become a museum. I was excited to find a framed poster of Lord Cochrane's, advertising for sailors:

GOD fave the KING

Doublons

SPANISH
Dollar Bag
Consigned to Boney

My LADS,

The rest of the GALLEONS with the TREASURE from LA PLATA, are waiting half loaded at CARTAGENA, for the arrival of those from PERU at PANAMA, as soon as that takes place, they are to sail for PORTOVELO, to take in the rest of their Cargo, with Provisions and Water for the Voyage to EUROPE. They stay at PORTOVELO a few days only. Such a Chance perhaps will never occur again.

THE FLYING

PALLAS,

Of 36 GUNS,

At PLYMOUTH,

is a new and uncommonly fine Frigate. Built on purpose. And ready for an EXPEDITION, as soon as some more good Hands are on board:

CAPTAIN LORD COCHRANE,

(who was not drowned in the ARAB as reported)
Commands her. The sooner you are on board the better.

None need apply, but SEAMEN, or Stout Hands, able to rouse about the Field Pieces, and carry an hundred weight of PEWTER, without stopping, at least three Miles.

To British Seamen. COCHRANE.

BONEY's CORONATION
Is postponed for want of COBBS.

J. Barfield, Printer, Wardour Street.

RENDEZVOUS, AT THE WHITE FLAG.

One of the Commander Nicholson's sons, Desmond, still lives near English Harbour. His house, on the top of a hill overlooking Falmouth, is a haven of civilisation. His wife, whom he met soon after arriving in Antigua, is a woman of great beauty; his daughter is a most talented potter. He himself is charming, erudite and generous with his time and knowledge. Although he has worked in the yacht-chartering business, he has devoted his spare time to history, archaeology and natural history.

143

It is his enthusiasm which, building on his father's start, has created much of English Harbour. He was kind enough to lend me books and papers of all kinds.

Going through these conjured up wonderful and sad pictures as I sat reading by the harbour, with all the creaking and winching sounds of boats around me and the splash of pelicans swooping down and flopping in the water. Imagine, in 1763, Rodney's great ship *Foudroyant*, 180 feet long with a beam of 50 feet, carrying eighty guns – the largest ship ever to come into English Harbour.

Rodney, despite his reputed greed for booty and plunder, had consideration for his men. The hospital in his time was up a long hill. When he saw sick men tottering, even crawling up the hill, he ordered that a carriage should always be waiting at the bottom ready to take up any invalid.

Think of poor Charles Pitt, aged twenty, commander of the sloop *Hornet* (fourteen guns). He died here in 1780. He was the brother of William, who was to be Prime Minister when only four years older. On Charles' grave is written: 'The genius that inspired and the Virtues that adorned the Parent were revived in the Son whose dawning Merit bespoke a meridian Splendour worthy of the name of Pitt.'

Then Nelson in 1784, coming in HMS *Boreas*, carving his name, it is said, on the wall of the catchment. It was not a happy time for him. The Antiguan planters and merchants disliked him for enforcing the Navigation Act, which forbade all trade with the young United States. In 1786, he wrote to his future wife, Fanny Nisbet, on Nevis: 'I am alone in the Commanding Officer's House while my ship is fitting . . . not a human creature to speak to, you will feel a little for me, I think. The moment old "Boreas" is habitable in my cabin, I shall fly to it, in order to avoid mosquitoes and melancholy.'

Picture the French ship *Egyptienne*, captured in 1804, lying in the harbour, gloomy and forbidding, renamed *Antigua* and turned into a prison hulk. Later she was removed to Grenada.

The following year came Sir Alexander Cochrane, as Commander-in-Chief of the Windward and Leeward islands, the uncle of my hero and evidently an equally eccentric figure. I came across this letter:

9 Jun 1806   Northumberland, just
                                        weighing to go off to Port Royal,
                                                        Martinique

Dear Commissioner,

I was much hurt to hear that the Hart [a 78-foot sloop] had been employed as a Watering Vessel, when I am in such distress for cruisers – I have given orders to prevent the like in future, and let me give you a little advice as to water – Oblige all your workmen to place Spouts around their houses and give them no water out of your tank, that have not.

The Tank at English Harbour was built for the Navy, so says the Deed – the ships are therefore entitled to the use of it – and those who are too lazy to catch water, should SUCK THEIR PAWS AS THE BEARS DO IN WINTER – I am glad . . . you are sending the St Lucia to sea, to prevent the horrid sin of – you know what.

Sincerely Yours,

A. Cochrane

Thomas Cochrane, the nephew, must have acquired his interest in pitch from his uncle at the same time. We find Sir Alexander already energetic in trying to promote pitch from Trinidad. In Desmond Nicholson's library, I was able to add to what I had learned about the Pitch Lake. Asphalt has been known since classical times. It was washed up on the shores of the Dead Sea which was known to the Greeks as Lake Asphaltites. It is not unique. Asphalt is found in California at Rancho La Brea. (This name comes from Trinidad, for Brea is the name of the village near the lake, being a Spanish corruption of the French word for pitch, *brai*.)

In 1805, Alexander Cochrane made a full report of his findings about pitch to the Admiralty and sent two shiploads to London. They said there was too much oil in it to be of any use. In 1850, Cochrane, by then 10th Earl of Dundonald, was using pitch in the boilers of HMS *Scourge*. Dundonald believed a mixture of two parts bitumen and one part coal was as good as pure coal and would lead to great savings, as mining pitch cost a quarter of the price of mining coal. Still no one else believed in his beloved pitch. The possible exception was Trollope who wrote in his *West Indies and the Spanish Main* of 'a great pitch lake of which all the world has heard, and of which that indefatigable old hero, Lord Dundonald, tried hard to make wax candles, and oil for burning.

145

The oils and candles he did make, but not, I fear, the money which should be consequent upon their fabrication. I have no doubt, however, that we shall all have wax candles from thence, for Lord Dundonald is one of those men who are born to do great deeds of which others shall reap the advantages. One of these days his name will be duly honoured for his conquests as well as for his candles.'

The charm of English Harbour lies to a large extent in the fact that it is used for its original purpose – as a haven for ships. That the ships are now there for pleasure and enjoyment, rather than for making war, seems to me only to enhance the charm.

Outside the precincts of English Harbour, we found little of interest. A British official on one of the other islands told me that Antigua is probably the least stable of the smaller islands. There were, it is true, many stories of corruption and of crime. A local pointed out a large house to us, built evidently for a minister's mistress. It struck me as an island which could ill afford any trouble. The dwindling of tourists, after a disturbance, on an island like Dominica does not have any disastrous effect, as there are only 220 hotel beds in the whole place. But for Martinique with 5,000 beds or Antigua with 3,250, a flight of tourists would be grievous.

We were now in the drier zone. Until we reached the larger islands we had left abundance and fertility. Nobody could say, as Miss Charles had done, that no one need be hungry. If tourism failed, Antigua would be hungry. The hotels, ghastly as many of them were with their barriers and sentry boxes and their hideous architecture, are vital for the economy, but they need not detain us.

Antigua was, however, the headquarters of Liat, the airline with which we were hopping up the islands, and we fell in with Ferdi de Gannes, their chief training and examining pilot. Ferdi was a most interesting man. He was born in Trinidad and became a champion bicyclist, often representing Trinidad in international games. When he was twenty-five, he thought it was time to have a more lasting career. His father had saved a little money for Ferdi's brother's education. Fortunately, the brother won a scholarship. The money could be put towards some training for Ferdi. He decided to be a pilot and, in 1955, he applied to British West Indian Airways. At that time, the idea of a black person becoming a pilot was considered bizarre, at the very least.

146

Ferdi went to England to take an aeronautical engineering course. Quite soon, the money ran out. His father mortgaged his house and his land. In 1958, Ferdi qualified as a pilot, with a commercial licence. He came home. There was no job for him. He spent a year selling lavatory seats. Then he got a job with Leeward Islands Air Transport, as it was then called.

It was a tiny company and the pilot had to do everything, including loading the baggage. In only two and a half years, Ferdi became their senior captain. He was offered a job by BWIA but turned it down. 'I enjoyed the little flights and the little planes.'

Eventually, Court Line bought Liat. Ferdi became an examiner in England, until Court Line went bust. By this time the little airline had become a social necessity. The governments of eleven islands clubbed together to buy it.

'We had taken air transport to tiny places. We were pioneers really. And we never lost a passenger. This short haul business is hard. The aircraft suffer a lot – the salt, the heat, the frequent taking off and landing.

'A pilot needs an analytical brain, capable of doing seven things at once. It is an insecure life, because every six months you have to have a medical and technical test. And in a small community like this, you always have to have good behaviour. That is, you can't get drunk at a party, because people expect pilots to be sober, even if they are not flying the next day.

'But I still love flying, even after 20,000 hours. Every day is different. It may be the same route, but the co-pilot is different, so is the hostess, and the passengers. And you may go a different way because of weather.'

We did not talk too much about the frights and scares of flying, but the weather of the Caribbean is sudden and erratic.

'If there is a hurricane, we just don't go up, but I have thrice been struck by lightning. The up-draughts and down-draughts can lift or drop you two thousand feet in a minute. The winds are always turbulent on the leeward side of an island. That is what makes Canefield on Dominica so difficult. It has a cross-wind. It is actually an aggregate of problems there. Castries on St Lucia looks easy but isn't. Looking back, I wonder how we got the B111 jet in there. Montserrat is by looks critical, but other things favour it.'

I hoped so, as we were flying there that afternoon.

Ferdi's house was a pleasing clapboard building. He had filled it with antiques and on the old pieces stood quantities of bicycling trophies. It was an extremely happy household. Ferdi's wife is a hostess with Liat. They have two children, a daughter at Miami College and a son of fifteen, who wants to be a pilot.

Ferdi's wife was very pretty and also very funny. We talked of the difference between West Indians at home, where they are undisciplined, late and often feckless, and West Indians abroad, where they are organised, punctual and industrious.

'You should see them on the planes,' said Ferdi's wife. 'When they check in, they have little luggage, but they have lots of relations nearby who load them up afterwards with what they say is hand luggage. The seats are tiny and half the passengers bring tape-decks that stretch across two seats. Then we have drunks who always want to pee during take-off. One did once and all the passengers had to duck.'

Under the new management, Liat (they dropped the old name, keeping merely the acronym, which wits say stands for luggage in another terminal) has changed from a social necessity to a viable business. It is one of the few co-operative efforts among the islands which actually works.

12

Montserrat

THE SHAMROCK ISLE

As our wing-tip seemed about to touch the sea, I was glad that Ferdi had told me that many things favoured the airport on Montserrat. Surely we could not be heading straight for that hillside. Of course, we landed safely. As usual, we had to attune ourselves to quite a different setting.

Montserrat is one of the inner chain of volcanic Leeward islands. (It is always hard to say which are the Leeward and which the Windward. Dominica, for instance, has been classed with both. For the Dutch, St Maarten, Saba and St Eustatius are all Windward. For us they are Leeward.) It is very small; eleven miles long and seven miles wide. It is mountainous, but the hills, which reminded Columbus of a saw, are unlike Dominica, for they are not clad in rain forest. Indeed, the large silk cotton trees were cut down in 1931 to rid the island of a pest that threatened the cotton crops, but there must have been considerable deforestation long before that.

The taxi drove us across the island, over bumpy hills and past deep ravines, known as *ghauts*. Very little seemed to be growing. There was only one field of sugar-cane. There were potatoes and sweet potatoes, but little else. There were few people about, but I saw two boys carrying cricket pads. We came down to the capital, Plymouth, which lay in flatter, coastal land. We had not seen so small a town: the total population of the island is only 12,000, of whom 1,600 live in Plymouth.

It was Sunday and an air of sleepiness pervaded. The car-hire place was in a private house. There were many cars outside. A child appeared.

'They're sleeping,' she said.

We rang the bell and we hooted. An upstairs curtain trembled and we sensed movement. We waited, but nothing happened. I had forgotten the ways of British Colonies.

The taxidriver had a friend who provided a car. We settled in to a rather grand hotel, the others all being inaccessible or shut. It had a pool, which suited Hamish. While he swam, I sat reading. An American came and sat beside me. He was small, dark and nervous, talking at enormous speed. He told me that his name was Philip Capobianco, that he was thirty-six, that he was a student at the private American medical college just outside Plymouth. Most of the students stayed pretty much on campus, but he liked to get away and he could afford to buy a drink in a hotel.

'The cadavers arrive tomorrow,' he said. 'They're big, you know. I thought they'd be tired old people from here, that kinda stuff. I think they order them big, you know. They come from Miami, the mortuary service. I think they say they're for the medical school, so they get big ones. The one I got's big.'

I wondered, for a moment, who but a medical school would order cadavers, big or small, but he was off again.

'I find it kinda hard, you know. That big guy lying there, maybe his arm hanging over the side. I still think we should show respect. The kids, well, you know, they are just kids, they do just terrible things. Throw a lung across the room and catch it. You know, that kinda stuff. But you'll never learn how a heart works unless you cut it open with an instructor.'

There are several of these private medical colleges in the West Indies. We had seen one in Grenada and there is one in Antigua which, according to Philip, comes and goes. They exist because medical colleges in the United States are few and small. The standards of teaching are high, although there is a campaign in the States for the profession to refuse recognition to their pupils. The course lasts only three years, as they have no holidays, merely short breaks. The fees are $18,000 a year.

The college on Montserrat is owned by a Chinaman, so how much of the fee remains in Montserrat is uncertain, but the colleges are a practical source of income for the island. In some ways they are better than tourism because, contrary to expectation, the students disrupt the life of the place very little. They are kept so hard at work that, as Philip said, they seldom leave campus, but inevitably spend quite a lot of money on everyday living.

Quite why Philip was a student was something of a puzzle. His parents emigrated from Naples to America. His father died when he was ten. He had uncles in the garment business. They made millions, but they died too. The family quarrelled. There was a $7 million lawsuit. Philip, I gathered, came out badly. Nonetheless, he got married to a Neapolitan girl whose family were in the Italian garment business.

'I travelled, you know, and made money. But she was dominated by her family. Her brothers. I couldn't survive. I didn't have to take that kinda stuff. Look, I worked, I got good money, but you wouldn't play along. You did what they wanted. Your brothers. I'm not going with that. You tell them.'

His voice grew louder. He kept on, as if I were his wife. It made me give little apprehensive laughs.

'Those brothers-in-law. Look, I was bringing in good business. You think I need to put up with this?'

Suddenly, I was the brothers-in-law.

'You think I'm gonna hand over my list of clients? You go and find them yourselves, like I did.'

More nervous laughs. Equally suddenly, it was over. I was careful to ask no more questions. Then he asked me if he'd be in my book. I said he would.

'Yeah? They'll be stunned. I'm in a book. You know what, my life'd make a book. Yeah. In the Savoia and Principe Hotel in Milan, I met two guys. I could tell they were American and I wanted to talk American. I'm at ease in Italian, but I was fed up with talking that. You know who one of those guys was and I didn't recognise him? It was— ' Philip named a pop star of whom I had never heard. 'There, you see. My life could be a book.'

Apart from the cadavers, everything on Montserrat was on a tiny scale. Plymouth was little more than a village, but it was attractive, with a little park by the waterfront. It had about it an air of innocence. In the Tourist Office, they provided visitors with a printed code of dress:

151

'In the Streets of Plymouth, Bars, Restaurants, Banks, Stores and Govt. Offices the following types of dress are undesirable: short shorts, bikinis, bra-type tops and topless outfits (men and women). On the Beaches the following are considered unacceptable: nudes and topless outfits (women).'

The southern third of the island is the most mountainous, with a still-murmuring volcano, gruesomely smelly, with an acid yellow pool of steaming water. Very little happens in the south, apart from Radio Antilles, with a 200,000-watt transmitter, which broadcasts in three languages and belts out reggae music and calypsos crackling with dubious innuendos, which do not reflect the innocence of Plymouth.

'Now,' says the disc-jockey, 'my favourite song about chickens: *Hold the cock . . . and pullet.*'

The northern end of the island was in many ways more interesting. Just outside Plymouth was St Anthony's Church, built in 1730 on the site of the original of a century earlier. It is agreeably plain. There is an evocative tablet in memory of Alexander Gordon, described as president of the island. '. . . he performed the duties of his station, hospitable to the stranger, generous to the poor, an encourager of whatever tended to make society agreeable or life ornamental, by a stroke of the sun, in the improvement of the roads, he met his fate and departed this life . . .' [in 1790].

In the graveyard is a memorial to thirty-one people who died a less useful death, in 1965, when a Pan-Am jet crashed on Chance's Peak. We sat by the grave of sixteen of them and looked at the peaceful sweep of the 3,000-foot mountain, rising Vesuvius-shaped behind Plymouth. The disaster was unimaginable. It was, I thought, at least a nice place to be buried – a few yards from Jumbie beach, under spreading mahogany trees, the air scented by a fine frangipani. Hamish insisted that if he were to die, I must promise to send his body home to Dorset. I decided that I did not care where I was buried.

Further north, we came upon another pop music connection. George Martin, the producer of the Beatles, has built a recording studio in a modern house high above the coast. Hamish goggled at the, to me, incomprehensible equipment which was being installed by an enthusiastic young engineer, called Paul. He was taking out a 52-track recording system and replacing it with a 60-track system, costing £200,000. Paul talked of the pop groups and stars who had come here: The Police, Air Supply, Duran Duran and Elton John. How incongruous it seemed, both with the lives of the donkey-riding peasants, tending their tomatoes and hot peppers, and of the retired gentlefolk in their villas and condominiums, which we could see below us, by the golf-course at Olveston.

The very northern end of the island became bare and treeless. In two bays, there were pleasant beaches of black sand. Then we climbed again to cross the island and the Emerald Isle, as Montserrat is called, began to seem quite like Ireland, with goats cropping the grass to the earth.

In one village, there was a funeral. The hearse was nearly blocking the road. We thought it more tactful to wait a while. The family would surely come soon. The driver of the hearse became impatient. He revved his engine furiously. Then he turned on the hearse radio at full volume, tuned to Radio Antilles: *Hold the cock . . . and pullet.* An old woman shouted: 'Toll de bell for de funeral, eet ha pas' tree. Toll de bell. Toll de bell.' A furious row ensued. We decided tact was not important and, before things became even more Irish, squeezed past the hearse, still blaring the chicken song.

Montserrat was originally populated by many Irish, sent by Cromwell to St Kitts and passed on. An Irish insouciance still prevails and the shamrock is Montserrat's emblem. There was broken glass all over the island, perhaps because they had lately given up returnable bottles. There was one deserted stretch of road on the far side of the island where some twenty or thirty bottles had been shattered on the tarmac. Officiously, I told a policeman, who had become a friend, about this.

'Ah yes,' he said, 'somebody mentioned that a while ago.'

Government House, guarded by a glorious figure in a white uniform and pith helmet, was not a very distinguished building, with a huge shamrock on the front. It was built in 1908, in the style of a plantation house, but mingily in some respects. When one reads of staircases on Nevis where ladies in panniered skirts could come down three abreast, it is a little disappointing to go through a front door and find the stairs rising abruptly and steeply in front of you, leaving little space to pass on either side of them to the back of the hall. The drawing-room was large enough, with two big photographs of the Queen and one of Prince Philip on the walls. The sofa- and chair-covers were of a hideous, floral print on a black background. It was gloriously British and it was here that I talked with the Governor, Mr Arthur Watson.

From what he told me, it appeared that almost everything militated against any hope of prosperity for Montserrat.

'Nothing works except for tourism. We do have a little success with vegetables, but America sits over us like a giant. It is cheaper to buy chicken pieces in boxes from the States than it is to grow them here.

'Transport costs across the island are very high. That is an old problem. In the days of sugar, it was difficult to co-operate with a central factory. Each estate had its own mill and often its own distillery.'

The Governor is responsible for all external affairs and for internal security, including the police. For other matters, there is a twelve-member council including the Governor, seven of whom are elected, two are ex-officio members and two are appointed by the Chief Minister (one with the Governor's guidance).

'It is rather an old-fashioned constitution, the original Chief Minister was quite content with it and no one seems in a hurry to change it. Nobody is really interested in independence. There is no strife here. After the slaves were emancipated, the philanthropist Joseph Sturge bought up several of the old sugar estates in order to benefit the people. This may account for the good nature of the people of Montserrat.'

Sturge, incidentally, was a Quaker from Gloucestershire, who came to Montserrat in 1836, two years after the abolition of slavery in all the British colonies. The estates which he bought up were eventually converted to growing limes. By 1885, there were a thousand acres of lime-trees and 180,000 gallons of juice were exported in that year. Limes became the mainstay of the island. As always, it was too good to last. In 1928, a hurricane destroyed all the lime-groves. The purveyors of juice abandoned Montserrat.

I sat in the little park by the sea front with Franklin Margetson, 'better known' as Fergus. He was a tall, very gentle person, with a grizzled beard, who had once been a member of the Legislative Council, but now runs the Land Development Department. (I hesitate to say that I cannot remember what colour he was, lest this sounds affected or, worse still, to him, offensive. My notes say he was pale. The interesting thing is that, after travelling for some months in the Caribbean, talking to educated people of all kinds, one literally becomes colourblind about people. It is only when prejudice or, for that matter, touchiness rears up that one again gives any thought to colour.)

'To be small,' said Mr Margetson, 'is a disaster, and Montserrat is very small.'

Recently, there has been a revival of cotton, one of those fashionable trends which so often give hope to the islands, only to fade some time later, crushing those enterprising people who have leaped at a chance. Sea Island Cotton used to be famous; here was an opportunity to revive it. The Japanese were eager buyers. Montserrat managed to put down 150 acres to cotton. It was not a lot, not enough, in the event, for it to be worthwhile for the cotton-boat to call at Plymouth. The Montserratians would have to make separate arrangements to ship their cotton to Barbados. This, at once, made the project uneconomic. Again, they could sell vegetables to St Maarten, but they cannot grow enough to be able to guarantee regular supplies.

Mr Margetson, when he was on the Legislative Council, belonged to the present ruling party, the People's Liberation Movement. Nonetheless, he feels they are not doing a good job, because they interfere too much and do not give the private sector sufficient opportunity. Yet he feared that the opposing People's Democratic Party was too conservative in its views. He believed that independence would come one day.

'Even the PLM have come round to it. The Chief Minister mentioned it today in a speech.' Then he added wryly, 'Of course, that may be the reason. When he found he was the only one in Caricom to be addressed as Chief Minister rather than Prime Minister, he may have changed his mind. If we were to become independent, it would put off investors.'

There were others who felt that the argument about investment was a weak one. Antigua and St Kitts get outside investors. Stability is not a guarantee for securing investors; nor, of course, is colonial status a guarantee of stability. There was a time when 'Associate Status' was in favour for islands of this sort. It did not work, not because it gave Britain, as one professor claimed, power without responsibility, but the exact reverse. The status quo suits the United States, and Britain is happy to go along with that. The cost is no greater than aid would be and it is reasonable to suppose that the people are perfectly happy, knowing little of other possibilities.

I fell into a ruminative mood on Montserrat. It was a charming place, but it had none of the feeling of adventure and excitement that I had both sensed in others and felt in myself in Dominica. It could not be just a question of landscape. Size does have something to do with it, Montserrat having one-sixth of the population of Dominica.

What must it be like, I wondered, to live in so small a place? Everyone knows everyone else. There is no escape as from a village in Britain to the anonymity of a big city. I saw, one morning, a work party from the prison. There were half a dozen prisoners in blue shorts and blue caps walking amiably along the road with an unarmed guard. Had they wished to escape, there was nowhere to escape to. The prison itself looked almost genial, with yellow stucco walls and, on the side presented to the street, white louvres as opposed to iron bars.

Everyone's day is spent in greetings. Automatically, strangers say 'Orright', or make that little hand movement as they pass one on the road, a gesture, perhaps, of sweeping aside anything disagreeable.

The inhabitants say that you live with it, this lack of privacy; but it must account to some degree for the emigration. Mr Margetson said that, when he was a young man, the population was higher by about three thousand.

I wrote in my diary: 'What a hell of a struggle this journey is. A battle of beliefs, if you like. Should all these islands become like Martinique? I want their lives to be improved, but what sort of improvement is it to have Capobianco when he gets rich? Remember how alive Dominica was. They had no condominiums, no golf-course. Montserrat gets more tourists, the only thing that works, as the Governor says. More villas. Is it an improvement to wreck all that is beautiful, by fitting it into a mould of vulgarity?'

It was high time to move on. In any case, it was not that bad. Despite the broken glass, there was one untidy thing missing. We had seen no broken-down cars on the roadsides. Round Montserrat there is no reef. They have found that if they pile up derelict cars on the sea bed, after a year, coral starts to grow on it. In the same time, forty new species of fish gather round it.

13
Nevis
GENTLEMEN AND PLAYERS

It was extraordinary how seldom we had an argument with anyone. I do not think that I am by nature cantankerous, but travel somehow fosters disputes. There are bureaucrats to deal with, who revel in recalcitrance. There are delays which fray the temper. There are rushes which stir the adrenaline. Air travel, in particular, with its treatment of passengers like cattle, almost sets out to exasperate.

We had flown back to Antigua and pondered about Barbuda, its dependent island. It was there that Sir Christopher Codrington, Governor of the Leeward Islands in the late seventeenth century, conducted experiments in the breeding of slaves. While the idea sounds revolting, he was in fact a worthy man. He conceived a great admiration for the Corramante tribe, who were unusually strong and finely built. Everyone else thought them difficult and obstreperous. Codrington thought them different from 'all other Negroes', and said, 'No man deserves to own a Corramante that would not treat him like a Friend rather than a slave.' The result is that, 300 years later, the people of Barbuda are astonishingly tall and handsome. However, we decided to fly straight to Nevis.

In the little Islander planes, I usually sat in a particular row of seats which was easier to get into. The pilot, a huge, grim man, said peremptorily that I was to sit in the back row. Hamish pointed out that it was difficult for him and painful for me to get in there. The pilot became rude and insistent. 'I always put wheelchair cases in the back.' Hamish asked him why.

'Because I say so. Otherwise, I won't fly.'

We had no choice. Hamish, spluttering, stuffed me, twisted and scraped, into the back. When we had landed and Hamish had hoicked me out again, I asked the pilot why he had not given his reason for condemning me to so awkward a position. He barked that I could have impeded other people's way out if we had had trouble. I thought that reasonable, but wondered why he could not have said so before.

'I am the Captain,' he said. It was an unusual attitude for the Caribbean. When I told people on Nevis about the incident, they all said: 'That must have been Killer Kelsick.' He had a reputation for contrariness, but also for remarkable skill as a pilot. 'He'd fly through a hurricane,' they said.

Nevis is even smaller than Montserrat by three square miles. The population is smaller, as well, by 2,000. An extinct volcano, rising to 3,200 feet, dominates the island. Its summit is usually obscured by a cap of cloud, looking a little like snow, which is why Columbus called the island Nuestra Senora de las Nievas.

We drove through the dark. There seemed to be hedgerows. I had a brief illusion of being back in England, driving through Cheshire on a warm summer's night. Even going through Charlestown, the capital, we might have been going through a little East Anglian or Kentish village, with wooden houses and larger buildings of stone and brick. The illusion faded as we turned down a bumpy track, past coconut groves, mango trees and, finally, clouds of bougainvillea. But it revived again at the English voices that greeted our arrival at my cousin's hotel on the site of an old plantation.

James Milnes-Gaskell came to Nevis in 1963. He bought a plantation called Montpelier. There were the ruins of the original sugar-boiling house and sugar mill, but little else. He set about building a hotel – a central block, with a dozen or more comfortable cottages. While waiting for his hotel, he became interested in local politics. At that time, Nevis belonged to a colonial grouping of three islands: St Kitts, Nevis and Anguilla. In 1967, this group was given near-independence by becoming

158

an Associated State of Great Britain. Appalling confusion followed, largely because of the wayward character of the Kittitian Prime Minister of the triple state, Robert Bradshaw. Anyone who chose to oppose him in any way ran a risk. Cousin James, than whom one can imagine no milder man, found himself in prison. He was not kept there long, a matter of seven weeks. But he was declared *persona non grata* and was not allowed back to his hotel until 1980, when the government changed. Two years later he married and he and his wife, Celia, run what Mark Ottaway thinks is one of: 'the foremost hotels of its class in the world.'

It does not really work like an hotel, more like a grand country house, with ancestral portraits on the walls, where the hosts have decided to have dinner in the conservatory for a change. I had hardly been there half an hour before I was involved in a deep conversation with Dr June Goodfield about the eradication of bilharzia in St Lucia and, not long after, another on the ethics of television journalism with the head of BBC television news.

I began to be afraid that this atmosphere, while pleasant as a holiday, would prove to be so seductive that I would learn nothing about the island. My fears were unfounded for several different reasons.

In the first place, Nevis seemed to me to be the first small island to have arranged its tourism rightly. Unlike Grenada and Tobago, where there are simply not enough well-run small hotels; unlike St Lucia where they favoured vast, impersonal hotels; unlike other islands which have introduced casinos; unlike Antigua where all the hotels except two are hideous; Nevis has several, really well-run, intimate, quiet, civilised, pretty hotels which might better be called inns.

The result is that the sort of people who go to Nevis are more civilised than those who go to other islands; they are also more inclined to get to know the Nevisians. And the Nevisians themselves have managed to maintain their values, especially their racial tolerance. (Their values, I need hardly add, do not include any lively regard for chastity. Young girls, I was told, usually have three babies before they get married.) Moreover, the Nevisians treat visitors as people of interest, rather than geese to be plucked.

The singularity of Nevis stems, too, from its past. It was said to have been settled largely by aristocratic younger sons, while its neighbour, St Kitts, was settled by people in trade. Whatever the truth of this, it was certainly a grand island, where the planters lived in huge Great Houses, with those majestic stairways wide enough for three, panniered ladies.

159

In the eighteenth century Nevis became a watering place, profiting from the mineral springs which flow just to the south of Charlestown. So popular was it that fashionable people from England would sail out to take the waters in the Queen of the Caribees, as the island was known.

We wandered among the evocative ruins of all the places of fashion, Ozymandias this time being endorsed by every pile of stones. The Bath Hotel, a tall building of stone, was first opened in 1778. John Huggins built the hotel for £40,000, an immense sum in those days. It was a splendid place with a huge ballroom and rooms for fifty guests. In 1825 a visitor complained that it was too big, but added that 'an invalid with a good servant might take up his quarters here with more comfort than in any other house of public reception in the West Indies.' At the end of the century, the Bath Hotel was sold for £40.

The building today is shuttered and bleak. Hamish managed to climb into it, but found it hard to work out where anything might have been, although there have been several attempts to restore it.

The Great House Eden Brown is gaunt and grey in its ruined state. Only a few walls with gaping, empty windows remain. It is tantalising because of the romantic legends about it. The story that most people told us was of a bridegroom challenged to a duel on his wedding eve by a rejected suitor of his betrothed. They fought. Both died. Even today, on the anniversary, anyone climbing to the ruins and spending the night there will hear the renewed cries of the bereaved bride.

Certainly there was one duel at Browne-Eden, as it was then called, in 1822. Edward Huggins, the younger, a relation of the Browne family who built it, was living in the Great House. He fought Walter Maynard. Maynard killed him and one can see his tomb near the old stables. Duels were quite common at that time. Usually they shot to miss. Huggins fired thus. Maynard aimed properly, according to some accounts because he considered Huggins to be lower-class. A girl later refused to marry him on the grounds that he was a murderer.

The child of the luckless Huggins may have been the original of the legend. George Juxon Huggins was born the year before his father was killed. In 1841, he was engaged to marry a girl from St Kitts, called Caroline Beard. Many people think he died in a duel with his best man, after an argument about a black girl. The legend has it that the house was abandoned forever after the duel. Nonetheless, there was a perfectly real Mrs Huggins, albeit a widow, living in the house in 1861 and it was inhabited until well into this century.

The tangle of Nevisian relationships is extremely confusing. Perhaps the grandest of all the Great Houses, Montravers, has connections with nearly every family of note on the island. The young heiress, who inherited this moated mansion in the middle of the eighteenth century, married John Pinney, a descendant of a far from aristocratic settler. Azariah Pinney, a Dorset refugee from the Monmouth Rebellion, arrived in Nevis in 1685 with only £15, a Bible, six gallons of sack and four of brandy. John was his great-grandson. When his estates were combined with Mary Helm's, they were worth £70,000.

John Pinney was a determinedly thrifty man, who was worth £340,000 when he died in England thirty years later. It is peculiar that so cautious a man should have decided to import camels to Nevis. Among the ruins of Montravers are the stables which he built for them. They did not thrive. A friend of James knew an old woman whose grandmother used to tell of the camels. She said one of them was called Neil – an unlikely name for a camel, until one realises that it was more probably an instruction rather than a name.

Montravers was sold for £35,650 in 1808, to Edward Huggins, father of the duel victim, whose other descendants lived there until the turn of the century. Then, when it was sold again, a manager married to a Maynard lived there until fifty years ago, when all its beautiful furniture was sold and it was left to crumble.

On the windward shore, we were drawn down to some less ruined buildings of beautiful cut stone, an old sugar mill. It looked romantic with the rough sea beyond, dark blue with white pinstripe waves. There were great outcrops of rock in the closely grazed links. Prickly pears with unusually small leaves were in yellow flower. They were spreading everywhere.

While we sat enjoying the spray-tinged wind, an old man appeared. He advanced with a kind of dancing gait. He was toothless and he had pink patches round the corners of his mouth.

'Melford O'Flaherty,' he said by way of introduction, repeating it a couple of times for reassurance. Did we want to see how the old sugar mill had worked? Yes, we did. Melford O'Flaherty plucked his cap off his head and then clapped it back on again. Then he began.

'Here, here is de standing. De standing it was called, de standing. And de kyarts drawn by mules, and de kyarts drawn by donkeys and de trucks drawn . . . no, not drawn. De kyarts drawn by mules and de kyarts drawn by donkeys and de trucks brought de cane here. What was it called?'

161

'How do you mean?' I asked, startled.

'I mean are you listening? I mean I told you what dis place where de kyarts drawn by mules and de kyarts drawn by . . .'

'It's called the standing,' I said, hurriedly.

'Dat's right, it's called de standing. Now you listen to what I say.'

And so we went round what was left of the rusting machinery of the sugar mill, one of the few steam-driven mills.

'Dere are tree kinds of sugar mill. De windmill driven by de wind. De mill with animals harnessed.' At this point O'Flaherty did a little dance to imitate a donkey. 'And de mill driven by steam. Tree kinds of mill, one wind, next animals, next steam.'

Every so often he would give us little tests to see if we had understood, for he plainly thought us very stupid. They were quite easy to pass, because he was never able to say anything fewer than three times.

Gradually O'Flaherty came to trust us, but it was more that he was so impressed by where Hamish could wheel me, than our attentiveness. When Hamish hauled me up a particularly steep and shaky stone stairway, O'Flaherty cried: 'The Lord be praised, praised be the Lord, praised the Lord.'

I learned more about the production of sugar that afternoon than I had in the whole journey.

On the original gateway of the plantation house of Montpelier there is a plaque:

On this site stood
MONTPELIER HOUSE
wherein
on the 11th day of March 1787
HORATIO NELSON
of immortal memory
then Captain of H.M.S. Boreas
was married to
FRANCES HERBERT NISBET

In Nelson's time, Montpelier belonged to Mr John Herbert, who was president of Nevis. Herbert must have been both upright and extremely amiable. If Nelson was unpopular on Antigua, he was loathed on Nevis.

Coming there in the *Boreas*, he discovered four American merchant ships, under a false flag, lying off Charlestown. They were laden with the American goods which were to be exchanged for the produce of many Nevisian merchants and plantation owners. Nelson ordered the vessels to leave. They refused. He then brought some of the crew to his ship and got them to confess that they were Americans. On the strength of these confessions, he impounded the goods on the ships.

The merchants sued Nelson for £40,000. Their claim was based on the notion that he was acting outside his jurisdiction and that such matters were, in peacetime, the concern of the governor, not of the navy. Nelson did not dare to leave the *Boreas* for eight weeks (except on Sundays, when no writs could be served) in case he were thrown in jail. Mr Herbert, who stood to lose money by Nelson's assiduous application of the Navigation Acts, nonetheless offered to put up £10,000 bail for the young, severe Captain.

It is hard to say whether Nevisian attitudes to Nelson changed because he married the widowed Frances or because of colonial love of royalty. Nelson's best friend was the future sailor-king, William IV, then Duke of Clarence, whose house we had seen in Antigua, looking down over English Harbour. He was captain of HMS *Pegasus*.

In a letter, the Prince wrote . . . 'From thence we all proceeded to Nevis. Here we remained a week. Nelson introduced me to his bride. She is a pretty and a sensible woman and may have a great deal of money if her uncle Mr Herbert thinks proper. Poor Nelson is over head and ears in love. I frequently laugh at him about it. However seriously, my Lord, he is in more need of a nurse than a wife. I do not really think he can live long . . . [Nelson] married Mrs Nisbet on the twelfth of March, and I had, my Lord, the honour of giving her away. He is now in for it. I wish him well and happy and that he may not repent the step he has taken . . .' The marriage actually took place on the eleventh of March.

The wedding was a grand affair, to which *le tout* Nevis came. The bridegroom and the best man wore their blue, white and gold, full-dress uniforms. The guests ate off a Royal Worcester service which had been specially made and shipped for the occasion.

Despite his treatment of poor Frances, Nelson is still highly regarded in Nevis. For twenty-seven years, Dr Robert Abrahams, an erudite Philadelphian, has collected all manner of things to do with Nelson. He has put his collection into the old sugar mill at Morning Star (where, incidentally, the militia surrendered, in 1706, to a marauding party of

French troops). Dr Abrahams has amassed an interesting variety of objects, including many letters, some plates from the Royal Worcester service, an invitation to Nelson's funeral, many pictures, prints and bibelots with appropriate associations. Rather surprisingly, the Doctor told me that he had come to the conclusion that Nelson, although of 'immortal memory', was a disagreeable man, somewhat in the style of MacArthur and Montgomery.

It was a pleasant comment on the pattern of life in Nevis that Dr Abrahams never locked the door of his museum and only once, two years before, had anything been stolen. Nor is colonial respect for royalty dead in Nevis. The clock in the museum is stopped at the precise moment at which the Queen came into the room on a visit in 1966. I did wonder, however, whether this is really a compliment she would appreciate. Even less likely to please her was the comedy on her more recent visit in 1985. She was asked to start the new generator which, it is hoped, will reduce the power cuts. Unfortunately, the new cables had not arrived. So men were sent to clean up the old generator and to give the sooty roof a new coat of paint. When the day came, everyone watched solemnly while the Queen pressed a button to restart the old generator. Let there be light.

We went, too, to another little museum, dedicated to Alexander Hamilton. Hamilton's story is one of those tales of perseverance and courage with which schoolteachers, thinking to inspire them, aggravate their more indolent pupils. Hamilton was born in 1757. His mother was the daughter of a Dr Fawcett who lived at Gingerland, in the south of the island. She must have been a rather erratic lady. She had married a man called Michael Lavien in about 1745. He had her convicted of adultery and jailed in Christiansted, on St Croix. When he judged that she had had time to reform, he arranged for her release. She rather sensibly ran away.

She returned to Nevis, where she had a house at the northern end of Charlestown near the sea, part of which is now the museum. She lived in it with a feckless figure called James Hamilton. Alexander was born in the house and lived there until he was five, when his father's debts drove the family to move to St Croix. Not long after they arrived, she died. Alexander worked in a hardware store and at sixteen went to America where, with the help of friends, he managed to continue his schooling in New Jersey. He fought at Yorktown against the English in the American War of Independence. After that he became a lawyer.

He prospered, rising eventually to be First Secretary of the American Treasury.

Alexander Hamilton's account of a hurricane, written when he was a boy of fifteen, in a letter to his father, is as vivid a description as any I have read and foreshadows his brilliance in later life:

St Croix, Sept. 6, 1772

Honoured Sir,

I take up my pen to give you an imperfect account of one of the most dreadful Hurricanes that memory or any records whatever can trace, which happened here on the 31st ultimo at night.

It began about dusk, at North, and raged very violently till ten o'clock. Then ensued a sudden and unexpected interval, which lasted about an hour. Meanwhile the wind was shifting round to the South West point, from whence it returned with redoubled fury and continued so 'till near three o'clock in the morning. Good God! what horror and destruction. Its impossible for me to describe or you to form any idea of it. It seemed as if a total dissolution of nature was taking place. The roaring of the sea and wind, fiery meteors flying about it in the air, the prodigious glare of almost perpetual lightning, the crash of the falling houses, and the ear-piercing shrieks of the distressed, were sufficient to strike astonishment into Angels. A great part of the buildings throughout the Island are levelled to the ground, almost all the rest very much shattered; several persons killed and numbers utterly ruined; whole families running about the streets, unknowing where to find a place to shelter; the sick exposed to the keeness of water and air without a bed to lie upon, or a dry covering to their bodies; and our harbours entirely bare. In a word, misery, in all its most hideous shapes, spread over the whole face of the country. A strong smell of gunpowder added somewhat to the terrors of the night; and it was observed that the rain was surprisingly salt. Indeed the water is so brackish and full of sulphur that there is hardly any drinking it.

Much of life on the island resembles the life of an English rural village. The fête at Government House, a hideous building of crazy-paving stone and corrugated iron, might just as well have been in a Bedfordshire backwater. There were rather few stalls, every one of them manned by white people, selling cakes, old clothes and all the rest of it. The white men wore yellow hats, which accorded ill with their red faces. The white women wore floral prints and large straw hats.

165

The brightest moment was the arrival of the band. They were called the Honey Bees. There were nine of them, led by a flautist who played brilliantly. The other players strummed on a banjo, a mandolin, two kinds of guitar, something that looked like a cross between a biscuit-tin and a cheese-grater, a long tube horn, like a didgeridoo I suppose, and presumably a drummer, though I don't remember him. Their hats were as varied as their instruments: a red cap, a green cap, a tweed cap, a white cap with a crest, a red floppy hat, a leather cap, a brown tea-cosy, one barehead and the flautist in a trilby.

The flautist's eyes slid round the crowd, taking in every reaction. Ten little children sucking iced-lollies, and looking themselves like iced-lollies in their sharp-coloured dresses, stood rocking to the music. In no time, the flautist had coaxed them into a real and happy dance, until their teacher came and, for some reason, ordered them away.

On another day we went to the cricket. The girls in the hotel would always discuss cricket at breakfast. They told us that we must go. It was the Leeward Islands versus Barbados. It was a Sunday and the ground was full – there were perhaps a thousand spectators. Everyone sat on the grass. There were just as many women in the crowd as there were men. It was a great outing, with tiny children taking a keen interest in the game. And the game itself was, it seemed to me, a sporting, good-natured game. The audience joined in with much shouting of advice and great roars of encouragement or disapproval. There was beer on sale, but there were only two drunks, one with a Maurice Bishop T-shirt, inscribed 'His spirit lives'. There was one man with a cow-bell which he rang at moments of excitement. Another man in a fawn suit gravely raised his broad-banded boater to me each time we happened to meet.

We watched Vivian Richards bowling at Joel Garner, whose sheer height looked astonishing. He seemed as tall as Nuestra Senora de las Nievas rising behind him, as he whacked boundaries off almost every ball. A small boy, sitting on the grass beside me, said he was looking forward to the test matches which were starting in Trinidad.

'We'll have to teach you how to play the game,' he said.

I said that, perhaps, we might do better this time.

'Well, I hope you win one,' he said, with Nevisian courtesy.

Not everything was as peaceful as this. There was much talk of a murder. A little old woman of eighty-two had been raped and killed. She

166

was a great bridge player and she had been expecting friends for a game of cards. They telephoned to say they could not come. It is assumed that she went out to shut the gate which she would have left open for her visitors. She was set upon. The first suspect was a man just out of prison, who said he was going to get anyone who could be blamed for his conviction, which in some way could have applied to the old woman. He was found to have an alibi. Gossip had a new suspect – a foreigner, who was said to have answered calls for many days saying his wife was out, when she was dead. It was whispered that he had taken her body out to sea and dumped it. The only basis for accusing him seemed to be that he lived not very far from the victim. The police were baffled.

On the third day we were there, the whole island had a different excitement. A party of people had gone up the mountain. When the time came to go down, three of them, a man and two girls, told the others to go ahead. They would follow. The man said he knew the way through the thick undergrowth. Quite soon, the three were lost. It sounds simple to walk down a mountain, but it is not. There are gullies and *ghauts* which cannot be crossed and many acres of impenetrable undergrowth. The two girls got fed up with following the man down so many false trails. They decided to climb back to the summit and wait to be rescued. Rescuers found them after thirty-six hours.

There was, however, no sign of the man. Everybody had an opinion as to what had happened to him. Everyone gave his opinion as fact. One of the most popular theories was that he was too ashamed to come out and that he would hide until everyone had forgotten about him. The most gruesome possibility was adumbrated by the ferryboat captain, whom we will meet shortly. He told me that there were many wild pigs on the mountain, the descendants of those brought by the conquistadores or by buccaneers and left behind. If anyone, alone on the mountain, falls and breaks a leg, he ends up as a pile of bones. After four days, the man walked out of the forest, weary but otherwise all right.

There is always a lively political feeling on all the islands, even those which are independent and unconnected with any other. On islands which are still colonies or partners with another, it is even more spirited. There is on Nevis an undercurrent of dislike for St Kitts, with whom they are linked and where the central seat of government is. This may be the natural unease of the small partner in any enterprise. It may be, as one Nevisian suggested to me, a relic of past snobbery, when the aristocratic Nevisian contempt for the Kittitian tradesfolk spread even to the slaves of Nevis, who came to despise the slaves of St Kitts. My own fancy was that the people of the Caribbean share with other people of charm, whose lives are precarious, a special individuality. It is a quality highly developed in Gypsies and Arabs, particularly nomads. They find it impossible to agree on anything, yet when an outside threat presents itself, they rally together and close ranks to defend themselves. But, as the Attorney-General on St Lucia said, where is the outside threat to the islands?

After the secession of Anguilla from the group, Nevis was given its own Assembly, which is really something like a County Council. The head of it is known as the Premier. In the case of the present incumbent, Mr Simeon Daniel, he is also Minister of Natural Resources and the Environment in St Kitts' Government.

I had been warned that Mr Daniel was outrageously unpunctual, so I took a book to my appointment and passed a happy hour reading Michael Foot's *Debts of Honour*. I was particularly struck by a passage referring to Hazlitt's mockery of the various splinters of the Dissenting Movement.

The people of the Caribbean are deeply religious, but I had been dismayed by the proliferation of preposterously-named churches, spreading from America. On Nevis, quite apart from the five Anglican churches, seven Methodist and two Roman Catholic chapels, there were buildings belonging to Seventh Day Adventists, Pentecostalists, the Wesleyan Holiness, the Church of the God of Prophecy, the Church of God of Mount Carmel, The Emmaus Chapel, all of which claim to be Christian, and a temple of the Jehovah Witnesses, who I trust make no such claim. In Charlestown alone, with a population of 1,200, I counted seven different churches. How Hazlitt would have shivered.

Even had I not enjoyed my wait, I would have at once been won over by Mr Daniel. I thought him decidedly cuddly, extremely polite, modest and calm. He was at pains to tell me how much he loved England, apart from the weather, and how happy Nevisians were in Britain. Most of them, he claimed, were in work. I had seen him at the cricket match and we talked of that. He complained that the last day of the match had been so slow simply to enable two of the players to get their centuries.

'The problem is that everyone plays for himself. They should have gone for it.' This seemed to echo my views of the individuality of the people of the Caribbean.

On the whole, the Premier is an optimist. He told me that the sugar plantations came to an end rather earlier than on other islands, because of the thin and rocky soil, unlike the rich volcanic earth of St Kitts, with the result that most of the land passed to the peasants in smallholdings. There is little real poverty. As opposed to the attitudes in most of the other islands, on Nevis, to work the land is not considered contemptible on the grounds of its being slave-work. Indeed, Mr Daniel said the first thing a young man wanted was a plot of land, however small. Of course, there is unemployment and most of the sixth-formers emigrate. I wondered what the genetic effect of this brain-drain might ultimately be on a small population.

Mr Daniel sees the future as 'myriads of small businesses, mostly initiated by foreigners with Nevisian partners.' In that way, he believes he can get Nevis on a sound economic footing.

'Then the question of secession won't arise, because they won't want to lose us and we won't be dependent on them for anything.'

Nevertheless, I did not detect in him any great affection for Kittitians.

His critics, however, believe that Mr Daniel is gullible to a dangerous degree, ready to listen to any rogue. I was told of a complete stranger's offering the Premier $100,000, without his ever inquiring as to where the money was coming from. They think him charming but woolly and believe that Nevis would long ago have broken away from St Kitts if he had only had more gumption.

One who disparages the Premier is Samuel Hunkins. This person of consequence is primarily a building contractor. It was he who built Montpelier for James. He is tall and languid. When I met him, he was wearing both a belt and braces to keep up his fawn trousers. He did not appear to understand when I asked if he were pessimistic. We sat in his funeral parlour. (He is a man of many parts.) On the wall was a certificate from The Great Southern School of Embalming, saying that 'Thelma Hunkins was qualified in both practical and theoretical embalming.' I took this to mean the theory and practice, 'theoretical embalming' not sounding a likely event. Thelma was his daughter.

Sam said he had started life in considerable poverty. He had started to learn his trade at the age of thirteen. He is now the biggest builder on the island, quite apart from his sidelines.

He had no opinion of the government and claimed that he was poorly treated in consequence. For instance, he is always being told to move his car, while others are allowed to park immediately in the place from which he has just been removed. He belongs to no party and, although pressed by friends to go into politics, he does not want that life – 'fame and travel to conferences, that is what they like.' But he would always want to join in anything that would make Nevis a better place.

Sam is unpopular, he says, because he does not say Nevis is the prettiest island in the world, where everything is peaceful and everyone is happy. He thinks it is badly governed by people who think only of self. And that is true throughout the Caribbean. He even believes there is corruption on Nevis.

'You know we had a murder? They say no one can find anything. Do you really think in a place so small no one knows anything? So is that corruption?

'If there are two girls, one is all covered in make-up, wearing a short skirt, and the other is demure and holy. Only when one gets pregnant do they say she is immoral.'

I looked a bit bemused at this parable.

'I mean,' said Sam, 'it is never corruption until they are caught. They go to church, are lay readers. Look at Pindling in the Bahamas. No one says anything until they are caught.'

Sam, of course, had quite a different opinion from everyone else on the subject of separation from St Kitts. He wanted to join the two islands together by a gigantic, two-mile causeway. He was much impressed by the news of the Channel Tunnel.

'Look at France and England. People must get together to do things.'

Another individualist of a different kind is Captain Anslyn, 'better known' as Brother. He is the skipper of the ferry which plies between Nevis and St Kitts. He is a large, jovial man with the resounding voice of an opera singer. His father was Dutch, his mother Nevisian. He appears to be the person to whom everyone takes his troubles. He runs a society for the fishermen of the island. He told me that Nevis exports fish to St Kitts, mostly bottom fish – grouper and snapper – and some migratory such as king fish and what they call dolphin, which is really dorado. He is not involved in politics, but he believes that Nevis will separate from St Kitts. He only hopes it will be an amicable parting, because there are so many families, half of whom live on one island and half on the other.

But it is the ferry which really matters to Brother. His father had been the ferry captain. Then another man took over. The ferry sank with fearful loss of life. When a new ferry was bought, Brother took over. He runs the *Caribe Queen* almost as if she were the flagship of a navy. She is spruce and clean. She always leaves at the appointed minute, never early, never late.

A year before, Brother had saved the *Caribe Queen* by a feat of extraordinary daring. The ferry was having an engine overhaul in St Kitts and was tethered to Deep Water Pier at Basseterre. The weather became unexpectedly rough. It was November. The usual hurricane season is from June to September, so there was little to fear. Moreover, there was nothing sinister in the weather forecast. Nevertheless, it was rough, so Brother untethered the boat, took it on its one working engine and anchored it in the roadstead, about two hundred yards off shore. He left three crew members on board and went ashore.

The next morning the weather was appalling. The swells had increased by ten or twelve feet. The wind was blowing at seventy-five miles an hour. The storm had become Hurricane Claus. Brother tried all day to get the police launch to take him out to the ferry. No one could find the officer in charge. His deputy would not take the risk.

'I think he would have made it, otherwise I would not have asked him, but I understand his reluctance.'

Brother used the same matter-of-fact phrase a little later. The weather got worse. He thought the ferry could not last much longer. Several boats broke loose and smashed on the rocks. The crew on board might die. Also, so many people's livelihoods depended on the ferry. The country could not afford another. He was responsible, he felt, for the safety of the vessel, the crew and its passengers. He decided to swim out. He radioed to the crew on the ferry to watch out for him.

'I drove to the home of one of my crew members who was ashore and told him that he and I would swim out to the vessel. His name is Alfred Gumbs, the son of Basie Gumbs. I asked him to come with me as I thought it would be safer for two of us to go. I am a very strong swimmer. Gumbs is also. I would not have asked him if I had not known this. I borrowed two pairs of swimming flippers.'

By now it was dark. Brother and Alfred Gumbs dived off the Deep Water Pier into the tempest sea. Debris was flying, hurled by the waves.

'We swam under the waves. Had we been on top, they would have rolled us over and the debris was more likely to hit us.'

The headlights of four cars on the pier guided them to the ship. How long the swim took he does not remember. It seemed endless. They reached the ship. The ladder had been torn away. Brother shouted

171

to his crew to lower a tyre on a rope. The boat was rolling so much that the propellers were lifting out of the water. It was nearly impossible to clamber on board, but at last they achieved it.

Brother hauled up one anchor and slipped the other. On their one starboard engine, they started to move. The *Caribe Queen* did not respond. The wild sea and the one-sided engine drove her towards the pier. Brother reversed his one engine. The boat shuddered and 'for the longest while' hung poised. Then gradually she started to back slowly out to sea.

All night, Brother and his crew rode out the storm. In the day, he brought her safely back and tethered her to the Deep Water Pier. He had saved his crew and the livelihood of his passengers and, of course, his *Caribe Queen*.

The days stretched happily on. We went sailing with a couple of gentle Americans, Fred and Mary Davis, in their yacht *Curlew*. They live on the yacht, doing day charters and dabbling in antiques. We sailed close to St Kitts, looking at Booby Island on the way, watching those strange birds which gave the rock its name. By some perversity, we were not allowed to anchor off St Kitts to picnic, because the Davises' licence worked only on Nevis. Mary gave us the best lobster salad of our whole journey and Fred sang to his guitar. He also had a tape of a Calypso which I had not heard since childhood:

> *It's love, love and love alone*
> *Which caused King Edward to leave the throne.*

There was so much that appealed on Nevis, perhaps because it, more even than other islands, represented the Caribbean philosophy that might be summed up by the phrase that nothing matters very much and very little matters at all.

Brother told me that, until recently, 'for the longest while,' the sterilisation unit at the hospital was broken. Every morning the instruments went over to St Kitts on his ferry and were brought back in the evening. Any major disaster in the daytime would have found them without a scalpel.

Mary Davis had told me that the Charlestown dentist was of the opinion that the Nevisian children living with two parents were more mixed up than those living with one parent.

172

I liked the idea of the secret stills in the hills, known colloquially as Hammonds after a local administrator who predicted, evidently correctly, that they would never be stamped out.

Above all, perhaps, I loved the lack of racial tension. The Premier had said that any such feelings were virtually unknown. (Other complained that he was inclined to go to too many American all-white parties.)

It would have been easy to stay, but we were already abusing James and Celia's delightful hospitality. So we boarded Brother's *Caribe Queen* and arrived in St Kitts.

14

St Kitts

FIRE AND BRIMSTONE

It could be argued that the British Empire was founded in St Kitts and that its founder was Thomas Warner, who landed at Old Road on 28 January 1623. Until that time, the British had been little more than pirates or brigands. The great Elizabethan sailors, Raleigh, Hawkins and especially Drake, were really intent on tormenting the Spanish and looting their treasure, rather than acquiring colonies.

Thomas Warner came of yeoman stock from Framlingham, in Suffolk. He was a soldier, who achieved the rank of captain in the King's Guard. In 1619, he joined an expedition to Surinam in search of Eldorado. During that voyage he conceived the idea of creating a settlement on a West Indian island, there to plant tobacco, spices and dyes.

Warner raised the money and took with him, initially, fourteen adventurous men, all from Suffolk, whose names read like Widdecombe Fair: William Tasted, John Rhodes, Robert Binns, Mr Benifield, Serjeant Jones, Mr Ware, William Ryle, Rowland Grasscocke, Mr Bond, Mr Langley, Mr Weaver, Serjeant Aplon and two other, nameless, figures.

174

They chose St Christopher's (as the island is still officially known) because it had water, a fine forest and very fertile soil. Notwithstanding these advantages, their first year was in many ways a portent of what all settlers' and planters' lives were to be over the next three and a half centuries. They built houses, planted corn and tobacco. They had plenty to eat. Rowland Grasscocke wrote to his family in England: '. . . all this while we lived well upon cassado bread, potatoes, plantanes, pines, turtles, guanas and fish a-plenty and for drink we had nicknobby.' Pines were pineapples, guanas iguanas and nicknobby something brewed from potatoes.

In September, a hurricane wiped out all their work, blowing away their houses and all their crops. They must have had fortitude. By the following February, they had harvested and packaged a whole new crop of tobacco. In March that year, more recruits arrived. In 1625, Charles I granted Warner the Governorship of St Kitts, Nevis, Montserrat and Barbados. It is true that it was not long before the King took them away again and gave all the Caribbean in perpetuity to the Earl of Carlisle, but respect for Warner remained.

Warner's example inspired hundreds of British people to emigrate to the West Indies and thus the first colonies were created. When the settlers switched their attention from tobacco to sugar, in about 1643, they began to make vast fortunes. Sugar was the seventeenth and eighteenth centuries' equivalent to oil in the twentieth century. It was a matter of great doubt in 1763 at the Treaty of Paris, whether Britain would decide to keep Canada or give that great country to France in exchange for Martinique and Guadeloupe.

In 1629, Warner was knighted. At the time of the ceremony, Queen Henrietta-Maria persuaded the king to give him also a beautiful, heart-shaped diamond ring. This ring had a romantic legend attached to it. Queen Elizabeth was said to have given it to her favourite, the Earl of Essex. When she gave it, she told Essex that, if ever he fell from favour and was in danger from her anger, he should send her the ring and she would remember her affection for him and pardon him.

Essex later was tried for treason and condemned to die. The Queen waited. The ring did not come. She decided that Essex was too proud. She signed the warrant for his execution.

Two years later, the Countess of Nottingham lay dying. She asked the Queen to visit her. She told Elizabeth that Essex had sent the ring, which she now gave to the Queen. She explained that Essex had passed

175

the ring through a window to a boy, asking him to take it to Lady Scroop, who would deliver it to the Queen. The boy took it, by mistake, not to Lady Scroop, but to her sister, Lady Nottingham. Lord Nottingham was an enemy of Essex. He forbade his wife to deliver the ring. She now asked the Queen to forgive her on her deathbed.

Elizabeth beat the dying woman, shaking her violently. 'God may forgive you, madam, but I never shall.' On returning home, the Queen sank into a decline, induced by grief and remorse. Within a month she died.

The ring descended through the Warner family to Charles Warner, the Attorney-General of Trinidad. In 1863, thieves stole it from his house in Port of Spain.

Sir Thomas Warner lived on until 1648. One of the first places I went to on St Kitts was St Thomas Church and graveyard, where Sir Thomas is buried. The church is in a very dilapidated state. The graveyard, sloping down to the village of Middle Island, is overgrown, but grand with royal palms. To one side, under a rickety, wooden canopy (I find that my notes use precisely the same words that Leigh Fermor used forty years ago) is Sir Thomas's tomb. A big marble slab rests on a stone base; three corners of the slab are missing, including some words from the uninspired poem to the good knight's memory. However, I liked one line:

> . . . hee still gave forth
> Large Narratives of Military worth
> Written with his swords poynt . . .

While I contemplated this tomb, an evangelist preacher was bellowing his message in the village beyond the graveyard. He made alleluia sound like the repeated slogan of a mad political speech. A gentle church-warden came to tell me of the efforts to restore the church. He produced from his pocket a cheque for $150 from a black Warner, recently returned from working in the United States.

Later, the Kittitian historian, Lloyd Matheson, told me a strange story of a visit by Sir Fred Warner, Britain's former Ambassador to Japan, to the grave of his ancestor. Mr Matheson took Sir Fred and his wife to the tomb. When they had looked at it, they wandered round the other graves and went into the church. They happened to notice that the huge bell of the church had been taken down. It was sitting, mute, on the floor of the belfry. When they were about to leave, Mr Matheson and Lady Warner walked towards the car, but Sir Fred went back alone to have one final look at the tomb.

At the moment that he reached it, the earth started to tremble and the air was filled with a rumbling sound. The shaking grew stronger and more violent. Stones fell crashing from the church tower. Then one clear, solemn note rang out from the churchbell.

What rage, one wonders, prompted the shade of Sir Thomas to conjure up an earthquake measuring 6.4 on the Richter scale and to clang inert bells, when confronted by his descendant. Or shall we say, what a coincidence?

Lloyd Matheson is the man largely responsible for the restoration of Brimstone Hill Fortress, known slightly ambiguously as the Gibraltar of the West Indies. I say ambiguously because it is perhaps best known for its defence, in 1782, against a siege by the French under the Marquis de Bouillé. The French, with eight thousand men, surrounded the Fort, where one thousand British troops held out for a month. It was one of those defeats which the British somehow convert in their minds to victories.

It is true that at the same time, as we saw earlier, Hood was dealing de Grasse's fleet a shocking pounding off Basseterre and that the whole war was shortly to be brought to an end by the Battle of the Saints. But equally, it is true that General Shirley, on 12 February, decided that 'it was expedient for the King's services to beat a parley and offer to capitulate for the surrender of the garrison upon terms honourable to His Majesty's arms and advantageous to the Colony'.

The siege had partly been lost because St Kitts merchants, furious at Rodney's destruction of their goods in the warehouses of the neighbouring Dutch islands of St Eustatius, had almost treacherously prevented guns and ammunition from being taken up to the Fort. When the French arrived, they found at the foot of Brimstone Hill, eight brass sixteen-pounders with 6,000 shot and two fifteen-inch brass mortars with 1,500 shell. These they used to breach the walls.

After the Treaty of Versailles in 1783, which restored the island to the British, new bastions were built to make the fortress truly impregnable. Thereafter it was never needed and, in 1853, it was abandoned by the military and its garrison sent to fight in the Crimea. The fortress mouldered. During the early part of this century, a few gestures were made towards preserving the fort but, in 1965, a society was formed, dedicated to restoring the whole site. They have done a remarkable job.

Brimstone Hill is an oddity. It rises abruptly to 800 feet, just inland from the northern end of the eastern shore. Geologically, it is quite unrelated to the mountains which stand behind it. It is, as it were, autonomous.

We drove up past various bastions, past the water catchment and past the arcade of the infantry officers' quarters, all built of beautifully-cut, dark, volcanic stone. The great Fort George was higher yet and the way to it was a steep ramp with occasional steps, perhaps a hundred yards long. It was more than I cared to ask even Hamish to attempt. In the café was a boy of sixteen, called Aldon. He was shocked that I was not going up to the fort. He told me that he so loved the place that he wanted to build a house on Brimstone Hill. He said he was strong and would help Hamish to get me up. By way of proof, he produced his thick, red tracksuit top. He said he walked great distances in this to get his body heated, which he thought was a healthy thing. Between them, he and Hamish dragged me up the precipitous ramp, Aldon declaring that I was the first person in a chair ever to reach the top.

Standing above the irregular pentagon of the courtyard, the view from the fort in all directions was splendid. We could see Nevis to the south, and to the north, barely six miles away, St Eustatius (known as Statia), beyond her Saba, and, a little to the east, and shadowy, St Maarten and St Barthélémy. More immediately, behind us rose Mount Misery, to nearly four thousand feet. Before us was the sea. From above, the sea looked calm, as it always does from a height. Yet it cannot have been, for a rainbow hovered over the water, formed by the sun shining on the spray. There was an unending variety of colours in the sea, spreading from the palest, turquoise shallows to the ink-dark depths, the colours enlivened by the patterns on the surface, created by flowing rivers, currents and unknown eddies.

We stayed and watched, too, the patterns on the land as dusk was coming. At first, a hundred different greens and, above, the dark of the mountain and, higher still, the grey and black of the clouds. Then the sky, with a pink and white tinge, while below, the last shafts of the sun mottled the huge green sweep with yellow. The cows stood out black, as their white egret attendants grew restless, anxious to fly to their communal nesting ground.

*　　　*　　　*

St Kitts consists really of two islands, joined by a narrow, flat isthmus. Basseterre lies at the southern end of the larger, fertile part. It is a town of some charm, although most of it has been rebuilt and rebuilt after the large number of disasters which beset the island, of which Sir Thomas's hurricane of 1623 was merely the first. In 1867 a great fire burned 500 houses, almost five-sixths of all the houses of the town. Hardly had it been rebuilt when, in January 1880, a great rainstorm hit Basseterre. In barely twelve hours, thirty-six inches of rain fell upon the town. Houses and buildings were torn from their foundations and swept into the sea. 231 people died. Fifteen bodies washed up on Statia. 115 were never found. Despite all this and later hurricanes, there are many pretty buildings, with stone for the ground floor and often two, even occasionally three, storeys with wooden balconies above.

It is a bustling town, with an air of energy which we had not seen since Guadeloupe, but it was a great deal more friendly. One morning, I was waiting in the street while Hamish performed some errand. A small boy on stilts asked me for seventy-five cents. He said it was to buy a tart. I was impressed by his skill on the stilts, which he had made himself out of junk. I gave him a dollar. In a few minutes, he was back, munching his tart. He offered to give me the twenty-five cents change.

We were staying not in Basseterre, but in a hotel on the isthmus with comfortable cottages. We had been met off the ferry by a gloriously bluff, ex-naval officer – Commander Reg Oldman DSO, OBE, a most hospitable and enthusiastic man. He had brought his enormous, American car right on to the pier where the ferry docked. He had some difficulty turning it among the mass of parcels, packages, window frames, motorbikes and vast collection of impedimenta which had come with us on the boat.

It was plain that everyone knew and liked the Commander. Some boys, fishing off the pier, had hooked a stingray. It had intelligently fastened itself to a post of the pier near the waterline. There was a great debate as to how they might dislodge the ray. For a moment, I thought the Commander was going to encourage the boys in their plan of taking the pier apart. Then it was possible to turn the car and we went.

Before dropping us at our hotel, Reg took us for a tour of Frigate Bay, and the isthmus, during which he contradicted everything which everyone on every other island had told me. He spoke with gusto of two- and three-hundred bedroom hotels. Anything less was, he said, quite uneconomic. He had no fear of crime or any interest by the Mafia.

The rest of the island, beyond the isthmus, is barren. It has the same clay soil as Nevis. In the centre is a large salt pond. There is no road on that part. Reg wanted a road to be built and a large number of big tourist hotels, as many as possible. He urged us to go to the casino, not far from our hotel. The bar in ours had no real food, so we walked towards the casino and found a simple, reasonably cheap restaurant or pizza bar, catering for the tourists in the four or five hotels already on the isthmus.

There was a sweetly innocent waitress whom Hamish was eyeing, until I restrained him. (He had not had enough windsurfing lately to absorb his energies, not that it ever made much difference.) Her mother had given her an autograph book and she asked me to sign it and perhaps write a poem to go with my autograph. I asked her name. It was Debbie. I could find no rhyme to Debbie, except possibly 'mebbe', but that seemed to lack verve. *Brebis?* I gave up.

We went across to the casino. It had the gloom of all modern casinos, which for some reason have to be dark, with only pools of light round the tables. All the gambling was conducted in US dollars. Hamish had never been in a casino before, so I bought him a few chips. Very few, when I found that, having only English money, they would give me less than one dollar in exchange for one pound.

Gamblers are depressing to watch. They never have any air of enjoyment. Moreover, I find it mildly provoking that they put on a face of consequence, as if they were doing something important rather than something foolish.

Any ill-humour of this sort was soon overtaken by a real indignation on learning that Kittitians were not allowed in. How can you not be allowed into something, otherwise public, in your own country? That alone seems to me to be patronising and unpleasant in a way which almost equals the old, colonial 'whites only' rules. Whenever I asked people about this, they said it was done to please the churches, but that the Kittitians would not want to go anyway. Hypocrisy was added to gross condescension. Hamish soon lost his few chips and we left.

In the next cottage at our hotel was a man evidently seething with nervous energy. He looked American, was aged about forty and bounced around like a puppy. He played music, very loudly: endless well-known pieces of Beethoven, Mozart, Chopin, Sibelius. While the music was on he would whistle or sing to it, sadly out of tune. When there was no music, he would whistle and sing even flatter, often confusing one piece of music with another, going off at unexpected tangents. What started as the 'Pastoral' might well end as 'Eine Kleine Nachtmusik'.

Eventually, we got to know him. His name was Rocky Soderberg. He came from North Carolina and spoke with what seemed to us, after months of West Indian voices, like a caricature Southern accent. He turned out to be a Quaker, full of unlooked-for compassion for black people, but with all of the Quaker reluctance to proselytise.

He had worked in Haiti in some way which he never made clear. He had an endearing *naïveté* and would declare his general disapproval of most missionaries, but add that he knew of some who did good work – like Mother Teresa. He recited a verse which he said he held dear. It went something on the lines of, 'If I could read your heart, and if you could read my heart, then we'd find we weren't so far apart.' We sat and were solemn for a bit after that.

Rocky also had that Quaker belief in business. The explanation of his presence in St Kitts was that he ran a factory in the industrial estate, making baseball hats. He invited us to visit it. When we got there, the place looked as if it were shut. There were no signs. The only entrance was a tiny door at one side of the long factory building. We crept in.

There were about fifty women, sitting in rows like a classroom, all stitching with nimble fingers. They oohed and aahed at the sight of Hamish who, with his dark hair and large blue eyes, has this curious effect on women, which I found decidedly aggravating.

Rocky appeared and allotted us a guide, who took us through every stage of the manufacture of baseball caps. The girls ogled Hamish. I learned a lot about hats. The girls were paid $37 a week. (I wondered how they lived when, for instance, a packet of washing powder cost $3.70. They use plain old soap, somebody told me. But everything is expensive.) They produced 1,300 dozen baseball hats a week.

There were sixty people working in all. Rocky had just started to make what he called 'lonjuree' and expected to employ 150 people the next year. Then he would expand into 'swimwear'.

Strangely, there was no music playing. I asked Rocky why not. He avoided the question twice. I suspected that he knew that the girls would want reggae. At last, a little shamefaced, he said, 'I rather like the quiet.'

The contrast between Nevis and St Kitts was so marked that I began to wonder whether the theory that Nevis was settled by aristocrats and St

Kitts by tradespeople might not have had some truth to it. Business certainly seems the keynote today.

Mr William Kelsick was perhaps an exceptionally powerful figure but his attitudes were, I felt, representative of the mercantile spirit of the island. He was chairman of a merchant group involved in every kind of business and managing director and chairman of St Kitts Breweries. He was a massive person of great courtesy and bonhomie, rising out of his cluttered office like some superman. He was deeply patriotic and wore a dark blue tie with the crest of St Kitts and Nevis on it. There was no question in his mind but that mass tourism was what St Kitts should pursue.

'Sugar has had it. You can perhaps get sixteen cents a pound for it in Europe, but it costs twenty-two cents to produce. All our savings have gone on supporting sugar, some £14 million. We have 2,000 unemployed out of a workforce of 18,000.'

'A woman sugar worker gets $18.50 a week. A cane cutter earns $92.50. In a hotel, she can earn $92.50 and he might make a little more, not much, but in both cases it would be for ten months of the year, not five.'

'You have to have numbers or you won't get the air service. To ensure regular Pan-Am flights, we have to have 1,700 beds. That's what they insist on.'

Of course, investors are hard to find and everyone is competing for them. A hotel room costs $60,000 to build. Mr Kelsick's hope is that USAID will give St Kitts both a road and a safe harbour for the barren end of the island, which is now accessible only on foot or by sea. Given those, they would hope for a mass of large hotels.

I felt some sympathy for this idea, particularly if it would provide better-paid work, as I had noticed what appeared to be greater poverty and definitely worse housing than on Nevis. Perhaps it would be possible to keep tourism to the isthmus and the barren end of the island, while ordinary Kittitian life could continue undisturbed in the prettier part of the island. As a means of survival, this kind of tourist *apartheid* might be acceptable, but it is hardly attractive.

Kelsick was very brisk about Nevis. He said that they could never find any solution other than being linked to St Kitts.

'When Simeon Daniel won a big enough majority to get rid of them, he should have done so. Instead, he took them into his cabinet.' By 'them', I took him to mean the separatists.

182

'They bleed us all the time. If they went on their own, Daniel would have to tax the people heavily and he wouldn't last long.'

We talked of Caricom, the Caribbean economic group. Trinidad, he said, was wrecking it. There was no end to Trinidad's mischief. For example, tyres from Trinidad cost twice as much as they did from Japan, although there was a duty of forty-five per cent on Japanese ones. Trinidad's wage-scale was ludicrous. Dockers were paid excessive wages, but did less work. (I had heard in Grenada of Trinidad dockers earning $60,000 a year.) The result was that ship turn-round was slow and consequently, freight costs were high. A bank employee's job, perhaps paying £15,000 in London, would be advertised in Trinidad at $40,000. It cost four times as much to produce a ton of sugar in Trinidad as in St Kitts.

'But Caricom has to work. Oh, if only the stupid politicians would forget their squabbles and let *us* get on with it.'

The one politician I did meet in St Kitts was Dr Billy Herbert. He was really a lawyer, but had been put in prison with my cousin James, by the corrupt Prime Minister Bradshaw. He is now St Kitts' ambassador to anywhere and everywhere, a system which works well and is economical. Dr Herbert is humorous and extremely flirtatious. We met in a bar and started to discuss cricket.

'Of course, we beat Trinidad. You know we have a world champion athlete? The world light heavyweight champion. And we won the basketball and the football. How, when we are so small, only 45,000 people? Because we have quality. You know Trinidad could have been the leader of the Caribbean if it were not for her profligate ways. Thank you, darling.'

This last to the girl who brought the beer and she looked at him with happy appreciation.

Dr Herbert's views coincided almost exactly with Mr Kelsick's, except that he had campaigned strongly against allowing the casino. He believed in big hotels and thought that they could keep the island divided with all the tourism confined to one end. He was not so worried about unemployment. It was, he thought, more a case of under employment. At about this point, he saw a girl at an upstairs window and blew her a kiss.

He told me that they had created 3,000 jobs on the industrial estate and that St Kitts, in the previous year, had produced $24 million worth of electronic equipment, equal to the production of all the other small islands added together. He blew another kiss to a girl in the street.

'I have been putting off going to New York, to the UN, for about two months. I told them when I took the job on that I would not represent my country in the cold weather. But I will take a risk with the cold and go to Japan to see if I could be the first to squeeze some aid out of them.'

We talked about Miss Charles's alarm about communism and infiltration.

'I like her very much, but it's an old record and I wish she'd stop playing it. Of course, it pleases Uncle Sam, so perhaps they'll give her more aid. That and women's rights. They'll need men's rights on Dominica soon or there'll be no men left.'

We moved on to the colour question. Dr Herbert said there was a complete mixing on St Kitts because there were so many indigenous whites. The French, in his view, were the most hypocritical, telling you how perfect it all was when in fact they were the worst racists. He agreed with me that Barbados was bad but had no explanation for this.

'St Kitts,' he said, 'is so much better than other islands.'

We said goodbye on the steps of the bar. He embraced a passing female. Then this glamorous figure strode off down the street. (Dr Herbert has recently been accused of some chicanery. I have not the least doubt but that he is innocent.)

I thought again of his last remark when, in the airport as we left, an American woman sat sobbing and wailing, 'I don't want to go home.'

15

The Dutch Islands

FROM GOAT STEW TO GAMBLING TABLES

Saint Eustatius is a Dutch island, one of the three they call their windward islands. Their leeward islands, Curaçao, Aruba and Bonaire, lie far to the south, just off the coast of Venezuela.

In her *Journal of a Lady of Quality*, Janet Schaw wrote, on 19 January 1775, a description of the Lower Town on St Eustatius.

'The town consists of one street a mile long, but very narrow and most disagreeable, as every one smokes tobacco, and the whiffs are constantly blown in your face.

'But never did I meet with such variety; here was a merchant vending his goods in Dutch, another in French, a third in Spanish, etc, etc. They all wear the habit of their country, and the diversity is really amusing.

'From one end of the town of Eustatia to the other is a continued mart, where the goods of the most different uses and qualities are displayed before the shop doors. Here hang rich embroideries, painted silks, flowered Muslins, with all the Manufactures of the Indies. Just by hand Sailors' Jackets, trousers, shoes, hats, etc. Next Stall contains most exquisite silver plate, the most beautiful indeed I ever saw, and close by these iron pots, kettles and shovels . . . I bought a quantity of excellent

185

French Gloves for 14 pence a pair, also English thread-stockings cheaper than I could buy at home . . . we purchased excellent Claret for less than two shillings a bottle, and Portuguese wines of different kinds very cheap.'

It was hardly like that on our arrival. The airport was small. Chickens wandered in and out. The prevailing mood was a domestic, rural one. We found a car and drove to Oranjestad, the only town.

There was scarcely anybody about. Never, as Janet Schaw would have said, did I see so deserted a place. In particular, there were no children. The population of the island in Janet Schaw's time was 20,000. Now it is 1,600. Many of the children are sent away to school in Curaçao.

The town was originally divided into lower and upper sections. The Lower Town was the one described by Janet Schaw and it taxes the imagination to try to conjure up any picture of Turkish, Greek and Jewish traders, or of eighty ships at a time anchored in Oranje Bay. There are fragmentary ruins, a little reminiscent of St Pierre in Martinique, but the strip of shore is so narrow between the cliff and the beach that it is nearly impossible to visualise so thronged a town, but easy to understand that whiffs would get blown in your face.

There were two hotels, reconstructed out of old ruins. They were quite pleasant but absurdly expensive, costing $220 a night for a double room. One was run by an American called Calder. It struck me as odd that both he and another American on St Kitts, called Leaman, who ran a rather similar establishment, should both have large portraits of themselves in their hotels. Mr Leaman was regarded as a considerable benefactor in St Kitts, a gentle, generous man. Mr Calder, however, seemed to lack that last scintilla of popularity, if those who described him as a 'grasping old turd' are anything to go by.

The Upper Town has its share of ruins. There is the old fort, built by the Zeelanders when they settled the island in 1636. The cannons were made in Amsterdam, 150 years later. There is the old Dutch Reformed Church, built of round stones known as 'face stones'. It was consecrated in 1775. Only the outer walls and the square tower remain. Originally, the north-west side of the tower was plastered white as a guide to ships. It was damaged in a hurricane in 1792, since when it has had no incumbent. There is the Honen Dalim, the second oldest synagogue in the Americas. It is somehow a more moving building. It is built of yellow brick. Inside the high shell, one can see traces of the upper-floor gallery where the Jewish women sat. Now there is probably not one Jew on the island.

The event which destroyed the amazing prosperity of St Eustatius, which was known in the late eighteenth century as the Golden Rock, hardly does credit to Britain. It is reasonable to argue that the island offered some provocation to the British. Then, as now, the obvious place for the islanders to trade was with the colonies in North America. The people of the West Indies, whose lives were hard even if the rewards were great, had strong sympathies with the spirit of independence which was burgeoning on the mainland. They, too, resented paying taxes to European powers who did nothing much in return. If the British islands objected to interference with their trade with America, how much more did a Dutch island object. Many of the weapons and much of the gunpowder used by the revolutionaries in the American War of Independence reached the rebels through St Eustatius, hidden in barrels labelled as rum or sugar. The profits to the Statians were large – up to 120 per cent on gunpowder, for instance. An even greater insult to Britain than merely trading with America came on 16 November 1776. The American brigantine *Andrew Doria* sailed by, flying the Grand Union flag. From Fort Oranje, the Dutch commander de Graaf fired a salute. It was the first act of recognition given to the new country. It infuriated the British.

When Britain declared war on Holland at the end of 1780, Admiral Rodney almost immediately attacked St Eustatius, before the Dutch Governor even knew war had been declared. Rodney's greed for loot was well known. He sacked the island, confiscating in the end between three and four million pounds worth of booty. Some of this was achieved by the scurvy trick of keeping the Dutch flag flying over the town for more than a month. By this artifice, he lured 150 ships into the bay and seized their cargoes.

The delay caused by this greed meant that Rodney failed to intercept de Grasse, who was crossing the Atlantic with a huge fleet. Had he done so, Alec Waugh argues by extension, Cornwallis might not have had to surrender at Yorktown.

Statia occupies only twenty square miles. The volcano called the Quill rises to 3,000 feet. The remoter parts are pretty but useless. Very little happened anywhere. A few cows, some vegetables, that seemed to be all. Some crumbling stone walls and shadows of ancient fields speak of a greater agricultural energy in the past. But what can so tiny a place do now? Tourism is, once more, the only answer. The people were all charming and welcoming. Eschewing the expensive hotels, we put up in a little courtyard of apartments, only half built. It cost only $40 for the night and had a television set.

We watched a psychiatrist giving a talk. He spoke a great deal about God, which I thought unusual for one of his profession. He also held the view, surprising in the Caribbean, that 'all kids live with their Mummy and Daddy.'

There was not very much to stay for, particularly as there was really nothing Dutch about the place, except for the occasional florin in amongst the American money. English was the main language and half the placenames were English.

We decided to fly on to Saba. At the airport, someone produced the carton of cigarettes which Hamish had characteristically left on the table the day before. Such honesty was touching and justified the sign in the place where one waited to leave: 'Be aware. There may be crime out there.'

It is ever a source of wonder to me how much nonsense people can talk about something they have just done. An American on Martinique had urged me to go to Saba, which I might well have decided to miss. It was worth it, he said, despite the terror of the landing strip. Saba, he explained, was just a volcano rising sheer out of the sea. Everyone lived inside the crater. The landing strip, therefore, had to be on the rim of the volcano, running across the rim at that, and was only 220 feet long.

In the event, the airstrip was at sea level and 1,300 feet long. Nonetheless, it was an alarming landing because the plane charges straight at a cliff, turns suddenly and then has to brake very sharply. It was not made much more reassuring by the sight of the pilot puffing at his pipe. (This was not Liat.) At least he was not so hypocritical as ever to put on the No Smoking sign. In the airport hut, the only noise was of people playing dominoes.

Saba is astonishing. It does rise sheer out of the sea, to nearly 3,000 feet at the peak of the absurdly-named Mountain Scenery, which the tourist brochures coyly say is the highest point in the whole Dutch kingdom. The total area of the island is only five square miles. There are four villages, all of them together producing a population no bigger than 1,050.

The landscape, although extraordinary for its steepness, is not very interesting. All the trees must have been cut down over the years for boat-building and firewood, so that the hillsides are covered with little more than tropical shrub. The villages, however, do look quite different and have something of a Dutch air, if only in their trim, clean look. Nearly all the buildings are of white clapboard. The windows and doors are picked out in dark green. The roofs are red. Everything had a doll's house look to it, except for the Catholic church, which is painted a particularly sickly yellow colour. Perhaps because of hurricanes, the houses are low and there is no space between the tops of the windows and the eaves, which makes for mean proportions.

The houses have neat, dreary little gardens. The Sabans seem very keen on Norfolk pines, which Captain Cook brought back from Norfolk Island in the South Seas. They look rather like plastic Christmas trees and bear about the same relation to real pine trees. The doll's house impression is magnified by the orange trees in many gardens, which are laden with an improbable number of vivid fruit.

It took a little while to get accustomed to the whiteness of the people, especially to the blond, blond children. I supposed that this came from their Dutch ancestry, but later learned that nearly all the people were of British descent. In 1685, only twenty-five years after some Dutch families moved from Statia to Saba, there were only three fewer Englishmen than the fifty-seven Dutchmen, and there were a number of Scots and Irish as well. In any case, in August of that year, Captain Morgan, the pirate, captured the island. He deported all the Dutch to St Maarten. Almost everyone on the island is called Hassell, Johnson or Simmons. In a list of ninety-nine captains – for the Sabans are great seafarers – I counted thirty-five Hassells, twenty-three Simmons and eleven Johnsons.

There were noticeably fewer black people on Saba, perhaps because the slaves had never outnumbered the white settlers as they had done on most of the other islands. There was absolutely no racial feeling. Again, this may have been a relic of history for, even in slave times, the white Sabans always worked side by side in the fields with their slaves.

The taxidriver who drove us up the zig-zag road from the airstrip told us that, although everyone could speak Dutch, most people used English. His family, at home, spoke Papiamento, which he thought was a mixture of Spanish and Portuguese, whereas it is a patois of African Dutch and Spanish and compounded with a little English and French.

We stayed in the one hotel in Windwardside, which was a touristy village. It was perhaps a little unreasonable not to like this village, as everyone was particularly friendly and welcoming. Perhaps it had something to do with the steepness, which tested even the patience of Hamish. To go to see anything meant pushing me up a one-in-three hill, and I was terrified on the return journey.

We took a taxi to The Bottom. This is the head village, the administrative centre, hardly worthy of the description capital. On the way, we passed a man with a gun. I asked what he was hoping to shoot. Gulls, the driver said. Could he have said that? I didn't like to ask him to repeat it a fourth time. I found the people very difficult to understand. An old man watering some flowers using a cup out of a bucket assured me that there was no water shortage and then talked for five minutes without my grasping more than one word in twenty.

The Bottom was so named because it was erroneously thought to be the bottom of an old volcanic crater, whereas it is merely a rare bit of flat land surrounded by hills and one side of Mountain Scenery. The descent to it is pretty, at first looking over the sea to the south, then down through palm-groves dotted with mango trees.

It is a tiny village, but we were drawn at once to Cranston's Antique Inn, a pretty, two-storey house where building was going on. Mr Cranston was a charming, gentle man, with a very humorous, very black face and greying hair. We sat in front of his hotel on a terrace, a few steps down from the road, and he told us that he also had a grocery shop and a bar. His son mostly runs the bar, he the inn, and they share the grocery work. The inn was being enlarged.

'They tell me I should have hot water. The Inn does not do very well. I have had it twenty-one years and I think it is beginning to pick up. About the hot water, what do you think? You see, if it's hot, they'll stay under the shower longer, thinking how comfortable and warm it is. Now they get out quickly and we save water.'

We all laughed to think of those nippy tourists. Remembering Sir Alexander Cochrane on Antigua, I asked about spouting. Mr Cranston thought he could spout the bar and grocery roof, but it meant bringing a pipe across the road.

While we talked, the young man, whom Mr Cranston had taken on the day before, made lunch. His name was Martin; a Hassell of course. He had a crewcut and wore both a large earring and an emblem of some sort round his neck. He cooked a goat stew. This is a dish of which I am something of a connoisseur. It was superb, something like a good *gulyas*.

Martin's story was unusual. His mother had died when he was six or seven years old. Some Canadians wanted to adopt him and his younger brother. The formalities of adoption took many years. When they were finished, Martin was seventeen. He and his brother set off for Toronto. The plan was foredoomed. For the Canadians, the boys were still the engaging little children they had seen long ago. They treated them as such. Martin left after a year, although his brother stayed for five. Martin had no reproaches for his adoptive parents, saying merely that it did not work out.

To come back to a tiny society, he thought, was difficult. 'You get mad, then you rise above it.' He liked his new job because Mr Cranston, although he was the boss, would do all the jobs that he asked Martin to do. He was happy; it was better than being shot or robbed. Had we noticed that in our hotel, to get a key for our room was a matter of making a special request? There was no need to lock anything.

The only problem was a shortage of girls. At dances, there would be crowds of men round the bar; some might even dance by themselves. It used to be the other way round. In the twenties, Saba was known as the Island of Women; in 1929, for example, there were 492 men and 916 women. For some reason, it evened up in the fifties. Many of the girls go away to school and come back . . . at this point Martin made a gesture of being pregnant . . . or they find a boyfriend on another island. Furthermore, intermarriage had led to there being many mentally handicapped children, which further reduced the number of girls. Fortunately, there were now many more inter-racial marriages.

After lunch, we walked through the village of The Bottom. It was peaceful, with beautiful trees. The quiet, plain Catholic church was bathed in the amber light of the afternoon sun. In the Anglican church were sad plaques, recording the fate of so many of Saba's sailors. I shuddered at this one:

'In loving memory of John Simmons, age 52 years. David W. Simmons, age 40 years. Richard R. Simmons, age 22 years. Isaac Simmons, age 16 years. *Lost at sea*, September 1918. We cannot, Lord, Thy purpose see; but all is well that's done by Thee.'

There was an old people's home, rather like an almshouse in an English village. A mad old woman beckoned us in, but we could not understand her. In another room, an old man was groaning, but no one appeared worried. Then we found a public library, a very modern building. Half the books were Dutch and the other half English. Many were classics, but I was impressed by the quality of the modern books, an intelligent selection. I was surprised, on this demure island, to see a book called *Sex in Religion*. It turned out not to be a purchase but a gift.

The librarian was a pretty young woman. While we were there, a number of children arrived and settled down round her desk. She started to read them a story about a giraffe in the forest. As we left, I thanked her and said, 'What a nice story.'

'At the beginning,' she said with a sinister look, which made the children wriggle. Then she laughed. It was a happy isle.

St Maarten is an island with very little history. Being virtually without water, it was of little strategic importance. It was quite early divided between the Dutch and the French and today the two halves, even though they have no physical signs of a border except for a small notice, have a very distinct atmosphere; and each its own spelling of the name.

The Dutch side was an instant nightmare. At the airport, the car renters pressed on us vouchers for free drinks in nightclubs, tours of 'resorts' where they try to sell you time-share apartments. For taking the tour, if you went with your wife (it did not specify that you should take a marriage certificate) and finish the tour, they would give you $50 off your car rental and $20 worth of casino chips. If you were prepared to join in this squalid conspiracy and spend an hour every two days on such tours, you could have a free car.

Philipsburg struck me at once as being deeply sleazy. The main street is called Front Street and is composed almost entirely of shops and restaurants. There is a Gucci, a Leda of Venice and, mysteriously, even a Marks & Spencer. Very few of the buildings had any elegance. The old courthouse, dated 1793, now the Post Office, has some distinction. There is a very pretty clapboard church with Gothic windows and one hotel which was formerly a government guesthouse. (It gave us a filthy breakfast.)

The price of everything was absurd. A good Italian dinner cost $87. We had a lot of trouble trying to find somewhere to stay. Curiously enough, this was the first time that we had had any difficulty, although we were travelling at the height of the season. I chose Lucy's Guesthouse from the guidebook, as it was one of the few places listed that I could conceivably afford. Their welcome lacked enthusiasm. 'We do not want wheelchairs here,' they said.

Mr Cranston had suggested another guesthouse called Bicos. A nice old woman showed us to a gloomy, long room with three beds rather like a prefabricated dormitory. We took the room because, by this time, we were desperate. The shower-room had no hot water. There were rules posted on the wall. No visitors. No alcohol. No washing of clothes. 'Anyone violating these rules will be expelled.' For this we had to pay $40.

As I was going to bed, I heard voices, near at hand. They came most clearly through the bathroom window. I looked through the louvres. The window opened on to the next bedroom. There, a young man was performing cunnilingus on his girlfriend, managing ingeniously to keep up a stream of conversation at the same time. She looked well pleased at this arrangement.

In the morning, we wandered about the town. The impression of sleaziness was confirmed. Tarts were beckoning to Hamish, even at 10 am. I wondered how it was, that expensive – which used to mean at least agreeable – has come to mean ugly, pretentious, vulgar. I suppose it could always be vulgar, but the old casino at Monte Carlo had an elegance. Nothing here has elegance – modern casinos, for some reason, are various hideous shades of purple and puce. In Front Street, there is a jeweller in puce, mock stone, its windows going up in steps. This next to what was once a pretty clapboard house.

We quickly realised that there was nothing to interest us in Philipsburg and so drove into the country. This was not much more inspiring. The island offers nothing but beaches. The rest consists of scrub-covered, conical hills of no particular interest. At the far end it is dry, almost desert, and rocky, a bit like Rajasthan.

The French half of the island is infinitely more pleasant, though the landscape is no more interesting. The capital of this half is a rather sleepy town called Marigot, but we decided to stay in the very simple village of Grand Case. It had a number of modest hotels with good restaurants. The one we chose had been owned by a M. Jean-Pierre Petra. He had sold the hotel but still ran the restaurant, where I had the best meal of our whole journey, well worth the $60 I paid for the two of us.

M. Petra had a Vietnamese wife, Hoa Hai. He was a slightly pathetic figure. He had been born in Indo-China. After the French were kicked out, he wandered from one disappearing colony to another – Morocco, Algeria, then Martinique and Guadeloupe. Once more, he was on the

193

move, still clutching his Vietnamese treasures. This time, he thought perhaps he would go to Florida. He had with him one of his sons; the other was at the Conservatoire in Bordeaux, having packed four years of piano training into six months. There are, in the islands, so many of these rather lost, almost stateless people, carrying with them a muddled culture which has entirely disappeared from real life.

The closer we got to America, the worse so many things appeared to be. The people on St Maarten seem to have no identity at all. Forty per cent of the population of the Dutch side are foreigners. Everyone talks in dollars. On the French side, there were vast properties which bore no relation to anything else on the island. These big properties have walls and fences, security guards and guard dogs – all the manifestations of the terrors of the rich. I longed for St Lucia or Dominica. Even Saba. How could it be so close and yet belong to a completely different world?

16
St Barthélémy
BRETON BREEDING

No one warned us about the landing at St Barthélémy. Usually the Liat pilots left the door to the cockpit open, so that one could see ahead. On the plane we took, belonging to another company, the pilot shut it. As we came close to the island, the plane plunged nearly in a dive. Through the windows on both sides we could see a steep hillside. We headed seemingly straight into the hill. There was no doubt but that we would crash. I tried to compose some amusing last words. Suddenly, the hill was on either side of us. There was a V-shaped gap in the ridge which we had been unable to see. By the time we had realised this, the plane landed, bumping onto the runway, the tyres giving a savage shriek. We stopped. The passengers gave a loud sob of relief. It was quite unnecessary, this fright, but I suppose it amused the pilot. (Furthermore, they had left our luggage behind, the second time it had happened with this company.) Hamish professed to have enjoyed the scare.

I began to wonder whether any apprehension is made better or made worse by exposure to whatever it may be one fears. I had never felt more than normal interest in the hazards of flying. Was I getting more nervous? I decided that it was a matter of pessimism or optimism. A savage fright would confirm a pessimist in his fear. Being optimistic I felt that, if one could overcome this fright, one could survive anything.

St Barthélémy is not much bigger than Saba, eight square miles as opposed to five. It has, however, many advantages. It has beautiful beaches in bays and coves. The capital, Gustavia, is clustered round an extremely pretty harbour. The town itself is not very interesting, although there are some attractive wooden houses, plainly influenced by Sweden, which once owned the island. Although the land is steep, with many conical hills, none is higher than 1,000 feet. The hills provide a greater feeling of space, the twenty-five miles of roads taking one to hidden places, whereas on Saba there was but one road, taking you up, then down and that was all.

There is little vegetation on St Barths. From my bedroom window, I looked out over the Anse du Grande Cul de Sac. Had there not been clusters of sea-grape and a few sodom apples, it might have been a bay in Scotland. In other parts there are clusters of coconut palms, but nothing on any scale. St Barths has never had the agriculture of the other islands. The people used to grow indigo but, for the most part, they grew only what they needed to survive and the population numbered only hundreds until the nineteenth century. It must, even so, have been a hard living, particularly on the windward side, where one can see, on the bare hillsides, traces of old stone walls, climbing up at an angle so steep that one cannot imagine cultivation being possible.

One woman, a taxidriver, told me that the island gets drier and drier every year, so that there is even less agriculture. Everyone has cisterns to store the rainwater but, she said, most people have to buy water at F100 (£10) a cubic metre.

One man, an American resident, told me that the island is not getting drier. It is far greener than it was thirty years ago, when he first arrived. This is partly because there are no more goats and partly because nobody now cuts wood for charcoal. He assured me that there was little cause for alarm. The St Barthians, when their cisterns get below three-quarters full, give up using any water. Then the rain comes and the cisterns overflow and everyone is happy.

It is of no great significance which theory is right. Agriculture, even in its limited traditional form, has been entirely superseded by tourism. The island is loud with American voices – not the interested travellers we had seen on other small islands, but the raucous variety, taking a couple of days off from the gambling on St Maarten, to look at a cute little island.

St Barths has an unusual history and it is the people who are interesting. The French first settled the island in 1648. The settlers did not last long: the Caribs ate them. Ten years later a group of one hundred Bretons, Normans and Poitevins arrived. They did better. They multiplied. By the end of the eighteenth century, the population had risen to 740. It was impossible to grow sugar on the island, so that the people lived the same peasant life that they had lived in France. There was neither the need nor the money to buy slaves. In 1784, Louis XVI airily gave the island to Sweden, in exchange for a duty-free warehouse in Gothenburg.

The Swedes made the island a freeport, and renamed Carenage, the capital, Gustavia, after King Gustav III. The wars of the eighteenth century brought an invasion and a fifteen-month occupation by the British, and a raid or two by the French, but in general the island flourished. By 1801, Gustavia had become a town of 5,000 inhabitants and there were 1,500 more people in the countryside.

This prosperity was short-lived. The end of the Napoleonic wars brought a rapid decline in the rather dubious kind of trading which brought these unexpected riches. Many traders left. In 1837, a hurricane destroyed half the houses. In 1849, 400 people died in an epidemic of yellow fever.

By 1879, the population had dropped below 1,000. Those who remained were mostly the descendants of the original French settlers. Sweden was by now anxious to be rid of this unprofitable island which, in any case, hardly suited the taste of the uncolonial Swedes. In a referendum, all but one of the inhabitants voted to be rejoined to France. The French bought the island back for 80,000 gold francs.

Whether the arrangement was good for either side is questionable. St Barths is regarded as a part of Guadeloupe and thus is a part of a *département*. The support the island receives is enormous. The housing is very good. The cars are tumbledown. I thought this a very sensible priority. Then it occurred to me that this was not the case on the French half of St Martin. Would these people, I wondered, have such good housing if they were black?

Today there are 3,400 people. As we went about, we kept on thinking we had seen people before in other parts of the island. Then we realised they all looked alike – sadly ugly, often red-headed, freckle-faced and cross-eyed. The young St Barthians had a strangely vacant look. Modern children's faces are etched with knowledge and sophistication,

197

sometimes too much of these dangerous ingredients. They were completely lacking on St Barths. The children's faces were as unmarked as those of Victorian nursery children – even the Victorians had Grimm, Struwelpeter and Alice. Their mouths were slack and their gait awkward, and both characteristics lingered in many of the adults.

It is a matter of inbreeding, which has left a worse mark here than on Saba, compounded as it is by quirks of custom. The complicated laws of inheritance meant that land was divided into tiny parcels. In order to have a workable piece of land, a boy was encouraged to marry a girl from the patch next to his. Most wives were chosen not from all the girls of the island but from those in the same tiny village. Either because of this separation or for other reasons, the people on the windward side of the island speak a rather different patois from those on the leeward side, another barrier to marriage, confining the possibilities still further.

Probably the most cut-off are the people of Corossol, although their village cannot be more than two miles from Gustavia. Some of the older women wear their ancient Breton costume, including a bonnet called *quiche-notte*. This is reputed to be derived from 'kiss me not', a rejection of an impulse which would hardly stir in a satyr's breast. Many of these people have never been to the other side of the island. The windwardsiders regard them as batty and are not inclined to marry them. So they have to marry each other and get battier still.

Monsieur Petra on St Martin had suggested that we visit a Madame Jeanne Audy-Rowland who, he said, had written a history of the island. She turned out to be an eccentric and rather fey woman from Normandy. She had lived on the island for fifteen years and had been married, at one time, to an Englishman. I judged her to be about forty-five. She was blonde and slightly blousy and she spoke in a breathy, affected manner.

The year before, she had brought over from Normandy a large, seventeenth-century, timber-frame barn. It had taken six people six months to erect. The floor, of irregular found-stone, had taken three months to lay. The roof was of shingles rather than thatch. In the barn was a collection of arty-crafty objects, both Norman and St Barthian, and Jeanne used it as her house. It looked wildly incongruous among the coconut palms, but it had the charm of the unexpected.

When we arrived, Jeanne was busy preparing for a dance to be held that night in a building on her land, but she was very welcoming. She produced copies of her book, which was an overblown fancy, improbably titled *Fils de Vikings à Saint Barth*. She said she had written it to teach the children of the island about their heritage. I fear they may be a trifle misled.

Jeanne showed us her collection of improbable artefacts and the huge ciderpress in the garden, which had come with the barn. Was she not worried about termites eating it, I asked? Nature, she assured me, must take its course. I decided that she was rather aggravating, with her latterday hippy approach. When I spoke about Calvados, she said she was a vegetarian. When I asked how many people there were on the island she said that that was not the sort of thing which concerned her. *'Moi, je suis paysanne,'* she added. How many *paysannes*, I wondered, could afford to ship barns across the Atlantic?

In the evening, when we went back for the dance, I revised my opinion a little. The dance was for local people. There were no tourists there; the only foreigners were a few people who lived on St Barthélémy. One of these was Michael Zimmer, a loquacious and eloquent, handsome American in his fifties. He spoke of the great difficulty outsiders had in getting to know the inhabitants, but she has achieved it. These funny, cross-eyed people, so sadly devoid of physical beauty, come to visit her and even invite her to their houses.

'Of course,' said Michael, 'she is covered in gold, unlike the *paysanne* she calls herself, and everyone loves gold – especially if it flows towards them. And she gives away gold. She doesn't hoard it. It rubs off on others.'

I felt somewhat more sympathetic to this genuinely generous and warm-hearted person, who had lent her garden and premises to the village for their carnival dance. For the party, Jeanne wore a white, floating dress and quite a lot of gold. She wandered round the garden a touch too ethereally, her arm linked through her lover's. Rather too often she would turn to kiss him, rather too intensely. Was it an act of love or a love act, I wondered?

Michael told me that at dances fifteen years ago, there were rows of chaperones sitting round the walls in case any boy made too bold advances to a girl. The consequence of boys getting off with girls was not so much that the girls got pregnant, but that they got married and moved in with the girls' parents. Any boy was completely discouraged until he had built a house of his own. And they all did, with their own hands (with the help of their friends), for a boy without a house was never going to have a sexlife.

199

The dance was a very energetic affair, far more lively than I had expected. The band of eight or nine musicians had come, especially, from Anguilla. They were indefatigable, playing reggae and some calypsos, in total darkness, for hours without cease.

I noticed that the black people, for there are a few on St Barths, did not mix with the whites. They even danced in a separate part of the building. Michael said that there is very little mixing. A woman in his village of St Jean had said to him with pride, 'You will never see a black head in our church.'

As we left the dance in our Mini-Moke, someone threw a bottle at us. It was a surprise, for the people all seemed polite and gentle. The young men, it appears, being denied girls, show their manhood by drinking.

But then I, too, was too drunk to care, having had a great number of rich *vieux rhums* to recover from the attentions of a tedious, aerobic woman at the hotel, who had earlier in the evening told me that I should not be so defeatist about having muscular dystrophy. I advised her to be a little more pessimistic about being an alcoholic.

As we drove to the airport, past St Jean church, its graveyard ablaze with artificial flowers, I thought that it was always the islands that still had a colour bar that I disliked. Then I thought of Jeanne who, when telling me that she would have to sell either her barn or her beach-house, had said, 'You must not write sad endings.'

I tried to be more enthusiastic. There was a lot really to be said for St Barths. I liked the way the people worked. If they had a day's task to do on a building, like laying a concrete slab, they would club together and start work at five in the morning. They would have no snobbery about what they did. An old man might shovel the sand, the tough, immature young men would do the heavy, gang work. The forty-year-old men would do the skilful work; the work which the old man used to do and the tough boys will do one day. The job, *la tâche*, would be done by ten, before the heat of the day. Then everyone would go home.

I liked the friendliness of the rather dim-witted waitresses, kissing the guests in the hotel goodbye and hoping they would be back next year. I liked the absolute honesty of the people, which meant that Jeanne and Michael never locked a door and had never lost anything. (The inhabitants, mysteriously, lock everything.)

Landing again in St Maarten, I knew that that was what I liked much less.

17

Anguilla

THE SEMI-ATTACHED ISLAND

Had there ever been any doubt in my mind that the only thing that really matters in a place is the people, Anguilla would have settled it forever. I had looked across at this flat, eel-shaped island from St Martin and thought that it looked dull. There appeared to be no hills and no trees.

We took a small ferry from Marigot, in the French half of St Martin, a swift boat which flew across the channel at forty knots or more. We arrived at Blowing Point at a simple jetty, to either side of which there were wrecked ferry boats, blown against the shore by hurricanes. Brother, I reflected, would never have allowed such a thing to happen. Yet the skipper of this ferry, a cool character in a Rasta hat, had told me, above the engine's roar, that Anguillians were great seamen and boatbuilders.

It was a shock of pleasure to recognise that we had, in a matter of five miles, exchanged the slick world of mass tourism and casinos for the sleepy, polite atmosphere of a British colony. The customs house was a simple shed. An old man in nautical rig said I need not bother to go up the steps to it merely to have my passport looked at. He would open a gate. The Governor's car, a modest affair, was there to meet some guest. No one paid it any attention.

We found a taxidriver, who said he would take us to some friends who would hire us a car. As we drove, I looked gloomily about. Anguilla is a coral limestone island, its soil is thin and rocky. All that seems to grow are a low scrub and clumps of sodom apples. There appeared not to be any planted thing.

Occasionally, I saw one stem of sisal or a solitary, fluffy cotton bush, presumably relics of some crop, a bit like guests who linger too long after dinner – though I began to wonder whether there ever had been a real dinner. At the last census twelve years ago, I later learned, there were only fourteen people on the whole island engaged in full-time farming.

Quite apart from the bleakness of the landscape, there were a great many unfinished houses dotted about, adding to the air of desolation. I asked the taximan about these, rather nervously, fearing that they might be the result of some economic disaster. He explained that this was far from the case. Every young man's ambition was to build a house. Usually his father would give him a plot of land. The land of Anguilla is divided into very small pieces, generally something between one and three acres. The total population is only 7,000 but, in 1976, there were 4,100 parcels of privately owned land. Only three people had more than 100 acres. The young man, having got his building plot, goes off to work, probably in St Maarten. When he has saved enough money, he comes home and lays the foundations of his house. Then he goes back to work until he has saved enough to build the walls. One day the roof goes on. It is a long process, but one which gives him great satisfaction.

The taxidriver's friends lived just outside the capital. I was reminded of Montserrat, but while there everyone was asleep, here everyone was wide awake with an eye cocked for any business opportunity. At the same time, everything was conducted on a basis of trust and with the greatest courtesy. At the bank in Montserrat, when they discovered I was over the limit on one credit card, they refused even to try another one, taking much satisfaction in saying in a voice which echoed: 'Refused.' The girl in Anguilla giggled when I told her it might happen again and she suggested that I just take the maximum amount allowed without reference by telex on as many cards as possible. Anguillians, I concluded, understood about business.

The island is only thirty-six square miles in area, so it did not take us long to explore every part of it. The capital, The Valley, was little more than a crossroads with a few buildings clustered round it, and held nothing of interest. There were only two other collections of houses.

The first, towards the west, had some hotels and restaurants and was called Sandy Ground Village, though it hardly warranted the title. But the bay it looked over was pretty, with ships moored and a little island. Further on there was the grandest hotel on the island, called the Malliouhana, which was reputed to have cost $16 million. It seemed to me, despite its three swimming pools and three tennis-courts and two miles of pure-white beach, to be just the sort of place I do not care for. No doubt, to paraphrase the theatre critic, those who like this kind of hotel will find it the kind of hotel they like.

The beaches of Anguilla are perfect, but I could not but be depressed by the absence of trees. There were only a few clusters of coconut palms and quite a lot of manchineel trees. These latter are a dubious asset, for they are so poisonous that, if you sit under them during a rainstorm, the water dripping from their leaves will blister your skin. Just before we arrived in Barbados, a friend on holiday, wandering along the beach, saw what she thought was something like a crab-apple. She picked it up and took a bite. It tasted disgusting, so she spat it out. Almost immediately, her tongue and throat began to swell. For many hours she could barely breathe and nearly had to have a tracheotomy.

There was nothing unusual to look at, except for an Amerindian ceremonial cave, known as the Fountain Cavern. It was closed to the public for fear that it would be damaged, although there are plans to develop it so that people can go in. The interest of it lies in the well-preserved and varied petroglyphs in the cave and a remarkable stalagmite carved in the likeness of Jocahu, the chief deity of the Arawaks.

We met Nik Douglas, an archaeologist from Harrogate with an extremely beautiful wife called Penny. He has spent four years in Anguilla, studying Arawak sites. He was a bearded, vigorous man wearing professorial-looking steel-rimmed spectacles. He had that wonderful enthusiasm for his subject which makes one want to learn everything about it.

The floor and every available level space of his office was covered with shards and stones and pots and figures. Theories bubbled out of him, leaving me dizzy. Some 50,000 years ago, Anguilla, St Martin and St Barthélémy were all joined together. They became separated when the ice melted after the last glacial climax. The sea level was 300 feet lower than it is today. Probably it achieved its present level about five or six thousand years ago. It was possible that man was living on Anguilla

203

then, because a tool was found close to the bones of an extinct giant rodent the size of a Virginia deer.

Caves, Nik said, that had a steady supply of water, as this one on Anguilla does, were surely sacred. He spoke of a Cuban tradition of a Fountain of Perpetual Youth, said to exist on one of the islands. He quoted a writer telling, in 1516, of an island, 'in whiche is a continual sprynge of runnynge water of such marvelous vertue, that the water thereof beinge dronk, perhappes with sume dyete maketh owld men younge ageyne.' Ponce de Léon, the companion of Columbus, whom we shall meet in Puerto Rico, believed in this legend and searched everywhere for the fountain.

No wonder, then, that the Arawaks carved this extraordinary stalagmite, more than fifteen feet high, in the shape of Jocahu Bagwe Maorocon – to give him his full name, meaning probably the creator – giver of cassava.

Nik's interests were not limited to Amerindians. As the Secretary of the local Archaeological and Historical Society, he investigates anything – even the rather tenuous theory that Captain Kidd may have buried some of his treasure on the island, which he visited not long before he was arrested in Boston, taken to England, tried and hanged.

The other interesting person we found was Smithy, who kept a bar for fishermen at Island Harbour, the second village, at the east end of Anguilla. The bar was in a grove of coconuts which grew nearly down to the water's edge.

The fishermen's boats, all painted in brilliant colours, were drawn up on the beach. Beside the boats were cages with lobsters in them. Nobody looked after these. This was a source of wonder to Margaret Zellers, who writes a most comprehensive guide to the Caribbean. She asked the fishermen whether nobody stole them. 'Somebody tried it once,' they said. 'We shot them.'

Smithy was a good-looking man, tall and powerful. I had noticed already that Anguillians were much more lucid and comprehensible than most of the islanders. Their standard of education was far higher. Smithy was a good example of a simple person with a far above average breadth of understanding.

He said that his family were all fishermen. But it was not a way of life which appealed to him at all, although it was very profitable. The boats usually set off at five-thirty in the morning and get back at any time during the afternoon. They go out about twenty-five miles to a hidden reef near Anegada, where there is a plentiful supply of lobsters. They are spiny lobsters rather than the kind with claws. The lobsters fetch $4 a pound. On a good day, a boat may bring back anything from a hundred to a hundred and fifty pounds. Against that, their boats and particularly their motors, are expensive. They need two outboard motors costing nearly $550 each.

While it is profitable, it is quite a dangerous profession. One of the reasons that the boats are so brightly coloured is that, in case of a disaster, they can be easily seen. It is only recently that they have taken to using compasses. In the old days, Smithy said, many boats were lost because the wind is usually so constant, blowing from the east. Everyone knew this and would steer accordingly. But, without their noticing, the wind would veer and they would steer a wrong course.

Smithy used to grill lobsters, and crayfish, from the reef off-shore. They were delicious. In the evening, the men would come and line the open-air bar and watch television while they drank. Sometimes, a couple of girls might come, but it was mostly a masculine outing. One evening, everyone was watching *Hart to Hart*. They loved it, cheering the heroes, booing the villains. When it came to the love bits, they laughed. 'Jonathan, he like a fuck. Ooh-hoo.' More laughter. In the middle there was a power cut. They were angry, not at the everyday fact of a power cut, but because the radio had said there would be light until 10 pm and now it was only 9 pm.

The Anguillians are a people with a very definite sense of what they think is right. They are people of immense independence, revealed, as the Governor pointed out to me, by their resolute decision to refuse independence from Britain. The recent history of Anguilla has not been easy. For entirely arbitrary, colonial reasons, Anguilla had for many years been administered in conjunction with St Kitts. When Britain agreed to set her Caribbean islands on the way to independence, this meaningless connection was perpetuated.

Within three months of St Kitts, Nevis and Anguilla being set up as an Associated State in 1967, Anguilla rebelled against the government in St Kitts and proposed to secede from the triple union. Being Anguillians, they decided that attack was the best means of defence. They invaded St Kitts.

The invasion was not a great success because, contrary to Anguillian hopes, no Kittitians rose to support them. However, it did prompt a lot of outside interest. St Kitts, under the odious Robert Bradshaw, wanted

Britain and various other islands to assist in a military operation against Anguilla. Instead, they formed a peace-keeping committee. All sorts of efforts were made to patch up the oxymoronic relationship between St Kitts and Anguilla. The Anguillians stood firm. An interim period was agreed upon, during which negotiations got nowhere.

In February 1969, Anguilla held a referendum and declared itself a Republic. Whereupon the British invaded the island. Everyone now realised that Anguillians would never revert to union with St Kitts. Nonetheless, it was not until 1980 that the final formal separation took place. Since then, the island has been a British colony – by its own choice.

The island could be said to be divided into two halves. At the eastern end, the Websters are chief; at the western end the Gumbs are supreme. The politics of the island swing between the two. Ronald Webster was the man who was mostly in charge during the battle for separation. Today, Emile Gumbs is Prime Minister.

I found Mr Gumbs to be a delightful person. He was a large man, sunburnt in a leathery sort of way, with crinkly grey hair and rimless spectacles. He had no trace of pomposity; indeed, he was very jokey and mildly indiscreet.

He told me that he believed that the independent spirit of the Anguillians stemmed from the days of slavery. Sugar was never a great success on this island. When it foundered, very early compared with other, more watered islands, the slave-owners used to let their slaves go off to work somewhere else until they had earned enough money to buy their freedom. And they used to come back.

'Who else would have done that? Why not run off and never come back? We still have the same spirit today.' All Anguillians are entrepreneurs. Every fisherman wants his own boat. The people own the land and their own houses. The Government owns only three per cent of the land.

'This spirit makes them very difficult people to govern. They hate paying property taxes. What has the Government done, they ask? It's my land, my house. You didn't build it. They are coming round to seeing that taxes pay for education, garbage disposal and so on.

'A St Kitts man once said that the difference between us was that, if you want something done on St Kitts you say "do it". To say "do it" on Anguilla practically ensures that it is not done.'

He said he could not understand Kittitians. They were so obedient that they might as well be slaves.

'They thought we would be obedient, so they tried to tell us what to do. For instance, we don't want casinos here. We want up-market tourism and small concerns.'

He told me that a leading Anguillian figure and former magistrate, Don Mitchell, thought that tourism would bring prostitution. 'Industry can bring more. On Aruba, there are 9,600 male employees and only 300 women. A thousand sailors in and out every day. They queue up, shouting, "Hurry up man, it's getting late".'

We talked of his policies.

'We have one and a half million dollars in aid. We deserve more because we asked to stay with Britain.' This last was said as a joke. He was planning a new air terminal, a new hospital and planning to enlarge the school.

Our talk came to an end because he had to go to see the Governor. The police were on his budget, but the Governor had total control of them. He wished to hand the cost over to Britain. It was a forlorn hope, as the Governor later confirmed, but the Prime Minister was a fighter for Anguillian rights.

I was left with the impression of a determined but gentle man, for we had also talked about birds. He told me that there were a hundred resident species on the island.

'I used to shoot a lot – white-cheeked pintail duck. One day I saw one swimming. I was just about to shoot when a little duckling followed her, then another and another. There were nine duckling. After that, I never shot again.'

Another day, I called on Ronald Webster. He was suffering because he had just had all his teeth out. This did not prevent his being both a highly entertaining host and a distinctly indignant politician.

What had become, he demanded to know, of his ten-year programme for the island? I asked what it had encompassed – a new air terminal, a new hospital, enlarging the school, better telephone system, improved electricity.

I protested that I thought all this was happening. Mr Webster was not in the least put out. The new terminal was to be on the site of the old one. It should be in a new place. The hospital was also in the wrong place. And so it went on.

'I think the Governor should take over and start all over again.'

Mr Webster would not start a revolution; one was quite enough. But he would organise a demonstration about the latest enormity. An American actor (was it Chuck Connors?) had been allowed to buy three-quarters of an acre of beach front, something forbidden to foreigners.

However wild all this might sound, Mr Webster is a most reasonable man. He fears corruption and the possible invasion by the Mafia. Think, he said, what an offer of $50,000 means to someone on Anguilla.

He does not want independence for the island. An American commission of inquiry came recently to Anguilla to consider the question. The people did not want the commission, let alone the independence.

Nor did Mr Webster see any chance of the islands of the Caribbean getting together in any way, if only because the smaller islands would be dominated. The larger islands would keep all the benefits for themselves.

'A stone rests where it lands,' he said, 'it certainly doesn't reach the tenth on the list.'

That afternoon we were to leave. For the first time, we were moving to an island which we could not see. It somehow made our departure sadder. We had had great fun on Anguilla, a wholly uninteresting place made wonderfully attractive by the character of its people.

18

The Virgin Islands

FLAGS OF CONVENIENCE

We were on the tarmac at Anguilla.

'Are you going to be violent?' the girl asked me. She was the co-pilot of the plane we were about to board, which had just landed. I had watched her going round the wheels of the aircraft, feeling how hot they were after braking sharply on the short runway. She approached each wheel warily from behind. If they do overheat, the nuts can sometimes shoot off sideways into your legs, like bullets. She was very pretty – in dark trousers and a white shirt with shoulder bars. When she had finished, she came over and asked me that question. She looked so normal and attractive. I could not think what she meant. I offered a cautious 'No'.

'Are you going to St Maarten then?'

'No, to Tortola.'

'Same thing,' she said with a laugh. 'Beef Island.' The airport of Tortola is actually on a small island joined to it by a bridge.

Columbus found and named the Virgin Islands after St Ursula, the daughter of a Cornish prince, who agreed to marry only if she could travel to Rome for three years, taking with her 11,000 virgins. Where she found so many virtuous girls in fifth-century Britain is a matter for conjecture. However, she trained them in the martial arts, and travelled with them to Rome, where she pledged allegiance to the Pope. While still on her journey in 453, near the Rhine, she encountered the Huns, who tried to seize her and to rape her followers. All died, preferring martyrdom to dishonour. (It was October the twenty-first – Trafalgar Day. A brave day in the British calendar, evidently.)

Columbus was unable to count the Virgin Islands and even today it is hard to establish how many there are, but he cannot have supposed that there were 11,000, when the truth is between forty and fifty. Another theory postulates that he found only women on the islands, the Caribs having killed all the Arawak men. This is unlikely, if only because the Caribs had surely reached these islands a hundred years before Columbus found them, on his second voyage in 1493. In any case, there is no certain record of his having landed.

After the flat islands of St Martin and Anguilla, here we were back in steep, volcanic land, reminiscent of that crumpled piece of parchment which the legendary explorer threw on the King of Spain's table when his sovereign asked him to describe the appearance of the latest island addition to his American empire – 'Like this, sire'.

Tortola, however, is nearly innocent of forest. Only one patch remains. The forest was cut first to clear the land for sugar, which grew uneasily on the hillsides. Then it was cut again for timber for ships. Finally, it was destroyed to provide wooden sleepers for the Puerto Rican railway. Much of the land is bare and bleak, untouched by rain.

I thought the beaches were far more attractive because, unlike Anguilla, they had at least a measure of vegetation and a few trees behind them. They were also more varied. Long Bay, for example, had rollers sweeping in, big enough for surf-boarding while, only a mile or two beyond, Cane Garden Bay was calm and placid. A group of American teenagers sat under the coconut palms singing to a boy's guitar. I noticed, with interest, that the village graveyards often lay unfenced between the road and the sea. It was a friendly arrangement.

As on Anguilla, nothing was growing to speak of. There was only one industry – tourism. On this island and all the Virgin Islands, the tourism was geared primarily to yachting. As we drove from one end of the island to the other, a distance of about twelve miles, we passed six marinas, each one bristling with masts like a ragged toothbrush. It struck me at once that two entirely separate ways of life were proceeding side by side.

When we drove inland up the steep hills, we found villages so far removed in feeling from the conspicuous wealth of the yacht marinas that we might have moved to another continent. The people must have been used to tourists in these hills but, when we paused in our hired Mini-Moke outside one village, a group of schoolgirls returning home in the afternoon leaped on Hamish, in a fever of girlish excitement. They fondled him, even stroking his genitals, provoked by his too brief shorts. He blushed and screamed, but could not drive off for fear of running over one of the girls. When, at last, he escaped, he would not speak to me for half an hour, because I had laughed so much at his embarrassment.

It had been quite difficult to find somewhere to stay. Margaret Oldfield, the co-pilot of the plane, had taken us to a pleasant little hotel in the hills, but we had no car for the first day or two, so we tried to find a room elsewhere. You could try Harry Vandermolen, people said in an unconvincing tone. Mr Vandermolen's establishment consisted of some primitive cottages perched on a steep cliffside. They were hardly suitable for me in my chair, quite apart from their being filthy. Mr Vandermolen, however, was an extraordinary character – one of those strange relics of colonial days, still hanging on in one of Britain's few remaining colonies. He was sitting at a desk in the huge room which constituted the reception, office and lounge of his hotel. He was watching the CBS news on television. A black woman wearing a hat sat in a chair, very close to another television set, watching *Rambo*. The room was full of books. There was a 1948 *Encyclopaedia Britannica* and the thirteen-volume *Oxford English Dictionary*. When he saw me looking at it, he said that he found it very useful.

'Only the other day, I proved to an American that we used to spell tyre with an "i", until they became pneumatic, when we changed to "y".' Harry Vandermolen said he was born off the Whitechapel Road in London. I never learned how he came to be in Tortola, but he was evidently unperturbed by a life which had, from all accounts, been filled with complications. Harry showed me a book of poems which he had had published. Apparently, the poems came to him almost as dreams in the night; every night for two or three months. Then, as suddenly as they had started, they stopped. This, perhaps, did not matter, as they had no great poetic merit.

'The poems were nearly all true,' Harry said. 'Yes, that one you are reading, that is what happened. Both my wives left me after fourteen

211

years of marriage. Each had a hysterectomy and left within three weeks.' It is an odd subject for a poem.

Now Harry is not married, but complications continue. He said that the woman watching *Rambo* lived down there, and he gave a vague wave to some houses below. She did the cleaning, he claimed. If so, the results of her work were hard to detect. She certainly caused trouble, for when I admired the three or four West African and Brazilian parrots which lived in a cage, Harry looked rueful. He used to have thirty parrots, many of them rare. One day, when he was out, the *Rambo*-addicted woman got cross with the birds. They were making so much noise that she could not hear the television. So she let them out. They flew away and Harry lost $2,000 worth of parrots. Harry merely sighed. The woman sat on watching the television, her face about two feet from the screen. I think we can be sure, despite the hat, that she lived there.

There were other permanent white residents on Tortola, a few of them extremely interesting. Jill Tattersall was married to a doctor who, in earlier colonial times, used to visit his patients on horseback and might be summoned urgently to Anguilla to perform an operation. It would take him sixteen hours to sail there. Mrs Tattersall, I thought at first, was a dry, earnest woman, albeit intelligent and erudite. On further acquaintance, she proved to be entertaining and full of *joie de vivre*. She had developed a fascinating and complicated theory about the languages of the early inhabitants of the Caribbean. Working on Taino, the language of the Arawaks (for some perverse reason, archaeologists are now inclined to call the people Taino as well as their language, but not Mrs Tattersall), she concluded that the vowels carried special meanings or associations. For example, 'a' would involve water, 'e' would imply strength. She noticed that so many words varied by only one vowel, but had, presumably in consequence, totally different meanings. Applying her theory to the Carib language, she found that it applied just as well to that as it had to Taino. A particular word in the two languages would be quite different and the road to its meaning quite different, but the vowel association would be correct. Thus a table in Taino would translate as a 'thing on which women prepare food', whereas in Carib it would be 'the place where a chief eats'. But the associations with the vowels turned out to be appropriate for each image of the table.

We talked also of colour in language. As is usual with more primitive languages, Taino has words only for colours at the red end of the spectrum. (Somali, I believe, gets no further than red and orange.) Mrs

Tattersall told me that the points of the compass have the same names as colours. Red is also the word for west and yellow or gold the word for east. Those are quite understandable. But why is south the same as black? Does it have something to do with dark mists? North is white, which seems logical to us for climatic reasons, but hardly to an Arawak. Nor would racial colouring have any meaning for them.

It was Mrs Tattersall, also, who drew my attention to the curious story of Kingston, a few miles east of Roadtown, the capital. In about 1834, after slavery had been abolished in the British islands, but while it still continued on the Danish Virgin Islands, a slave ship on its way to St Thomas was wrecked on Tortola. What was to be done with the survivors? It was thought wrong to send the slaves on. No one thought of sending the unfortunates back to Africa. Eventually, they were given a village, called Kingston. There they lived, distinctly separate, despising the other blacks on the island for having been slaves, and despised themselves by the local blacks as having just come out of the bush, still practising their primitive rituals, while the ex-slaves were by now all Christians. Even today, there can be residual, almost atavistic, animosity between the people of Kingston and others, so that they are reluctant to intermarry. In this attitude Tortola was different from almost every other island, where great importance is attached, as we have seen, to African origins. Indeed, if you ask a Tortolan where his roots may have been, he is quite likely to say, 'Nottingham, I think, is maybe where my family come from.'

Despite the fact that we were getting closer and closer to the United States, that US dollars were now the only currency anybody considered, that three-quarters of the yachts in the marinas were American, Tortola managed to remain supremely British. One morning we awoke to find the Royal Navy had arrived – HMS *Battleaxe*, a frigate named, so the wits had it, after the Admiral's wife. Soon Roadtown was full of pale-skinned sailors. The officers looked so decently clean in their whites, after all the tanned yachtsmen in 'torn shorts'. The men looked about twelve years old. We went down to see their ship at the quayside. It looked much like any other ship to me, but Hamish bubbled with interest. As we left the docks, two able-seamen stopped us at the gate. One of them, in a barely intelligible Scottish accent, asked us how to get up the hill. He wanted to take a photograph of his ship from above. We offered to take them.

The Glaswegian, Scott, wore only a skimpy pair of shorts made of shiny, Union Jack material. Neil, who came from Barnsley and was covered in alarming red, scabby spots, wore track-suit trousers and a T-shirt.

Scott kept up a steady stream of information and observation. He described the ports they had visited – Mobile, Charleston, Karachi. He gave a vivid account of the prostitutes in the windows of Amsterdam, adding with pride, 'I've never paid for it.' He had joined the navy at sixteen and cannot get out until he is twenty-two. He was not sure that he would want to when the time came. What would he do? His speciality was electronic warfare. That, I thought, would be a great help if he did leave the navy. Scott looked sceptical. 'There are not that many people on land wanting to count how many radar machines there are within sixty miles.' Neil was a quieter boy. He told me that most of the lads had those Union Jack shorts, but they were not allowed to wear them in America or other foreign countries. Most of the crew of 250 were, he said, keep-fit addicts, doing exercises and jogging round the deck; thirteen laps of the deck equalled a mile. Once ashore, on the other hand, all they wanted to do was get drunk. Often the bar nearest to the dock gates was all that they would see of a port.

After a drink at our hotel, Hamish took Scott and Neil back to *Battleaxe*. They invited Hamish on board. There was no one checking who boarded the vessel. As far as he could judge, they went all over the ship. The boys let him play with the guns. Hamish thought it was merely ill-luck that the door to the operations room was locked. So happy-go-lucky an attitude to security struck me as charming but a little rash. Another sailor later told me that, really, they were very conscious of security. There were areas of the ship Hamish could never have seen, but he did agree that perhaps they worried less on Tortola than in Puerto Rico or Charleston.

One day we took a ferry to St John, one of the three main American Virgin Islands; the other two being St Thomas and St Croix. The United States bought these islands from Denmark in 1917 for $25 million. The purpose was to protect the Panama Canal from the Germans. The journey was pretty, as the boat wove its way through the islands – out from West End and Frenchman's Cay, where frigate birds swooped over the yachts, past Great Thatch and Little Thatch, past what I thought was a chapel, as it had a wooden cross beside it, but later was told was an old, Danish customs post, then along the coast of St John and round into the harbour of Cruz Bay. We had to have visas for this little excursion but, for once, US Immigration was not a terror.

Nearly half of the island of St John is a National Park, largely due to Laurance S. Rockefeller, who bought up some five thousand acres of unspoilt land in the fifties and gave it to the nation. Gradually, the park has been added to and it will eventually cover two-thirds of the island. The result is worthy, but dull. As one drives through the centre of the island, it is a pleasure to see the huge mangos, the mass of mahogany and some fine kapok trees but, somehow, the regimented beaches, with large plastic rubbish-bags every hundred yards, and the streams of visitors and campers lend a falseness to what should be natural. The Annaberg plantation ruins are probably the best arranged and explained example of the workings of a sugar estate in the whole Caribbean, but somehow I longed to be back on Nevis with Melford O'Flaherty giving his dancing, dramatic account of how things were done. Indeed, I began to wish that the hordes of tourists would settle down for a picnic among the extensive groves of manchineel trees.

I far preferred the late eighteenth-century church built by the Moravian missionaries, gentle followers of the teachings of John Huss. They campaigned with passion and courage against slavery. It was an odd building with a pink roof, white gutters, pale ochre upper walls, dark red lower walls and pale, blue-grey shutters. Strangely, the wall of the external stairway was painted on the outside with steps, corresponding to the actual steps on the other side of the wall. Here the missionaries taught the slaves to read and write and also the craft skills which they themselves practised. The Moravians had two churches on St John – one called Bethania and this one called Emmaus. Emmaus was built on the site of the Great House of the Caroline plantation. There, in the great slave revolt of 1733, the rebels murdered the owner, Judge Sodtmann and his twelve-year-old daughter. So raw a deed naturally created a *jumbie* or ghost, which haunts the site, coming each full moon in the guise of a large billy goat.

On our way back to the ferry I realised that, as we neared the American continent, we were seeing many new birds, ones we had not seen before, most of which I could not identify. I particularly admired a thrush, speckled like ours, but not so plump and with a far longer beak, much more elegant. As we went back on the rattly old ferryboat, I reflected upon the absurdity of borders and visas. Here we were, day-trippers, requiring, as we hopped from one little island to another, to have passports duly stamped by officials in London for the sake of officials in Washington. That absurdity, as we passed again the old Danish customs post, led on to the absurdity of all those changes of ownership in the eighteenth century. Twice St John had been British, once for as long as seven years. Of course, then it was a matter of economics, but were those economics worth all those lives? Who cares now if one of those minute specks was once Danish or Dutch, or Spanish or French, or English or Swedish. No one, but it still affects the people's lives without their knowing it.

We took a ferry to Virgin Gorda, another British island. The boat took us past more islands, some with exotic names – to starboard lay Norman; Peter; Dead Chest; Salt, where lives old Miss Clementine Smith, who promptly pays rent to the Queen of one bag of salt a year, although she grumbles that nobody comes to collect it. At eighty-six, she was coshed by a marauder, but was soon back on her island; Cooper; Ginger; and Fallen Jerusalem, a weird assembly of vast boulders of granite. To port, Beef; Scrub; a glimpse of Great Camonoe; and finally, the Dogs. I sat at the back of this ferry in the place where they pile the luggage. A young man, working on the boat, yelled at me above the noise of the engines and the spray. 'The Lord wants you to be well and to walk.' I tried to discourage him politely, but he shouted that I must write to Brother Schambrack in Pennsylvania. He would help me to walk. Did I know it was demons? Demons who were against the Lord and wanted to trouble the world. I must write to Schambrack – a personal letter. He said Schambrack liked personal letters. Or I could go to his office. 'The Lord wants you to go.' He looked to be a normal young man. I encouraged him to get married. I thought it might take his mind off these things.

Virgin Gorda is dry and barren, its hills covered only with a drab scrub. Where the ferry set us down, there was nothing but a hut. There is no town on Virgin Gorda, only a conglomeration of houses grandiosely called Spanish Town. A taxi took us up a steep road along the ridge back of the islands, so that we could see the sea on either side. We soon reached the eastern end of the island and looked down over a bay or sound encircled by islands. The sound was full of yachts, one a huge, elegant motor yacht. Over the sound, parasailors floated like cloud-spiders. Grey boobies plunged into the water. On the other side we could see Trade Winds, the hotel where we were to stay, a collection of cottages with an Indonesian look, dotted on the hillside. They looked well, especially when compared with the neighbouring yacht club, which had red corrugated-iron roofs, making it look like a shanty town. A boat took us across the bay.

Our stay at Trade Winds was virtually a holiday. This hotel and another even quieter one, a short boatride away, were run by a man called Tad Michel, a person of astounding energy, who came originally, he told me, from 'the free city of Danzig'. As a young man he went to Australia, then joined the British army and finally ended up here, married to an American wife from North Carolina. Trade Winds catered for a reasonably popular market (if $225 a day for a double room can be called popular), but everything was in good taste. It was wonderful to do nothing for three days. Hamish water-skied and windsurfed and I read.

To look at, the islands round the bay could have been in the drier part of the Mediterranean, except for the lack of rocky outcrops and the almost total absence of trees. (All the water for the hotel came from desalination plants.) It was a pleasing prospect. In the evenings, the sound became even more attractive. Just before dark, the hummingbirds would flit feverishly round for one last sip of nectar from the red bell flowers or the yellow allamanda beneath my window. One evening, I watched a banana-quit and a hummingbird feeding from the same bush. One flitted, the other hovered. The banana-quit often made a muddle of trying to reach into the flower, being too heavy for the branch. How could they have taken such different paths of evolution? Could one be said to be better adapted to its environment than the other? And why was one so timid and the other so bold, when their experience of human beings must have been identical? I always find Darwin difficult.

As the light faded, the hills softened to look like bobbly cushions. The smooth sheet of water acquired the same steely tone as the darkening sky. Then for a short few minutes, both sea and air went pink and the last parasailor floated back to earth like a giant bat. Finally, the stars appeared, echoed by the lights of the yachts below us on the water.

The large yacht looked at night like a pier. It belonged to a man who called himself the Prince Léon de Lignac, Duc de Soveria Simeri, Ministre Plénipotentiaire de la Maison Royale d'Este-Bavière, Chevalier Grand Croix de l'Ordre de Malte. All this fal-de-rol, which can never have been intended to deceive anyone really, was the alias of an enormously rich Dutchman who made his fortune from a mail-order business. The yacht, which is called *New Horizons*, is said to have cost $48 million. She is 197 feet long, carries a helicopter and has a crew of fifteen good-looking young men. While the exterior of the yacht is splendid, the interior, to judge from some photographs that I chanced to see, is of an ostentatious vulgarity not seen since Caligula, all gilt and marble. The 'prince', according to rumour, never invites women on board. One evening he came ashore, bringing his guests for a drink at Trade Winds. He was sorrowfully uninteresting and not one whit patrician in appearance but, such is the lure of even pretence princedom, that his epicene companions, one of whom Hamish took for a woman, treated him with supreme deference, which he accepted with solemnity. I concluded that he had a wry sense of humour.

On one day, we went to Necker (formerly Nicker) Island, which lay just outside the sound. This again was just a lump of rock, extending perhaps to ten or fifteen acres, covered in scrub and sea-grapes, but having good beaches. It belongs to Richard Branson. It was amusing to compare the taste of this millionaire with that of the spurious prince. Where the latter had indulged a love of the flashy and meretricious, flaunting his riches in flamboyant ornamentation, Mr Branson, at probably comparable expense, had exercised a fastidious liking for cultivated simplicity. The style of his house was Balinese. The main room was about one hundred feet long and forty feet wide. The roof rose to about thirty-five feet. Everything was so large that a billiard table in one part of the room looked quite small. The doors were of Chilean oak and the beams of Brazilian timber. Oddly, each of the beams was stencilled with the word 'Fuck'. This, it was revealed, was the name of the Brazilian lumber man who had provided the wood. He was said to pronounce it Fouquet. The size of the room had tempted Mr Branson into making some of the Balinese furniture in a larger size than its original inspiration, which looked awkward. The bamboo dining-chairs were so big that girls sitting on them looked like children allowed down from the nursery, their legs dangling above the floor. The bedrooms were pretty, with Balinese quilts and Haitian primitive paintings chosen to match the colours of the quilts. The bathrooms were of stone. There was a lot of water – a pool with water on one side level with its rim, and a fountain on the terrace which flowed into a jacuzzi and then on into the pool.

From the outside, the house looked modest, having a Canadian shingle roof and resting on a stone base which melted into the land. In the garden there was a 350-year-old Balinese ceremonial hut and the tennis-court had a copy of a similar hut beside it. The tennis-court itself was of astro-turf, which apparently required seventeen-and-a-half tons of sand to make it stand properly – special sand from Florida, that is. The only disappointment was the garden, with no plants of any interest. A young man from Selkirk had been brought to plan and plant it. I became quite enraged by both his lack of enthusiasm and his ignorance. He maintained that the spray prevented most things from growing, but had not been to see any other Caribbean gardens – Andromeda on Barbados, for instance, which thrives in the full bluster of the Atlantic. Of course, it rains more on Barbados, but Mr Branson has a huge desalination plant, perfectly capable of watering at least enough to be of some interest.

There is so much that is vulgar and ostentatious in the Caribbean that I was much impressed to find a place which was created by a rich man's fancy and yet had about it nothing which could possibly offend anybody and might give pleasure to many. Indeed, I was intrigued to learn that the practical Mr Branson was perfectly prepared to let his island for $5,500 a day.

After a few days at Trade Winds, I realised that on Tortola and Virgin Gorda, we had really met none but white people. Tad Michel told me that the people of Virgin Gorda live lives quite untouched by tourism, except economically. They go to work and return in the evening to their villages, where the important things are the family and the church. White people, particularly tourists, have no occasion to go to the villages, where bikinied women and men in brief shorts would not, in any case, be welcome. This confirmed what I had felt on arrival, that two separate strands of life existed on these islands, each quite removed from the other. Here were the yachtsmen and the tourists – privileged, rich and white. There were the blacks – waiters, deck-scrubbers, menials, all poor.

Yet without the tourism, what would there be? I had a fantasy that Tourism is a vast nation with huge armies that march across continents, destroying just as effectively as conquering, armed hordes like the Mongols, Huns, Vandals, Visigoths or whatever. The Tourist Empire will grow to be the biggest ever known. Unlike the Greeks or the Romans or the British or the French, it will leave no cultural mark. Its buildings, flimsy and transitory, will not stand as monuments. It has no religion save some primitive, undeveloped worship of the sun. It has no art, no literature, no law.

I had not been able to get to the extraordinary granite boulders on the south side of Virgin Gorda. These amazing rocks are often as big as houses, sometimes fluted, sometimes pierced with sculptural holes, sometimes balanced like a funambulist's trick. The pilot of our aeroplane made a detour so that we could fly over these strange geological formations. They lay below us, some on the land, others in the sea, looking like a gathering of giant seals and whales basking in the morning sun.

Our sadness at leaving the amiable atmosphere of Trade Winds was exacerbated by the airport on St Thomas, where we had to change planes. I had not much cared for the look of the island from the air. It looked as built-up as the French Riviera. The airport was like a Hieronymous Bosch painting. It was impossible to move. The ramshackle buildings were filthy and noisy. When we battled our way through the mad crowds to the check-in desk, an hour before our confirmed flight to St Croix, the Pan-Am man laughed at us. We would be lucky to get onto the flight after that, he said. The echoing doubt of St Thomas was whether we would ever get away from this hell. Eventually, we did, taking a jumbo jet for a fifteen-minute journey, which seemed like the proverbial sledgehammer to crack a nut.

The airport at St Croix at least bore no resemblance to St Thomas. It was quite peaceful but all the hire-cars had already gone. We waddled along the smooth roads in an enormous, wallowing Studebaker taxi. At first sight, I thought this flatter island was depressing, a little like the poorer areas of Louisiana. Then we came to Christiansted, the capital. After the jumble of the British Virgins, the non-existence of a town in Anguilla, and the sleaziness of Philipsburg, this town was a surprise. Arcades and churches and a market square – real architecture. Architecture that was both familiar and yet different; eighteenth-century in feeling but not like St George's or Basseterre or Plymouth. It was Danish. How different from our classical heritage are the flatter arches, the lower roof pitch, the plain shutters. I longed to explore, but we had nowhere to stay.

I sat in the bar of an hotel called The Charte House. It had a pretty facade and an arcaded entrance, but was very simple. It was, the reception said, full up. Hamish ran all over the town and could find nothing. He came back to ask how much we could spend as there was no reasonable room to be had, and then ran off again. I ordered another old rum and wondered about towns built by one group of people, but inhabited by others. St Croix had lived under seven flags in its time – Spanish, British, French, Dutch, the Knights of Malta and American, but for nearly two hundred years it was Danish and it was the Danes who built Christiansted. Florence, I thought, no matter how many coachloads arrive from Wigan or jumboloads from Sacramento, remains Italian. In the cool of the winter, the city reverts to its true owners, whether Corsini princes or the taxidriver descendants of the Medicis' grooms. But what have these people to do with the Danish planters who built the Great Houses or the Danish sailors who used this Charte House?

The lady who brought me another glass of rum told me that she was from Jamaica. She was friendly and I explained our plight to her. 'Of course there is a room,' she said. And she went to infinite trouble moving guests around, so that we could have a convenient room on the ground floor. I began to feel that St Croix had promise after all. But I never came any closer to solving my conundrum. That night we went to a restaurant a hundred yards up the street. The waitress came up. 'My name is Apryl and I welcome you to Rumours. Have you all had a good day? It'll make my day if you have.'

'Could you stop all that?' I asked.

'Yeah, it's terrible isn't it? I mean, I could ruin both our days in no time.'

Could this pretty, black girl, with a steady stream of backchat, be a St Cruzan who might enlighten me? I asked her where she was from. California, she said.

The predominant colour of Christiansted is a pale ochre, perhaps to match the colour of the hard, yellow Flensborg bricks of Fort Christian, which the Danes built soon after they bought the island from the French in 1733. These same bricks, originally brought as ballast, were used in many of the houses. There are several fine buildings, some of clapboard, some of stone, but mostly stucco. Not far from the harbour and the modern marina is the house where Alexander Hamilton was supposed to have worked when he was a youth. That, at least, made an earlier American connection. However, one morning was enough to exhaust the interest of Christiansted, with its unreal feeling, reminiscent in a way of Williamsburg. We set off into the countryside.

The island is not large, not much more than eighty square miles. Driving round it, there was little to give one any clue as to the culture of the place, if any. The first thing I noticed was a complete absence of agriculture. This fertile land was once a huge producer of sugar. It has a reasonable rainfall of forty-five inches a year, but in two or three days of exploration I saw one herd of sheep, a small number of cows and a few acres of maize – no more. Even the rather good Cruzan rum owes nothing to Cruzan agriculture. All the molasses used in its manufacture is imported from other islands. I found it curiously disturbing to look at such wonderful land doing nothing, although it did mean that there were parts of the island which had not yet been developed and which were attractively wild, with lost patches of forest full of splendid mahogany. We spent a long time in one such patch, studying a termite nest up in a tree. These horrible creatures build huge nests twice the size of a rugby-ball. As they cannot stand the daylight, they build covered ways up the trunks of trees and along the branches. If one destroys a section, the creepy things repair it the next night. Hamish punctured the nest itself and we were surprised to see how thin its covering was. For some reason it gave me the shivers. It was odd to leave this unsullied hillside and, ten minutes later, eat fast-food in a MacDonalds.

The other town on the island is Frederiksted, built originally by British settlers, at the western end of the island. Like Christiansted, it is laid out on a grid pattern, but its houses are less solid, being mostly of clapboard. The Anglican Church, St Paul's, was built in 1812 and came, for some reason, under the jurisdiction of the Bishop of London. When the United States bought the island, the church was transferred to the Episcopalian Church, in the diocese of the Bishop of Puerto Rico. Now the island has its own bishop.

Not far from Frederiksted, we found the Whim Great House, one of the stranger architectural fancies of the Caribbean. It was built in 1794 by a planter, Christopher MacEvoy Jr. It is supposed to be modelled on a European manor house and is grandly built of stone and coral, the mortar being bound with molasses. However, it has only three, large rooms. One end of the single-storey building is curved into a bay, with three windows. Down each side are seven more windows, each capped with either a classical pediment or a recessed arch. The shingle roof follows the shape of the building, incongruously with no ridge at the front but a smooth curve. The whole building is surrounded by what the St Croix Landmarks Society, who own it, are pleased to call a moat, but is in reality an area, like in a London house, designed to give light to the basement, where presumably slaves lived. The three rooms are well furnished with a mixture of Danish and American furniture, including a planter's chair, designed for lying back with one's legs up, but in the outhouses I found it disconcerting to see the everyday objects of my childhood, a mangle or a knife sharpener, displayed as antiques, as bizarre to young eyes as a slave-chain.

James Rodgers is the headmaster of the John H. Woodson Junior High School, set for some reason in a field a long way from either town. He had his foot in a cast, having broken his ankle playing some ballgame with his pupils. He amazed me by saying that he thought only fifteen per cent of the native population of St Croix was white. I had been struck by how few black people I had seen in Christiansted; but then Mr Rodgers said that only half the population was native and that, by way of compensation, there were more Virgin Islanders living in the United States than there were in the Virgin Islands.

On the whole, Mr Rodgers said, the majority of people were reasonably content. Change was coming rapidly. Ten or fifteen years ago the blacks hated the whites. 'Now the kids see no difference.' Their whole identity, he maintained, is in the melting pot. Danish was spoken only by the very old. 'Nobody knows who's who any more.' When tourism started, only the whites benefited. Now that was changing. Any talk of independence was nonsense, an assertion of false pride. What the people did want, however, was the abolition of their colonial status. The US Virgin Islands have their own elected legislature of fifteen members who sit in St Thomas. The governor is also elected. But Congress has the power to change any laws that it may make. The islands send one delegate to serve in the US House of Representatives, but he has no vote. On the maps, Point Udall is marked as being the easternmost point of the United States. But what does that mean if the islanders do not have full representation?' 'The people want all or nothing,' said Mr Rodgers. 'The things we want mean a lot but cost very little – for instance, the right to vote for the President.'

It was a cry along those lines that was heard elsewhere in 1776.

'Going to Puerto Rico are you? Yeah, well I lived there eight years. April '85, I got mugged fifteen times in two months. I was shot. I was stabbed. So I moved to St Croix. You know what happened last night? I was mugged twice, by the same kid. Second time, he shook me and shook me and said "You're an old man, you must have more money than that." The police took me to a house. Said was it these kids? No, I said. I'd know that kid anywhere. And I'll smash his skull.'

Tom was indeed an old man, an ex-policeman, all shaky and bruised. He was staying in the Charte House. He wore torn shorts of some felt material in a disagreeable saffron colour. They were stained and had holes in them. Above, he wore a T-shirt saying US Army; below, a pair of sandals. His whole appearance was grizzled and grubby. It was hard to make out whether he was bearded or merely unshaven. His eyes were very blue, with the smallest pupils I have ever seen.

He showed me where the bullet went into his hand and where it came out by the elbow. He showed me the front of his hand – fourteen stitches; and the back – twenty stitches. He showed me the wound on his finger which his attackers had slashed to get a ring off – the blood eased it off.

Tom gave me a list of hotels and places to eat in San Juan. He advised me to meet a particular priest. The priest had suggested to him that he should leave Puerto Rico as it seemed that the muggers must kill him, sooner or later. 'If they do, Father, Jesus, I'm going to take one of the Spics with me, all the way down the line.'

We set off with some apprehension. Tom had advised me not to take the seaplane. He recommended another airline which would save me $14. Tom knew the price of everything. I found the idea of the seaplane irresistible. They take off from near the centre of Christiansted. The planes are Grumman Gooses – lovely squat, safe-looking things. Inside, it is somehow cosy when you board, much more substantial than an ordinary twenty-seater plane. The Grumman Goose roars a bit and waddles to the water's edge and flops in like a contented duck. The take-off is wonderful – no fear of running out of runway. The plane gradually gathers speed; spray flies past the window. The change from sea to air is hardly noticeable. The cheat was landing at San Juan airport – on the land. I was looking forward to swooping down onto the sea, like one of the boobies.

19
Puerto Rico
ANCIENT FOOTBALL AND MODERN COCKTAILS

The impact of Puerto Rico was a many faceted affair. After Tom and his dire warnings, I had expected to dislike the island and to go in terror. But it was not that. The first surprise was how our perception of everything had changed in four months. It was true that things had been becoming more and more Americanised as we drew closer, leaving memories of St Vincent and Dominica far behind. Nonetheless, even St Croix was Caribbean, we now realised. The sleepy politeness, the jokes which always solved everything, the real interest which people had as to whether Hamish was my son, the unimportance of time or whether you really had a ticket for something, all this and so much more we had come to think of as normal.

Now, with savage abruptness, all was changed. The customs' men had guns. The surly hell of officialdom glared at us. No one cared about anything except that you should park the car in the right place and should not stay there more than ninety seconds, or whether your ticket was blue or yellow, or why you hadn't filled the form out right. There were the familiar but forgotten signs, Howard Johnsons, Pizza Huts, banks built of glass, used-car lots surrounded by wire fencing hung with

226

bunting, cables and telegraph wires hanging everywhere, screaming hoardings. In town, a boy bicycled the wrong way. A motorcycle cop snatched him up, flung him against a wall, cosh at the ready.

We found a hotel next to one Tom had recommended, a little more expensive too, which would have shocked him. It was still early in the day. Feeling confused, we drove out into the country. Traffic-jams, expressways. After half an hour we turned off the highway up into the hills. Soon the houses thinned and we were in a tropical forest – one of the most spectacular we had yet seen. The trees seemed like comforting old friends: fern-trees; that deceptive *cecropia*, its pale leaves making one think it was a flower; superb bamboo; creepers like curtains. Even the forest held surprises. Every so often the winding road would come out on the ridge of a valley and our astounded eyes, almost out of control, swept over wide views stretching for miles, not having focused so far for weeks. The further we went the more San Juan seemed like a momentary aberration. We came down out of the rain forest to find ourselves in agricultural land. The terracing on the hillsides climbed higher than we had seen anywhere. Here, plainly, were a people who valued their land and tended it. They were not poor by the standards of other islands. Their houses were simple, but outside most of them was a car of sorts. The beauty of the Cayey Mountain Range drew us on and on, past a lovely lake near Patillas, until we found we had gone right across the island to the southern coast, about forty miles. We had to drive back over the mountains in the dark, gazing with amazement, when we reached the northern heights, over miles and miles of twinkling lights – all white or blue, not yellow, as Hamish observed.

Then we were back in San Juan. We dined in the restaurant under our hotel which was, mysteriously, run by quite different people. It was unexpectedly fashionable, the clientele being very smart compared with the guests in the hotel above. I began to think old Tom had a point when I noticed that the headwaiter unlocked the glass door every time someone arrived and quickly locked it again once they were inside. When I asked him about this he said, 'You know, is if someone come not dressed correcto, I can wave him go away.' I came later to think that this was really a sales gimmick, although there have been rare cases of bandits holding up restaurants for the guests' money and jewellery.

Of course, one re-adapts extraordinarily quickly. The next day, San Juan did not seem so formidable; we were already used to the rushing traffic and the confusion of a city of half a million people, surrounded by suburbs with probably another million. Old San Juan is a place of great charm, although nearly destroyed by the motorcar. It is at the end of an island or a spit of land and is protected both from land and sea by a big fortress at each end of the town. As one approaches, before reaching the walls, one has to pass a regrettable Capitol, built in twenties dictator-style, all sugar-white marble. The too-squat dome topped by a cupola sits on a hexagonal base. The columns below are too close together. It is an ugly building, which is sad, when all the ancient buildings within the city itself are rather understated, with the frolicsome exception of an Edwardian-style casino. The two great forts, San Cristobal and El Morro, are wonderful, wave-battered examples of Spanish solidity, bristling with cannons, while the lightly-decorated, stucco houses in the narrow, cobbled streets reflect centuries of knowledge of how to build in a hot climate.

El Morro, on the very tip of the island, rises 140 feet above the rocky shore. Sir Francis Drake failed to get through its defences in 1595, though the Earl of Cumberland later managed to invest it from the landward side. It did him little good as he and his men were attacked by dysentry and had to abandon the fort fairly soon after they had occupied it. It never fell again until the Spanish-American war of 1898, when it was attacked by Admiral William Sampson, to whom the Spanish navy surrendered at Santiago de Cuba.

San Cristobal was built about 230 years after El Morro and is interesting for its ingenious system of fortifications. It is so intricately designed that in order to penetrate the main section, an attacker would first have to capture five separate buildings connected only by tunnels and divided by dry moats.

Hamish loved the fortresses but was less pleased by my interest in the cathedral, particularly as we had one of our perennial arguments on the subject of his shorts, which were really swimming trunks. I pointed out that this was a Catholic country. He had had a Neapolitan girlfriend, so I thought he might understand. Nonsense, he said. We went into the cathedral, both sulking. It was a building of simple beauty, built originally in 1540, on the site of the first church of wood and thatch, which was destroyed by a hurricane. The Earl of Cumberland's troops, I fear, did much damage to the new building, and so did more hurricanes. What stands now is good nineteenth-century restoration, although there are four rooms with glorious stone-vaulted, Gothic ceilings and an unusual spiral staircase dating from the sixteenth century. Feeling soothed myself, I noticed that Hamish had cheered up. I could not think that it was the tomb of Ponce de Léon, the first governor of Puerto Rico, at which we were looking, that had produced his triumphant smile. It was not. It was three other people in shorts as offensive as his own.

The Americanisation of this island at first sight seems complete. When we left the cathedral we went over to the other side of the street to what was once a convent, and which was now an hotel. It was not a particularly distinguished building, but it could have had a measure of charm. Instead, the courtyard had been filled with what might have been a roadside fast-food joint, with a squalid wooden bar and ghastly plastic chairs. Hideous music blared out. On the menu I noticed Nun's Brochette and forbore to ask what it was, for fear of appearing amused.

I discussed the point with an official of the Ron Bacardi factory, Señor Mario S. Belaval (for a while I thought Ron was a name, but in the end worked out that it was the Spanish for rum). 'We are not truly Latin anymore,' said Señor Belaval. 'The US has had too great an influence on us for too long – our sense of justice, for instance, that's not Latin.'

Puerto Rico has a different relationship with the United States from that of the Virgin Islands. It is termed a commonwealth, with full powers of local government. All Puerto Ricans are US citizens. The Legislature is a bicameral assembly. The governor is popularly elected. They have, too, an elected Resident Commissioner, who sits, but may not vote (except in committee), in the US House of Representatives. Thus their autonomy is greater than that of the Virgin Islanders, but it is still extremely limited. The Puerto Ricans themselves are happy enough with the arrangement. They are too Americanised to want independence. Although Puerto Rico is much larger than any of the islands we had been to so far, they look without envy at comparable countries that are independent – Haiti, the Dominican Republic, Cuba and Jamaica. At the same time, they are not eager for statehood and full integration with the United States like Hawaii. 'Ask a man in the hills, "Are you American?",' said Señor Belaval. 'He will say, "not at all".'

We set off to explore the island. We drove first westward, along the north coast on another highway, crowded with juggernaut trucks, past tinselled used-car lots. We might have been in Florida. After an hour or more, we could see to the south, beyond the coastal plain, knobbly, indented hills and, behind them, higher mountains blue with mist. We

229

turned towards them, losing at once all touch with America. We started to climb, the road twisting through forest – magnificent kapoks and mahoganies and great splashes of flame-of-the-forest, with their brilliant red flowers and dark, dark green leaves. Then came a lake, giving an almost alpine feeling to the steep mountain setting, a feeling denied by the nodding bamboo. We were now approaching the Cordillera Central, a ridge of mountains which runs for three-quarters of the length of the island, reaching, at its highest point, nearly 4,400 feet. We passed a house which had stood on the edge of a low cliff overhanging a river. The cliff had collapsed and the house, still nearly intact, lay at an angle just above the water.

On our first night in the country, we stayed in a hotel high in the mountains, called the Hacienda Gripiñas. It was not easy to find, partly because of its remoteness, but more because its name contained two of the hazards of Puerto Rican Spanish. Quite often, Puerto Ricans change 'r' to 'l'. Nearly always they drop 's's' altogether, saying *ha'ta la vi'ta*. My struggling Spanish contended ill with these vagaries – I had been taught to roll my 'r's' and to lisp thick 's's'. However, we found the place eventually – a wooden house on the side of a hill. It was painted dark green and white, reminding us of the older houses in the Dutch islands. Here we heard our first *coquí*. This creature is a tiny tree frog, *Eleutherodactylus coquí*, which has become a symbol of Puerto Rico. The biggest of these frogs is never more than an inch long, but on average, they are half that size. They have large, bulging eyes. Their feet are scarcely webbed, but have suction caps at the ends of the fingers or toes, being adapted for tree-climbing rather than swimming. They are stupendous jumpers, considering their minute size. The most unexpected thing about these little frogs is the prodigious volume of their cry. They do not croak, but pronouce quite distinctly ko-KEE, with great force. They sound more like a bird, which gave rise to one legend that it was once a bird deprived of flight but granted the power to climb trees to its nest; or even a boy whistling, which produced another tale that the original *coquí* was a punished child. The male looks after the eggs and guards them, and looks after the hatchlings as well. They are so intriguing that someone has been studying them for ten years and still has not reached the end of their interest.

Everyone assured me that the *coquí* only lives in Puerto Rico and the immediately surrounding islands. That in itself might not be so odd, but I was told that most attempts to move it anywhere else have failed (though they have been bred in Louisiana). It will not survive in any zoo abroad, however carefully its home habitat is recreated. Hamish hunted for ages in a tree which grew in the hotel grounds, trying to see a *coquí* which was calling there. It was too small and well-camouflaged. As the night wore on, I decided that I was glad that the *coquí* was resistant to export. Dozens of them called their single, repetitive cry all night. I thought it could drive a person mad. Back in England, I learned that this particular species of *Eleutherodactylus* had only been identified in 1967. A couple of them were taken to Essex University and were kept in a fountain in the zoology department. There they multiplied to the point of being a nuisance.

The hotel was certainly proof that America did not penetrate into the interior. There was a mixture of prettiness, incompetence and friendliness and there was little that the American would demand. The beds were shamefully uncomfortable, the bathroom tatty. We had to wait nearly an hour for our dinner. When it came, it was not bad, but it was faithfully Spanish. The veal was not veal but beef. Everything was in breadcrumbs – *empanada*.

About an hour from the hotel was the most interesting Arawak site. When Columbus arrived in Puerto Rico, there were some forty thousand Arawaks on the island. The Caribs, who moved gradually up the islands from South America some hundreds of years after the Arawaks, had never established themselves on Puerto Rico, although they made persistent raids on the island from Viaques off the east coast of Puerto Rico. The Arawaks have always been regarded as a gentle people, although they were probably not as soppy as early historians made them out. Their initial acquiescence may well have stemmed from a belief that the Spaniards were sent by Yocahú, the great god in the sky, and were therefore immortal. After a while, the *cacique*, or leader, Urayoán decided to test the validity of this belief. When a conquistador, Diego Salcedo, was being carried across the Guarabo River by Urayoán's men, the *cacique* told them to hold him under water for a long time. The Arawaks were much relieved to find he was dead. But the discovery was also their doom. Emboldened, the Arawaks rebelled in 1511. The start of the revolt was so surprising to the Spaniards that the Arawaks killed a young Spanish captain and his men with no difficulty and destroyed a Spanish village. These were the last battles that the

231

Indians won. Juan Ponce de Léon picked off the *caciques* one by one in a series of battles, starting with the greatest leader Agueybana the Brave. The tactics of the Arawaks, the leader at the head of his forces, painted red and black and wearing the glittering gold emblem of his office round his neck, were child's play for the Spaniards. They concentrated on killing the chief. When he fell, the Arawaks fled. By 1550, there were only sixty Arawaks left on the island.

The Arawak religion was simple. Apart from Yocahú, there were tutelary spirits, known as *cemis*, whom they modelled in clay, stone, wood, gold and even cotton. The chiefs used to consult with these *cemis* by taking powdered hallucinogens, which were blasted up their nostrils through special pipes. The effect, according to a friend who tried it, was quite devastating. The very least that could happen was that the *cemis* would become chatty. The Arawak religion encompassed many elements of fun. There were frequent feasts and, more unexpected, there were ball-games that were partly religious and partly merely sporting. Each village had a flat pitch or court, sometimes several, on which they played their version of football.

Caguana lies in a wonderful landscape, surrounded by sharp, cragged hills like those in a Chinese painting or the background to Leonardo's 'Virgin of the Rocks'. The trees stand in clumps among the rocks. Below, the land slopes down to the Tanamá River. The site itself is like a park, with tall, royal palms and fine guava trees. There is no naturally flat place for miles around, but here there are ten courts in all, nine rectangular and one circular. The largest one measures fifty yards by thirty-five yards. It is absolutely flat and must have been a great labour to make. Round it stand stones, a little like gravestones, between two and three feet high. On them are carved faces and figures and symbols. Some are vigorous, but mostly they are like a child's drawings. The Arawaks played a quite difficult game on these grounds, as described by early Spanish chroniclers. There could be any number of players from about ten to about thirty on each side. The ball was made of rubber – incidentally the first encounter Europeans had with rubber. The pitch was divided in half. One team threw the ball at the other side. The object was never to let the ball fall to the ground without bouncing. The players were not allowed to use their hands or feet. They could use their heads, elbows, hips and knees. The ball could bounce, but if it fell dead the team on whose side it was lost a point. Interestingly, there was a great deal of betting on the outcome and the score; not in money, for they used no money, but in ornaments, weapons and tools.

It must have been a happy life, although the Arawaks had some less agreeable customs. It was their practice to pull out every hair on their bodies except on their heads and their eyebrows. Even less pleasant was the rule that the *cacique*'s favourite wife should be buried alive with him.

Half a mile from this idyllic place, we passed a house which had in its garden a Puerto Rican version of the garden gnome – a very big figure of a *péon*, leading a donkey and cart. How pathetic that the lands of the brave chief Guarionex, who razed the village of Sotomayor in the uprising of 1511, should have passed to someone who could choose to put up such a monstrosity.

We drove on through country of spectacular grandeur. The spring-flowering trees were in their prime, quite a number of yellow poui (once called *Tabebuia serratifolia* but now *Cybistax donnell-smithii*, presumably to confuse the amateur) and another tree which bore brilliant orange-red flowers, also before the leaves came (*Bucayo gigante* they said it was, perhaps an erythrina) and the pink poui (*Tabebuia pentaphylla*), called by the Spanish white oak (*Roble blanco*) because of its hard, heavy wood. The yellow poui, too, has very heavy wood, a cubic foot weighing as much as eighty pounds. There were so many varieties of tree that I despaired of ever learning what they were. It was not just trees, but everything that grows – giant bananas, tree-ferns, wild citrus, and an abundance of flowers. There was one flower which intrigued me by its variations, which I conclude must have been *Impatiens*. It could grow close to the ground like a creeper, covering whole banks by the roadside, or it could be two feet high. Each clump had plants with different colours, ranging from a pink so pale as really to be white, through various shades and tones of pink to quite a deep mauve, almost violet. Beside it often grew a deep yellow flower with a jet black centre. Wild grapefruit and wild oranges, or untended ones, lay on the road, no one even bothering to pick them up.

As we came lower in the mountains, we found coffee growing and I regretted that an archaeologist had said it was not possible for us to visit a coffee and corn plantation near where we were, which he plans to open to the public. I especially wanted to see a machine that he had found there – a Scotch S-turbine, I think he said – which he claims will revolutionise the history of hydraulic engineering.

233

Up and down valleys we went, through this glorious landscape, so that I wondered more and more how it could be that all the average person, even the average American, knows of this island is *West Side Story*. The truth is so far removed from that image, that I became quite indignant on behalf of these delightful people, whose courtesy and friendliness outshines that of any New Yorker. If some of the people in the city are rough (and in the end I concluded that, despite old Tom, San Juan is no rougher than many American cities) it is because of what they have learned in America. The young men of Puerto Rico flock to the United States in search of work. When a recession hits America they come back; for who would not prefer to be out of work in this island rather than in Pittsburgh or Chicago? They bring with them the drug habits, the violence, the thieving tricks – the things they acquired in the States.

Gradually, we came down to the southern coast at the west end of the island. The vagaries of guidebooks and tourist offices led us to a dreary hotel near Guánica. It could only have been recently built, but was already in decay. No bath plug nor any chance of getting one. The desk fell when I tried to write on it. Everywhere was dark. Everything was enclosed by a high wire fence so that one could not get to the beach. The swimming pool had a long list of rules beside it. The dining-room was icy with air-conditioning. There was a plastic yellow flower on each table; this after a day of more flowers than one could imagine. There was no fresh juice; that after the bounty and abundance of the forest. I wished that we were back with the real cool of the hills and even the *coquí*.

Guánica lies in a bay. It is not an interesting town, being an inconclusive mixture of a tourist resort and a potential centre of industry. On the tentative promenade by the sea is a plaque which reads:

Puerto Rico
National Society of the Daughters
of the American Revolution
Placed this tablet to commemorate the landing
of the American troops under General Nelson A. Miles
on Guánica Beach, July 25th 1898.

Under the plaque is a stone which says:

This stone prepared as Pedestal by the Municipality of Guánica bears inscription graven by American soldiers during occupation of the town. July 25 1955.

234

The soldiers had cut the letters:

3rd BAT

1st U.S.V. ENG. R.S.

SEPT 1898

By coincidence, I had just been reading, for want of anything better, Steinbeck's dreadful *Travels with Charley* and had there come across General Miles fighting against the Indian chief Joseph and the Nez Percés.

Looking at this plaque, I reflected on the meaning of the Spanish–American war. The United States, in 1898, was in an expansionist mood. It was all very well for President McKinley in his inaugural address to forswear wars of conquest and territorial aggression. Within months he was grabbing all that he could get – the Philippines first and, two months later, Cuba. There was a plausible excuse for Cuba, which the Americans had had express designs upon ever since John Quincy Adams had, in 1823, claimed it was joined by nature to the United States.

In 1895 the Cubans had rebelled against Spain. The struggle mouldered on, Spain being unable to control it. The US sent the battleship *Maine* to Havana. While in the harbour, she blew up, killing 260 sailors. The Americans said she was sabotaged by the Spanish. The Spanish said it was an internal explosion. Congress declared that Cuba should be free and independent, and disclaimed any intention of exercising sovereignty over the island.

She promptly occupied Cuba and imposed on the island a right of intervention in her affairs, which continued until the coming of Fidel Castro, and claimed permanent bases there, one of which, Guantanamo, she still holds. In the same way that America swiped Hawaii, as it were, on the way back from the Philippines without any justification whatever, she merrily annexed Puerto Rico at the same time that she drove Spain out of Cuba. She incidentally abrogated at once the self-governing constitution which Spain had granted to Puerto Rico the year before.

The people of the Caribbean have always in the background the pronouncements of John Quincy Adams, of Theodore Roosevelt, of Assistant Secretary of State Loomis who said in 1904: '. . . no picture of our future is complete which does not contemplate and comprehend the United States as the dominant power in the Caribbean Sea.' Time after

235

time, the United States has intervened – in Cuba, Puerto Rico, Haiti, the Dominican Republic and most recently Grenada. It may, according to your point of view, feel like a perpetual threat or feel like having a guardian angel. But I could not help wondering, as I sat gazing out over the bay where the Americans landed, whether the history, certainly of Cuba and possibly of Puerto Rico, might not have been a happier one both for them and for America, had McKinley kept to the promises of his inaugural address.

We made expeditions from our dismal hotel. First we went to Mayaguez, a port and university town on the west coast. Primarily, I wanted to see the botanical gardens, which were said to be superb. They came under the US Department of Agriculture so, it being a Saturday, they were shut. 'Federal' said the University guard. Driving round the outside of the gardens was tantalising. Inside, I could see all the trees I wanted to identify. Two immensely tall yellow pouis, at least fifty feet high, were in full bloom. They are quixotic trees, flowering copiously, the flowers coming straight out of the leafless branches. They last only a few days, then fall in a wide pool of yellow round the base of the tree.

There were few other attractions in Mayaguez, the original town was almost entirely destroyed by an earthquake in 1918. I was baffled to find that not one of the three students from whom I asked the way in the University could speak any useful English, yet eighty per cent of the population are said to have been to America. Rather shamefacedly, we went to the zoo. I hate zoos. This was no exception, indeed was worse than most. At least the poor creatures should be plainly and accurately marked, so that one could learn something. Many of the cages had no labels. Of the few that there were, none said where the animals came from. A Puerto Rican child might reasonably suppose that there were Amherst pheasants on the island, as these shared a cage with an indigenous dove. The poor condor looked bedraggled and miserable, as did the cassowary. The only animals which looked at all content were the capybara, like labrador-sized hamsters. They were breeding famously.

On another day, we explored the south-west corner of the island. It was dull after the wonders of the interior. Mostly it serves as a middle-class holiday resort. The beaches are nothing to speak of after the Virgin Islands, but they are obviously popular and there are inlets with unspoilt bays. The large holiday complex at Boquerón filled me with despair with its high fences and lists of rules. These fences cannot be the product of fear, for there is nothing to fear. It must be some obsession with 'exclusivity'.

There was one wholly unexpected area, stretching for several miles, perhaps a couple of hundred feet above sea-level. It was strangely barren, virtually treeless and covered in savannah grass. All sense of being in the Caribbean faded. I felt as if I had suddenly been transported to Africa. Round and about I could see only pale brown, dry grass and low thorn bushes. Overhead, vultures circled. It was the sort of country where a lion might lie up, waiting for the night.

There were herds of Friesians and Bramahs for milking and some Aberdeen Angus. We stopped to talk to one farmer who looked almost comically like a *gaucho* in the movies. He wore jeans, a western shirt and a wide-brimmed hat. His horse, still saddled, stood hitched to a post. The stirrups were broad and made of leather. He told me that he had a herd of 180 Holsteins, which he grazed over two thousand acres. He never made silage nor did he cut hay. Not surprisingly, his cows on average yielded only ten pints a day, but both he and they seemed happy. Actually, I suppose, it was surprising that they yielded that much, as they lived only on this wispy, dry grass and nothing else grew on the land, except flat-topped thorn trees and sodom apple. How incongruous this farmer was in this lonely landscape when one thought that barely more than a mile away were beaches crowded with urban Puerto Ricans on happy family outings, lovers kissing, children playing ball and grand-fathers sleeping.

We had been invited to stay at Palmas del Mar, a grand resort at the opposite end of the island. It was a journey which could have been made in three or four hours on the super highways, but we could not resist another drive through the mountains. We first went along the coast to Ponce, the second largest town on the island, in order to go to the art gallery there. It was another of those odd shifts of dimension to find ourselves looking at European paintings, and equally odd to wonder how some of them got there. The first picture I saw was a Reynolds of someone called Charles Vernon. 'Dashwood heirlooms', it said in large letters on the frame. Did someone steal it from West Wycombe? There were sculptures by Bernini, Nollekens, Rodin and Epstein. Most peculiar of all was a large collection of Pre-Raphaelites. There was a huge William Edward Frost of Diana surprised by Actaeon, a marvellous Burne-Jones and the best Leighton I have ever seen, of a woman in a brilliant tangerine dress entitled 'Flaming June'. Of the Puerto Rican painters, the one who sticks in my memory is Francisco Oller, a late nineteenth-century artist, obviously influenced by contemporary French painting. An exhibition of Puerto Rican works of the last twenty-five years was striking, I thought, not for any great originality but for a deep and miserable pessimism. It made me uneasy, but I was in any case angry with the architect of the building – Edward Durrell Stone. It was a lavish building, good in many ways, if a little pretentious, with talk in the guide of its being the 'Parthenon of the Caribbean'. There was, however, absolutely no provision for wheelchairs, the curve of the staircase being almost designed to inhibit them. A small lift would have added little to the cost of this new building, far less, I dare say, than one of the fancy gardens which have little to do with the viewing of pictures. I therefore never saw half the museum, the better half I need hardly say – the Spanish, Italian and Dutch works.

We took then to the mountain roads. It was once again an afternoon of incomparable beauty, through the forests, up and down valleys splashed with the vivid reds and oranges of the flowering trees, past lakes, over rivers, stopping every so often to gaze at superb vistas to the sea.

Palmas del Mar is on the east coast, an enormous and grand resort covering six or seven thousand acres, with a golf-course, a little harbour, two or three miles of coastline varying from long sandy beach to rocky cliff. There are at least three hotels, several restaurants, shops, groups of apartments, clusters of villas.

It is not the sort of place that I would ever have chosen to visit, had it not been for an introduction to Estéban Padilla, the architect designer of much of the complex. Steve, as he is known, is a cosmopolitan figure of exceptional charm, who went to university in Florence and Paris. He is a plump and jovial person in his forties. His engaging, crinkly face crumples up when he is amused, his eyes totally disappearing, so that he looks like a laughing frankfurter. Any lingering doubts I may have had about the Americanisation of Puerto Rico would have been dispelled by Steve. He is not American, nor is he Spanish. He is what I came to recognise as Puerto Rican. An amalgam perhaps, but by now a quite distinct nationality – far too easy-going for an American (the Americans use the word relax more than any other people, but will never learn that it is only those who do not have to think about relaxing who do so), far too self-mocking for a Spaniard. 'The spirit of Puerto Rico,' Steve said to me one day, 'can be summed up in the phrase *hay bendito*.' Roughly, one might translate it as 'bless my soul' or 'mercy on us', but it is far more vulgar or camp than that. They say it to one another all the time. If you say it to a speed cop, he laughs and lets you off.

Seeing this resort through Steve's eyes, much of my prejudice faded. It was all so intelligently done. The little harbour with its marina will be very agreeable when it is completed. In order to get it right, they had consulted with M. Spoerry, the architect of the successful Port Grimaud, near St Tropez. The intention is to have close-knit clusters of houses, each with its own shops and perhaps restaurant, giving the feeling of the village.

We lunched together one day, at the place where the fishermen bring in the fish, sitting on rough benches at bare tables, looking across at the harbour. We might well have been in the Mediterranean. Beyond the little port we could see Candeleero Point. It was there that, in the last century, when Spain had forbidden all trade with the United States, smugglers would light a light to guide the illicit traders in.

I was glad that we had come because these resorts are a part of the new Caribbean, and I now learned how much thought and ingenuity went into them. I certainly would not wish to live in one, but then I would not wish to live in a Maasai menyatta or an Eskimo igloo. I tried to analyse why I found the idea of a resort so unattractive. I think it was largely because it was a false society. In real life, one has Belgravia cheek by jowl with Pimlico or Third Avenue a minute's walk from Park Avenue. It is the problem of new towns that they are all one class and one age-group. Somehow the particular level of riches is not an appealing one to make into a group. In the country, walking to the post office, you pass and greet a farmer, a teacher, a butcher and a doctor. Time will be the remedy in a new town, but is there any remedy behind barriers and guards?

Another problem is the transient nature of the inhabitants. Of the 700 houses so far sold, only 200 belong to fixed residents. One day there could be 11,000 houses. More probably, there will be 6,000. Proportionately, that would mean 1,700 lived in while 4,300 would be empty or only temporarily inhabited.

Perhaps I was wrong to think about it this way. I remember once becoming enraged by Arnold Kettle's *Introduction to the English Novel*. He claimed that it was so much harder to write about a modern shop, say Marks and Spencer, than about Poll Sweedlepipe's shop. What nonsense. Poll Sweedlepipe's shop must have been far drearier than Marks and Spencer, until Dickens' art lifted it to the sublime.

There was drama enough at Palmas del Mar. The harbour was seized by Citibank when the recession nearly closed the whole enterprise. They sold it to X who sold it to Y. (X remained as manager and milked Y.) Now it is once more with Citibank. Probably the original promoters will buy it back, for they have at last started to make a profit. Another drama was unfolding with a group who had bought one section of the land to develop. They had decided to kick out one of their number, but he was the one who had all the share certificates in his safe.

In any case, Hamish and I had a thoroughly enjoyable time. There were all the amusements Hamish liked and there were pleasant excursions and restful places to watch the sea and to read. Hamish, furthermore, was seduced by a woman of forty-five, whom I had planned to seduce. My consolation was to be found in a restaurant for which Michel Guérard had designed the menu. The food was delicious and the Catalan family who ran it were entertaining.

On our last night, Steve gave a party. It was a good one. So good that I did not notice that I had dropped my wallet in the road, full of money and full of credit cards. At three in the morning, one of those guards knocked on our door. He brought my wallet.

20

The Dominican Republic

FAVOURITE OF COLUMBUS

Seldom is one more than mildly surprised. Photography, television documentaries, every form of modern communication, have robbed the traveller of those moments of wild surprise that colour the pages of nineteenth-century travel books. One may feel awe, as at the Grand Canyon, or a kind of relief at finally understanding, like putting in the final piece of a jigsaw, on seeing Venice for the first time, but not surprise.

In Santo Domingo, I was astonished. No one had ever told me about it. Never had I seen a picture. I suppose I must have read something, but I did not remember it. For me, the Dominican Republic was just a place which had once had a disagreeable dictator, called Trujillo. Oh yes, it was the other half of Haiti. Together they made up Hispaniola. That was all I knew.

Now here I was looking down a street in which nearly every building had been built when Henry VII was on the throne of England. At the airport, I had picked up a leaflet which described the Dominican Republic as the 'craddle' of the Americas. As we wandered through the streets of the colonial quarter of Santo Domingo, it gradually dawned on

241

me that it was true. Here was the first church and also the first cathedral, the first university, the first hospital, the first convent, the first fortress in the western hemisphere. Here indeed the Americas were born.

Columbus established his first real settlement on Hispaniola on his second journey, in 1493, at Isabela on the north coast. It was a swampy place and the Spaniards had to abandon it after three years. They chose instead the site of Santo Domingo, because of the wide mouth of the Ozama River and because it was only ten miles from Haina, where they had found deposits of gold in the river. Real building did not begin until the arrival of the first governor of the island, Nicolás de Ovando, in 1502. The hotel we were staying in was built in that year as the Governor's house, joined to another two, also built by him. He must have been an obsessive builder. Almost next to the hotel is the Ozama fortress, which Trujillo used as a prison, renaming it, with a dictator's talent for euphemy, the Tower of Homage. The Governor started it as soon as he arrived. In 1503, he started to build the Hospital of San Nicolás de Bari, although it was not finished until 1552.

Where Nicolás de Ovando left off, Columbus's son, Diego Colón, continued. He laid the foundation stone of the cathedral in 1514. The building was finished in 1540. It has been much altered since then, so that the north side of the building, facing the square where Columbus's statue stands, looks like a patchwork quilt. The north entrance goes straight into what was a chapel where, one is ashamed to read, Sir Francis Drake slung his hammock, while he sacked the city in 1586, destroying many of its most dignified buildings. The interior of the cathedral is calm and cool, with soaring columns, high vaulting and grand arches which do no harm to the simplicity of its style. Unfortunately, this plain peace is marred by a huge and hideous tomb donated by the Spanish government, in 1892, to house the supposed bones of Columbus, discovered during restoration by the French some twenty years earlier. The poor man's remains are supposed to be in at least three other places.

Diego Colón's other important building was the Alcazar, the viceregal seat of the Spanish crown for at least sixty years. Of course, it was destroyed by Drake, but it has been rebuilt in the austere style of the original with only a five-arched loggia on the ground floor and a matching balcony above to relieve the solid rectangular block.

All these buildings and so many more were built of heavy stone. By the solidity of their architecture, the Spaniards demonstrated their intention to stay, claiming this new world as theirs for all time. I loved the thickness of the walls and the way, in the evening as one passed by, they threw out the heat they had gathered in the day from the sun. I loved those long, white-washed walls, with so few windows, perhaps just one wrought iron balcony and a single doorway – the only colour being the red tiles over the one window and one door – all suggestive of luxurious privacy inside. Most of the buildings are restored, but there is nothing dead about them; they are in some ways more real than the more genuine ones we had seen in San Juan.

My favourite, to which I wish I could return again and again, was the Church of the Convento de los Dominicanos. This convent was built in 1510 and, in 1538, given the status of a university by the Pope. The first time that we went, the church was shut. There was a woman at a side door, cleaning. She asked if we wanted to go in, pleased by our interest. It was always a delight with these buildings, having looked at their dark exteriors, to step inside and find that same coral stone so pale, where the sun could not burn it to a sombre grey, giving an extra lightness to the fine stonework. Drake apparently did not destroy this building – not, one imagines, out of any respect for learning (he had quite demolished the Franciscan Convento dedicated to teaching), but perhaps because twenty-four days of pillage was not enough to destroy every building. The church had three sections; first a delicate but plain vaulted roof at the east end, then a barrel roof and finally, below a gallery, a nearly flat vaulted ceiling which defied gravity. The woman with her young daughter led us to the Capilla del Rosario, a chapel with an enthralling carved stone dome. It was a combination of pagan and Christian symbolism reflecting the comfortable way the medieval church embraced and adapted to its own uses the beliefs of earlier religions. In the centre of the dome was a flat sun, representing God. In each corner was a large figure representing both Matthew, Mark, Luke and John, and Jupiter, Saturn, Mars and Mercury. Below came the twelve apostles in the form of signs of the zodiac, some in high relief, others in bas-relief.

The charm of the Dominican Republic was not just in its architecture. The difference between this island and Puerto Rico struck us almost as a physical blow as soon as we emerged from the airport customs. At once there was a crowd of people hustling, trying to hire us a car. There was a difference from anything we had seen which took me some time to identify, but I did notice that the young man from whom we hired the car gave me a Bible on which to rest the form while I signed it.

The poverty was a part of the physical shock, and yet I thought guiltily that it was somehow like coming home after the riches and tidy-mindedness of Puerto Rico. Why, I wondered, does poverty always seem more alive? I concluded that the simple answer was that it is. It was a conclusion that was to be much shaken later on, in Haiti. Hamish looked in horror at the shanty towns at the outskirts of Santo Domingo. He had never before seen that hopeless huddle of corrugated iron and boards all brown and grey-brown like a rusted cubist painting.

As we walked through the streets, I kept wondering what it was that felt both so familiar and yet so odd. Hamish went on being shocked. To me the place felt vibrant. There were shoeshine boys, a man selling tiny unweaned puppies on the pavement. There were money-changers and scores of little boys begging, rubbing their tummies. There was one deaf and dumb one who was begging not for money so much as for a smile. In the shops one could buy guns and leather pistol holsters.

The new city sprawled for miles, a modern city in patches, with slum areas of shanty town, next door to grand suburbs of villas surrounded by high walls. All along the seafront ran a broad road, the Malecón, brightly lit with restaurants and lined with palmtrees. At one end of this promenade stands a vast statue of Fray Antonio Montesino who, in his Advent sermon of 1511, made an impassioned plea for human rights and in particular for the rights of the Indians. When the Spaniards arrived, there were between two and three hundred thousand Indians in Hispaniola. In 1510 there were 46,000. Montesino's plea was of no avail. By 1512, there were 20,000. In 1570, there were only two Indian villages remaining, the last handful of those of whom Columbus wrote that, 'there is no better nor gentler people in the world'.

On Saturday nights, the whole city turns out for the *paséo* on the Malecón. People walk up and down, groups of them sit on the balustrade, the waves breaking on the rocks below. Carriages ply to and fro, drawn by Rocinante horses, their ribs and haunches sticking out like springs on an old sofa. Everyone is laughing. Music blares from all the cars, playing merengue. It must be one of the liveliest streets in the world. Not all is so guileless. The *South American Handbook* had said that one hotel was, 'not for the squeamish as it does a brisk "trade" in young boys.' Mischievously, one night I sent Hamish in to see what it was like. He came out pale, followed by an importunate 'gay'. When we had got rid of him, I took Hamish for a drink to recover his composure. A man in a white suit came and sat at our table. He spoke English and was interesting about the city. After a few minutes, Hamish jumped up and begged to go back to the hotel. The man, he told me outside, had put his hand on his thigh. 'I'll never go out again at night. It's not safe. Something terrible could happen,' he said.

It was at that moment I realized what it was that made Santo Domingo so different. Of course, it was safe. It was safe in the way that Nice, even Naples, was safe fifty years ago, unless one courted disaster. Everything about the place belonged to a forgotten time. There was so much that was recognisable, but that has disappeared from Europe.

Much of it was dreadful. There would be children at midnight in the streets, offering to clean the windscreen of one's car. The style of begging and the distance for which they would follow one, with a persistence which you never find in countries where begging still exists, say India or Africa, were unnerving. There was no doubt that one could have bought young boys and probably young girls. It was noticeable that there were no household aids, and in the hotel, the maids did the cleaning on their hands and knees.

Much that was not dreadful belonged to that seductive class of luxury which the presence of poverty affords those who are less poor. The streetsellers would peel an orange for you. Servants earn only $15 a week. Some of the forgotten things were merely delightful, such as there being no question but that fruit juice would be fresh, the size of drinks being not measured but generously poured, the feeling of solidity about the furniture in quite cheap restaurants, the fact that so much was made of genuine materials – real leather, real cotton, unfrozen food.

There was much that was plain old-fashioned. The young men in discos would wear ties and black trousers. They would dance the merengue, a kind of Latin-American reel. Virginity was still essential for the young girls. If her parents knew that their daughter had slept with a young man, they would insist on marriage. The girls would kiss like vampires but that was that.

Of course, the disparity between rich and poor was deeply offensive, but I felt, perhaps nostalgically, that there was a simplicity which we have lost. The sin, for the most part, was unsophisticated sin, less distasteful to my mind than what can be found in London or New York – if only because it was openly acknowledged for what it was and not hypocritically dolled up as liberation or emancipation.

*   *   *

After a few days we set off westward along the coast. Once we were free of the sprawling suburbs and past the town of Cristóbal, where I was glad to hear that the odious Trujillo's famous Casa de Caoba (mahogany) had been much damaged by Hurricane David, it was plain that here was another island where agriculture is still of paramount importance. Sugar still represents half the nation's exports. There were sugar mills, but also fields of plantain, cassava and sweet potato. Up in the hills to our right, there was coffee. At Azua, about seventy-five miles from the capital, we turned down to the sea to a beach called Playa de Monte Rio. It was, by Caribbean standards, not a very interesting beach, but it was Sunday and there were crowds of young people. There were three restaurants or bars which served food. In the first, the music was so loud that I could not stay there. The second was nearly as bad but had another section with no loudspeakers actually directed at it. The restaurant was right on the beach a few yards from the sea, just a roof really, open on all sides.

The young people paraded up and down the beach, swam, drank and danced in the first half of our restaurant. There was one girl in a green bathing-dress. She wore pants underneath it for some reason. She danced provocatively with her companions, but kept looking at us. Suddenly, she darted over and said to Hamish, 'I like you. Will you dance?' He wouldn't. She then tried to persuade him to swim. I said that we were about to eat lunch. Every so often, she popped back to ask some question. Where were we from? How old was Hamish? Then she went to swim. She must have lurked nearby, because as soon as Hamish set off to swim after lunch, she appeared, took him by the hand and led him into the water.

They played together in the sea for quite a long time. When they came back, Hamish looked somewhat embarrassed, but produced the surprising information that her pubic hair was shaved. Altagracia, for that was her name, now plied me with a stream of questions. 'I love him, does he love me?' It was easier to say yes. Where were we going? How long for? Could she come? I evaded most of these. She said she was a music student from San Juan de Maguana, a town to the north-west, and that she was fifteen. She wrote down her name and address with great labour, her writing being wholly uneducated.

Altagracia was a puzzle. She was extremely pretty, nearly black but with European features. She was not very intelligent, indeed rather stupid in that, when I could not understand what she said, she would

246

treat me as seriously deaf, leaning forward and shouting close to my ear. I could not think she was a prostitute, but what was she doing, evidently unattached, fifty miles from home? When we made to go, she asked for a lift into Azua. There, she said she would go on with us as our road went in the right direction for her. This was true, but at the junction where she should go north, she asked if she could come with us. Hamish thought it a good idea. I did not. We gave her money for her bus. She then said she would go back to the beach – about fifteen miles. We had planned to go to San Juan, but somehow we never did and we did not see Altagracia again. But by then Hamish's heart was otherwise engaged.

The road after leaving Azua ran through country which became progressively drier. The agriculture stopped. People at the roadside sold what looked like packets of reeds but were, I discovered later, broomheads made of palm leaves. Soon there were no villages, just rolling hills covered in cactus and century plants with spiky orange flowers. Then the road turned south and the landscape changed again, to the lusher vegetation and canefields once more. The Dominican Republic is far more varied in appearance than Puerto Rico which, with the exception of that one patch of dry grassland, must have a far higher rainfall.

Barahona, where we spent the night, is a dull town, with a passable hotel where the local dignitaries had drinks in the evening, looking out over the Bahía de Neiba to the Sierra Martin Garcia, reminding Hamish, as the light faded, of the Whitenose Cliffs at Weymouth Bay. The locals wisely did not dine in the hotel. I was surprised to see a large party of Americans of late middle-age in this out-of-the-way place. Before they sat down to dinner, they stood while one of them boomed grace. They were missionaries.

We had planned to drive round the Barahona peninsula and up over the Sierra de Baoruco, along the border with Haiti, to Jimani. The dirt road ran beside the sea. There were great rollers coming into pleasant coves and palm-fringed beaches. To our right, cliffs rose sharply – the end of the sierra. Every so often there was a village of small huts, some thatched, some with corrugated iron roofs. The houses were often prettily painted in pink and green or blue and pink. Many of the doors were carved with patterns. The people were much blacker here and living was meagre, despite more rain. I was constantly reminded of Africa.

At length, we came to a larger village, called Enriquillo after the Indian *cacique*, who was the first Amerindian to lead a revolt against the invading Europeans. He had been educated by Franciscan friars at their Convento in Santo Domingo and was at first inclined to co-operate closely with the Spanish. Unfortunately, the governor's son seduced, or even raped, Enriquillo's wife. Enriquillo did not want real bloodshed between himself and the Spaniards, but he shot the governor's son in the arm. Nobody believed Enriquillo's story as to why he had shot him and the Spanish wanted to try him. Enriquillo took to the hills. For thirteen years, he hid in the Sierra de Baoruco and made harrassing raids upon the Spanish settlements. The conquistadores could never capture him but eventually they killed him by the loathsome device of poisoning the well at which they discovered he drew his water. The little town called after this hero lay at the beginning of a wide, dry plain. It was dusty. There were some feeble attempts at new housing, little more than cheerless shacks of concrete. The schoolchildren were dressed in khaki, perhaps in the hope that the all-pervading dust would not show on their clothes.

The plain was dreary. There were two dead cows on the road, one had just been hit by a car. The road itself was appalling, having some long time ago been paved, but now crumbling away. There is no worse surface than this. We came to Oviedo, which we had hoped might be a town where we could get something to eat. We found, instead, almost a ghost-town. There were many uninhabited houses and even an unused stadium. It must have been some abandoned project. It was hot and miserable. The desert land was dull and the road got no better. We looked forward to climbing up into the sierra.

At last, after another forty excruciating miles, we reached Pedernales, marked on our map as a large town. It was sited on the river of the same name, which forms the border with Haiti. It was a forlorn place, without any focus. We asked a group of three people where the centre was. They all pointed in different directions. The most we could buy to eat was a packet of biscuits and an orange. We headed for the road over the sierra. We had gone only half a mile when a lorrydriver told us that the road was impassable. Of course, we did not believe him and we started to climb. The road was not too bad to start with, but soon we came to a village where they said it was difficult even for four-wheel-drive cars. There was nothing for it but to drive back the hundred bumpy miles of the way we had come.

An abandoned enterprise is always miserable. On the outward journey the potholes are cushioned by optimism; on the return, each one is a reproach. As we left Pedernales, the military stopped us; a smiling young boy with a rifle told us to open the boot, presumably to search for illegal Haitian immigrants. The two dead cows still lay on the road. There were evidently no vultures here. Indeed, there were very few birds of any sort – one like a magpie and otherwise only doves. When we reached Enriquillo and the sea, we cheered up. The town looked less dusty Everyone was out on the streets in clean clothes. From every bar came the click of billiard balls. The children were playing hopscotch and I wondered what the Spanish for that might be. The older boys and girls were mixing more freely than I would have expected. I was startled to see a father pick up his naked baby son and kiss him on his genitals.

We were still determined to get to Jimani, on the north side of the sierra. The road, such as it was, lay in a wide, wide valley between the Sierra Baoruco and the Sierra de Neiba. At first it ran through thousands of acres of cane. The harvest was in progress. There were trains carrying the cut cane to the mill; one lost its waggons, which trundled on downhill in pursuit of the engine. The driver had to judge nicely how to stop them. Then we crossed mudflats, where the telegraph poles were made of trees with wiggly trunks, so they looked as if they were Victorian rustic. As we neared the foot of the Sierra de Neiba, we found palm groves watered by the mountain streams. Naked boys and girls swam in the crystal pools.

Near the town of Neiba we came to Lake Enriquillo. We saw some flamingoes striding on pinkish legs over the muddy foreshore. This lake is remarkable in several ways. It is the largest lake in the Caribbean; it lies about 140 feet below sea level; it is inhabited by crocodiles, most of which live on the island of Cabritos, flamingoes and a great many iguana. We drove the whole length of the lake, stopping every so often to go down to the shore to see if we could see the crocodiles. Masses of boys followed us each time. They always said the crocodiles were just over there in the next bay, but they never were.

The houses in this area were nearly all very poor, though many of them were painted – plenty of pink and green and also darker red and blue. Some, often the newer ones, were just of plain wood, with neat lattice work under the eaves and good, carved doors. Nearly all the houses were thatched. It was interesting, when we tried later – but were prevented by the military – to cross the Sierra de Neiba, to see the army housing up on the ranchland of the mountains. They made me realise that the traditional ones, old or new, look like houses, while the modern ones, of roughly the same size, look like sheds. Beside the road, I saw three brand new rocking-chairs and, after that, I noticed that nearly every house had one. Is the Dominican Republic the last outpost of the rocking-chair?

It was a slow but enjoyable drive, through country which had nothing to do with anyone's picture of the West Indies. At moments I thought I was back in the Sahel, beside the River Niger. The feeling was not merely geographically different. Here there was no echo of history; none of that keen sense of the beginning of colonial empires which informs Santo Domingo, nor any of that plantation nostalgia created by ancient sugar mills. The village people round Lake Enriquillo have reverted to an African way of life and yet they have so much that is Spanish in their looks, in their customs and, of course, in their language.

Jimani is a border town. The army is there in force. The two sierras come closer together here, one to the north, the other to the south. To the east is the lake, to the west Haiti. As the border is closed, not many people have any occasion to come here except for a few more intrepid tourists who come for the wildlife. There was only one very simple hotel. Chickens wandered in and out of the dining area. There were goats in the garden. One was tied to a log which it dragged round after it. The goat crossed the corner of a cracked, old swimming pool that was filling with water. The log fell in. The goat bellowed with indignation. A soldier was playing dominoes by himself on the terrace. A languid man offered to show us a room. The best one was taken by another soldier, who lay on his back asleep, his door open. His hand held a lighted cigarette. The room the man showed us had two beds which took up practically the whole space. There was a stained sheet on each bed. The room shared a combined lavatory and shower with the room beyond. The lavatory flushing system was broken, which had deterred no one from using it. Hamish became as indignant as the goat with its log. 'We cannot stay here, it's terrible.' I said that I thought it quite adequate. 'But look at the sheets,' he howled. I explained that one could turn them over and hope. I was enjoying myself. The young, I said, were spoilt. There was nowhere else, in any case.

We went in the car up the village, towards the border. At the barracks they stopped us. We chatted for a bit with a young soldier who eventually said we could go to the border itself. There was a large gateway with high, iron gates. To one side were more military houses, mostly deserted. The guards at the gate said that it was very quiet now, after the deposition of Duvalier six weeks before. It was possible to get permission to cross the border here. It would take about three months to obtain. We said we would try to come to wave to them from the other side long before that.

On the way back, we came across a cockfight. It took place in a rough, circular edifice made of wood and corrugated iron, a little like a small version of Shakespeare's Globe Theatre in a bad movie. The pit, which was about fifteen feet in diameter, had a three-foot barrier round it. Outside that was a single row of chairs with their backs to the structure. Above, there was a gallery with four tiers of seats under the iron roof. We sat below. The bookies kept pressing me to bet, though I had no idea what to bet on or how the system worked. They carried sheaves of pesos and looked at me with contempt. The first fight was about to begin.

The owners brought their birds. The first belonged to a soldier. The other owner was a grey-haired man of angry mien, in a pale yellow suit. The cocks were plucked all the way down their backs and under their wings, to make them more vulnerable. Their thighs, too, were bare of feathers. They had extra spurs strapped to their legs, and a coloured band, which was the only way I could tell them apart. The owners sprayed something from a beer bottle under the birds' wings. Perhaps it was just water to cool them. Then the umpire dabbed something from a tiny bottle on the cocks' spurs. Alcohol possibly, to wipe off anything the owners might have put on to enfeeble their opponent's bird.

The owners climbed into the pit holding their birds and thrusting them at each other to foster their fury. At a sign, they threw them together on the ground and left the pit. The birds arched their wings and pecked. They would dash forward in little rushes, flap together and fall back. The fight dragged on and on, the birds leaping with little zest and giving weak pecks. I thought it was mildly nasty and uninteresting. The crowd shared the second view. They were not very excited, shouting a bit and betting without much enthusiasm. The owners yelled most, leaning over the barrier and clapping their hands at the birds to encourage them. Eventually, the older man's bird sank to the ground. After a long wait, the umpire pronounced in favour of the soldier's bird.

251

The owners picked them up. One spur on the soldier's bird was hanging loose. He gave it to our neighbour. The cocks, even the vanquished one, seemed to regard the affair with equanimity, going away bright-eyed, if bleeding.

The second fight was much better, which is to say nastier and bloodier. The two birds leaped around the pit, often flying two feet in the air, at which the crowd gave a yell of thrill. Before this couple of cocks were put in, I noticed their legs trembling uncontrollably. One of the owners was in front of me for most of the fight. His legs in his cheap pink trousers trembled as the bird's had done. The crowd yelled their bets, shrieking at each scrum of feathers. Those at the top beat on the corrugated roof. The people's faces were twisted and unpleasant to see. There were only three women in an audience of, say, eighty but their mouths, too, made obscene shapes of excitement. The bird with yellow spurs fell and lay prone, its head on one side, its wings spread, its whole body heaving. The white-spurred cock stood, heaving too, as though unconcerned. This time the yellow bird rose again. When it rose, they fought again with renewed leaps, the crowd howling. The yellow sank once more. And rose again. They pecked and clawed. Blood streamed from their lacerated backs. Then down the yellow went again. The white stood. At last the umpire counted the beaten creature out. We left.

Back at the hotel, there was a choice of beef or chicken for dinner, with fried plantain. There was nothing else in the shops. We drank rum and soda. The smallest measure one could buy was half a bottle. In the morning, the man said we would have to buy bread if we wanted it. He gave us thimblefuls of very sweet coffee. The bill for everything came to $19. Hamish said he had not slept at all, thinking all night of the sheets and the lavatory.

We spent another few days in Santo Domingo before exploring the rest of the island. We had become fond of the Nicolás de Ovando hotel, despite its shortcomings. The water was rarely hot, but uncomplaining maids brought scalding buckets for my bath. In two of the rooms we were given, the air-conditioning spurted out dancing fountains of water, once drenching Hamish's bed. Most of all we had become fond of the girls who worked at the reception desk. They were always anxious that we should miss nothing. They sent us to the Museo del Hombre to study pre-Columbian art. They introduced us to all manner of interesting people – architects, professors, artists, businessmen and rum producers. The girls were all young and attractive, if only because Dominican women are probably the most beautiful in the world and it is hard to find a plain one. Every one of them was far better educated than a receptionist would be in Europe. Of course, they were all wide-eyed with love for Hamish. There was one called Yosa. She was undoubtedly the prettiest and one of the brightest. I found it was hard to lure Hamish out of the hotel when Yosa was on duty, and his conversation became tedious as he asked my opinion of her every feature and characteristic. I explained to him the difference between a carefully brought-up Spanish girl and the sort of girls he was used to. I pointed out that her brothers might become stiletto-happy if he were to overstep the mark. The only response was an idiot grin. I decided that we should move on.

To the east of Santo Domingo, the country was dull, flat and dry. By the sea there were palms and a little green vegetation. Inland, it was nearly desert, though towards the town of Romana we crossed wide rivers, fed by the hills to the north.

Our destination was Casa de Campo, a resort much on the lines of Palmas del Mar in Puerto Rico. Originally it was a 7,000-acre sugar estate, which was bought by Gulf and Western. They decided to make much of the land into a smart holiday area for rich Americans. The main part of it was dismal. Almost everything was ill-conceived. Horrid little bungalows sprawled about, instead of being arranged in village clusters. The long airstrip lay between most of the houses and the beach. The sugar mill, noisy and smelly, chugged away not far from the main complex. None of this really concerned us as we were to stay at Altos de Chavón, a most curious addition to the resort.

The late Charles Bluhdorn was chairman of Gulf and Western. He had the idea of building a mock-Mediterranean village on the top of the high cliffs looking over the valley of the Chavón river. Bluhdorn had in mind quite modest little whitewashed houses. However, he had as a friend Robert Capo, an Italian filmset designer, who had worked with Fellini and Visconti. He had more grandiose notions as to how the funds of Gulf and Western might be employed. He prevailed upon Bluhdorn to allow him to build in stone and to build not just a simple peasant village, but to create an arts centre. The idea grew. Building started in 1976 – an amphitheatre for concerts, an art gallery, an archaeological museum, a church, an hotel, many workshops, several restaurants, a swimming pool and much else.

Altos de Chavón, as it is called, strikes so peculiar a note that I was exercised to know what I felt about it. As we wandered round on the first evening I kept thinking of Remy de Gourmont's observation that any reproduction is an act of cowardice in imitation of an act of energy. But then the village was not really a reproduction. It was neither Greek nor Roman. It was not Italian. It was fantasy, classical baroque – a filmset. But was a filmset the place to teach students about art, for that was the express or expressed purpose of the place? I worked myself up into a rage about it, until I felt a dark antipathy towards it all, a horror that anyone could create anything so spurious, meretricious and empty as this in the name of art, only eighty miles from those solid acts of faith and courage that had so awed me in Santo Domingo. How could these people have so lacked the spirit of their age and failed to build a modern home for artists? How could any self-respecting artist or craftsman live with the bogus? Think what a modern amphitheatre of stone might have been. And the church. What can St Stanislas make of his final resting place? What could the Pope have been thinking of when he gave the remains of his national patron saint to Gulf and Western? Whatever would the students learn?

On the next morning, I felt calmer. Two of the staff of the place, Vevita León, the administrative manager, and Santiago Fittipaldi, the marketing manager, were so demonstrably devoted to the educational purpose of the place that, as they took me round, I smothered my objections, and averted my eye from the sentimental tricks the architect had used to create his sham effects. They were insistent on the quality of the teaching. Eighty of the hundred students came from the Dominican Republic, many of them went on to Parsons School of Design in New York where, without exception, they had done well. Vevita assured me that they did not teach the students to admire the buildings.

The work that was going on in the workshops was perfectly worthwhile. The archaeological museum was a positive delight. But I was still inclined to agree with one of the visiting academics who maintained that the place was too commercial ever to be taken seriously. The streams of tourists from Casa de Campo, the glossy restaurants, the boutiques of such trendy figures as Oscar de la Renta hardly fostered an academic atmosphere.

Charles Bluhdorn had died in 1982. Gulf and Western had recently sold the whole estate. There had been considerable difficulties with some of the visiting academics. One Scots writer had inspired the students with revolutionary ideas, which did not accord at all with the organisers' notions of how things should be conducted. Throughout all these changes, Bluhdorn's daughter Dominique had been in charge of Altos de Chavón. She was only nineteen when her father made her the administrator of the village. I hesitated to meet her, feeling that it might be rude or offensive to question the wisdom of her recently dead father, but Vevita encouraged me.

Dominique was not exactly pretty, but had an amusing face with a large forehead and an erratic, slightly shiny nose. Her small eyes were alight with interest. Her fair hair was held back by a white band. She wore white trousers and an orangey-pink shirt. She was elegant and decidedly attractive. She had a wonderful confidence that was in no way arrogant. She was not in the least put out by my reservations about the place. She believed that modern buildings would not have suited the landscape, a view which revealed little understanding of architecture or of what I was talking about.

'My father just wanted to evoke an atmosphere. It is not a reproduction or a copy of anything. We always say it was designed by a film designer. People often think it is a re-creation and say, "Oh you've made it just what it was like in Columbus's time." We explain it was a fantasy, just an atmosphere.

'As for being commercial, sure. It's meant to be commercial. We are not trying to train fine artists. There are too many of them in the country, doing nothing. We want to train people for jobs, for work in design and in crafts.'

Dominique was so enthusiastic, sincere and industrious about her work and so winning in herself that I felt my objections melting. On balance, I decided that it was better that Altos de Chavón should exist than otherwise. But I do not think it will be the Bauhaus of the Caribbean.

We could not head directly north, they told us, because the roads were too bad. So we had to go back westwards to take the main road to the north coast. The road climbed high and the land became richer and greener, though there was no forest, all the trees having been cut down at some time. To our left, there was wilder country towards Pico Duarte, Dominicana's highest mountain, which rises to 10,000 feet, where it sometimes freezes. We attempted a track up into the high

Cordillera and found ourselves in a different kind of forest with pines, but the way became too rough and we had to turn back after admiring the political dedication of one mountain village, where the members of the PLD party had painted many of the boulders in the river above the water line in their party's lilac colour and inscribed them with their symbol for the coming elections. The elections were six weeks away, but everywhere slogans had been neatly painted on the roads. Whole walls, embankments, any flat surfaces were taken up. Signposts were few enough, but they were covered. Loudspeaker vans went bawling by in the remotest districts.

About half way to the north, we stopped for a sandwich at an elaborate modern snack bar. Chickens and pieces of meat were turning on spits. There was a wide selection of juices and ice-creams. Over the bar was a large picture of Jesus Christ.

We got more and more the impression that this was a country, in a way that it had been difficult to conceive on other islands. It would have taken months to reach every point on this island. This was the only place where we could have had to retrace a hundred miles as we had done on the Barahona peninsula.

The road went through the town of Santiago de los Caballeros, where the restoration of the Republic was proclaimed in 1863, after a period of re-occupation by the Spanish. We had time only to drive round a preposterously ugly monument to the occasion that took the form of an ill-proportioned building in dictator-classical style, topped by a barley-sugar column with a huge statue of the Angel of Peace. As we went round, a loudspeaker inside blared forth a drear Latin-American moan.

The hills before the sea were pleasant. There were cows grazing in what looked like parks with palms instead of oaks or elms. We reached the coast near Puerto Plata. I had had great hopes of this city, which was said to have many fine colonial houses. It was one of the few disappointments in the Dominican Republic. The old part of the town was sad because so much was in decay. Those few of the nineteenth-century, balconied, clapboard houses that had been preserved looked splendid, when painted and clean, their windows and doors often picked out in a pleasing dark red. The cathedral was shut, but it was a fine twenties building with Gothicky windows and two towers, at first sight traditional but really very advanced. The town hall and other official buildings were in the same genre, but were interspersed with later and uglier buildings. The whole town was made hideous with the roar of

256

motor-cycles and scooters known as moto-conchos, which serve mostly as taxis, the Dominicans managing to make these ghastly machines even noiser than the Italians.

We pressed on, past the outskirts, with dreadful hoardings and ugly, ill-set buildings, the worst aspects of tourist development. And past another golf-course resort, then on along the coast road until we came to Sosúa. Here was something completely different from anything we had known anywhere. It was a small town, modern but quite attractive, with many small hotels and restaurants. It had a markedly European feeling, like a small Mediterranean village forty years ago. The hotels were all full until, at last, we found a delightful, open-air Italian restaurant with only five tables and a similar number of rooms to let behind. The owner, Alfredo, and his wife were charming. He gave us an apartment with two bedrooms and a big sitting-room, apologising for charging so much for it – $30. Admittedly the arrangements were simple and the water went off many times in the day, but Alfredo's cooking was supreme.

Sosúa has an unusual history. On 2 October 1937, the dictator Trujillo ordered a massacre of all Haitians in Dominicana, in revenge for a border dispute with Haiti in which a number of Dominicans were killed. The slaughter lasted thirty-six hours. The number who were murdered is not known, but it was estimated at something in the region of 20,000, many of them illegal immigrants from the even poorer half of Hispaniola. This barbarous act did not attract the condemniation it deserved. Nonetheless, Trujillo felt a need to redress the balance, public opinion abroad regarding him with loathing. In 1939, he offered to give a home to 100,000 Jewish refugees. He proposed to give them some little-used land on the north coast of the country. There may also have been in Trujillo's mind a mad notion of altering the genetic stock of the island. It would not, as we shall see, have been the first time a Hispaniola dictator had entertained such a plan. Not surprisingly, not many Jews wished to come, seeing the exchange of one totalitarian, murderous regime for another as a poor one. Only about a thousand arrived.

The owner of the hotel next door to ours was one of those who came late. His name was Joe Benjamín, a gentle, hospitable man. He came to Sosúa from Shanghai in 1947. His father had been in Buchenwald, but his mother was not Jewish, so she managed to escape from Germany in 1939. Somehow, she also arranged for Joe's father's release. Joe told me that the thousand came mostly from Germany and Austria, but there were some Czechs and French as well. Nearly all of them were

German-speakers. One might have thought that they would have been delighted to find themselves in such an enchanting place, with a grand, sandy beach and many rocky coves, the spray whooshing up through blow-holes in the coral, like so many fountains.

Alas, most of them were city-dwellers and did not much care for it. Nevertheless, they made the very best of their circumstances, taking to farming, that being the only possible work. A New York Jewish association bought the land cheaply and sold it on long and easy terms to the refugees. A *terea* (750 square yards) cost them $100. The refugees went in principally for dairy farming and sausage-making. Soon Sosúa was the best organised place on the island. There was an excellent medical and veterinary service. Joe remembers two Jeeps, one with a red cross and the other a blue one. They were the first vehicles. The refugees built a synagogue and the community prospered.

The feed for Joe's cows is supplemented by molasses. He believes in a low cost, low yield approach, so that his cows give about three gallons a day. (I thought ruefully of the dairy farmer on Puerto Rico.) Most of the refugees moved away after the war, preferring to revert to a city life. Now only about fifteen families remain. They live well. The land they bought so cheaply is now extremely valuable. Urban land, once fifteen cents a square metre, is now worth $100. Even farmland sells for $15. To some extent the people preserve their customs and individuality. Joe said that it would be unthinkable for him not to go to see his mother every afternoon for coffee and cakes.

I had seen a signpost saying Sinagoga. We went along the road and saw nothing. We met a woman whom I took for a resident, but who was an Italian, possibly a tourist. She said the synagogue was on the other side of town. She had tried to go, but it was always shut. It was, she added, dedicated to St Anthony of Padua. The synagogue?

'*Si, certo la sinagoga, sempre chiusa. San Antonio di Padova.* Bye-bye.'

'*Ciaou*,' I said.

A little further on, I met an unlikely American of some age, all in white. White crotcheted cap, white beard, white shirt, shorts, stockings and shoes. 'The synagogue? Why, you just passed it. You know it's shut. The Rabbi went away. I took a service there yesterday. I'm not a Rabbi, but I tried to help, you know.' He was Mr Rabinowitz, he said, on holiday from the States. This delightful old man must have brought a lot of cheer to the rather enclosed remnants of the original community.

As we walked back to our hotel, I saw why we had missed the synagogue. It was a tiny, insignificant wooden building, reminding one of the struggling beginnings of this place. It may be a little sad that the community has for the most part dispersed (although leaving a legacy of wonderful cheeses and sausages and the best milk in the Caribbean), but there is another thought which Joe Benjamín expressed.

'It was as well,' he said, 'that the 100,000 Jews that Trujillo invited did not come. It would have turned the place into Israel; they would have made slaves again of the Dominican people.'

The northern coast became more and more attractive the further east we went. The first part of our journey was through verdant countryside, pastureland for cattle, dotted with palm trees. Later, the cliffs to our right closed in, narrowing the plain. Here the palm groves were denser. Every so often the road went down to the sea, where there were long beaches of fine sand, ending in rocky promontories, all deserted. Here, too, there were paddy-fields, brilliant emerald, spotted white by egrets – Garga they called them. The road was new, built to encourage tourists. The peasants spread their grain on the tarmac to dry and not just grain, but beans and other crops. It was an unlooked-for bonus for the farmers. How much there was of beauty: the land, the prettily-painted houses, the infinite variety of feature and of hue of the people, the little girls in their flouncy dresses, their hair in bunches, tugging at one's sentiment.

We stopped at the lighthouse at Cabo Francés Viejo and gazed out to sea towards the Silver Shoals. It was out there that, in 1641, the galleon *Nuestra Señora de la Concepción* ran onto the reef. She was one of the richest treasure ships ever to sail, for in that year the Spanish admiral lost his head and crammed the whole year's treasure onto two ships, instead of disposing it among several so that at least some, probably the majority, would get home safely. I knew all about the *Concepción* because, many years ago, I had, with a number of friends, funded an expedition to look for that glorious hoard of gold. The planning and the dreaming had been fun. I am not sure whether any of us really believed the treasure was there, but the question became academic, because the captain whose boat we had equipped ran off with all the money. We consoled ourselves with the thought that there had probably been nothing there.

Some years later, an American group found the treasure. I had been to see the part they gave to the Dominican government, which is on show in Santo Domingo. There was much fascinating material, as well as piles of pieces of eight. There was not much gold on show, but then who knows how much there was originally. The government officials, who did the deal with the treasure hunters, may not have felt it necessary to pass it all on to the museum.

I was intrigued now to see the place where the survivors must have scrambled ashore, other greedier ones drowning with the armfuls of gold and silver that they attempted to bring with them. I also reflected upon the greed of our captain, who would have been far richer had he used our money for the task he was meant to perform.

For those who like a coincidence, I was listening two days later to the BBC World Service. I heard that a Captain William Sutton had been arrested in Brest. A hoard of arms, destined for some African coup, had been found on his ship. I hope it was the same Sutton.

It seemed hardly possible that the Dominican Republic could produce any more surprises or any greater pleasures. Yet the peninsula of Samaná provided both. The peninsula lies at the extreme north-east corner of the island. After the town of Sánchez there was a subtle change in the landscape. It was hilly rather than rugged and the road passed through exquisite palm groves, the grass beneath them dappled by filtered sunlight. The villages were poor, but gave me again that feeling that here the people were living a life that was natural to them, uninfluenced by the colonial past.

The whole peninsula was the perfect embodiment of people's ideas of the Caribbean. There were long untouched beaches, magical secret coves. Inland the hills were green and rolling, with tall trees in the deep hollows, places where the lordly ones might have dwelt. We had seen nothing which so combined gentle and wild natures since Tobago. The people were amiable and cheerful, even when we waited discreetly behind a long funeral procession, the body, wrapped only in a sheet, being carried on a litter, they waved us by, smiling. But once I saw a woman, desolate with fatigue as she carried home her provisions up a long hill. Behind her trailed one daughter, tired and resigned and, some way back, another, about four years old, also carrying some cassava. Her face was twisted beyond crying, by a kind of active despair I had never seen in a child before. It was a reminder not to be deceived by the illusion of tropical paradise.

It was the town of Samaná which produced the unexpected. Tourism has made it more prosperous, though the government ran out of steam in their plans for it. The hotel was extremely simple, with a restaurant which had appalling 'Vood', as the English menu spelt it. I pondered for a long time as to who Mr Blur might be, who had inspired a dish called 'Filete Gordon Blur', before I realised what it meant. A small boy came to the door of the restaurant, begging. The waiter gave him a plate of chips, which he ate sitting on the doorstep.

After a while, as we sat in the restaurant near the open doorway, it came to me that many of the passers-by were speaking English. They were not tourists. They were local people, blacker than most of the islanders. When we went out to look at the bay a man came up to us, offering in perfect English, to guide us. He gave me his card, which read, 'King George Esq'.

George (he had, for effect, reversed his names) was a tall, handsome man with chiselled features, but quite different in appearance from other Dominicans we had known. He explained proudly in his strong, vibrant voice, that he was of English descent, as were most of the townsfolk of Samaná. They all spoke English, he said, rather than Spanish. When he saw how interested I was, he said he would introduce me to his friend Kelly, who was an authority on the history of Samaná.

Kelly lived in a dingy part of the town a little up in the hills. He was merry and plump, not so dark-skinned as George and wearing a little moustache. Almost the first thing he told me, again in perfect English, was that he gave his life to the Lord Jesus Christ. It was a long time before we got to the story of why the people of Samaná spoke English. We settled down on the terrace of a Chinese bar and restaurant. It had a spectacular view over the bay of Samaná and the almost too perfect little island of Cayo Levantado. There was a Chinese youth working just below us, on some building extension.

'You know,' said Kelly, 'those Chinese really work. Wherever they go they work. They don't respect time. They work all day and they do anything themselves. The two brothers came here in 1963, as poor as anybody. Now look at them. They own all this. The land, the buildings, the business.'

As if to bear him out, an elderly Chinese, presumably one of the brothers, came out to look at the work. He moved a big oildrum across the site. Kelly and George did not really approve of too much work, though

Kelly opined that George might do a little more. More importantly, he thought George ought to come back to the gospel. We talked of their families. Kelly had four children and had adopted a fifth.

'They are all at school. That means five school uniforms and so many books and notebooks. I could spend two hundred pesos [£19] on books every three months.'

King George had seven children.

'But I closed that factory, now,' said George.

'We must educate our babies,' said Kelly, in a severe tone.

'I've got four in school,' George replied, with some indignation.

'I know,' said Kelly, giving him an affectionate pat on the knee.

I wondered whether we would ever get to what I wanted to know.

'When I was a soldier,' observed Kelly, 'and I was a soldier for fifteen years, a big man said to me, "All soldiers know is drinking." Some people are different, I said. "All they know is drinking and women." Sit down, I said. He sat. Do you know who was the first president of the Dominican Republic? "Oh," he said and he didn't know, so I told him the history of the Dominican Republic and he said if I had all that in my head I wouldn't be a soldier.'

Kelly then proceeded to tell us the history of the Dominican Republic and of Samaná. He told us that Columbus arrived here on 12 January 1493. He was on his way back to Spain when he saw the bay and came to investigate it. The natives were hostile, but Columbus waved a white flag, which convinced them of his peaceful intentions. But when they landed, the Indians soon decided that the Spanish were treating them as slaves. Majobanet, the *cacique*, attacked the Spaniards. This battle, known as the Battle of the Bay of Arrows, was the first fight between the Spanish and the Indians in the New World.

All Kelly's stories had a mythic quality about them, making them a pleasure to listen to, even if some lacked verisimilitude. We listened to tales of Enriquillo lurid with blood and treachery. Kelly even brought us up to recent years under Trujillo when, he said, shoeshine boys would act as *agents provocateurs*, egging you on until you said, 'Times are hard these days.' At that, the shoeshine boy would whip a pistol from his box and arrest you for spreading sedition.

He saved what I wanted to know until the very end when he said, 'We must go back to 1822, when Dominicana was under the rule of Haiti and President Jean-Pierre Boyer.' This president decided to bring runaway slaves from Philadelphia to populate the empty areas of Dominicana.

Other authorities than Kelly suggest that Boyer was anxious to make the population blacker, to dilute the Spanish blood in this side of Hispaniola. He wanted 6,000 new black people.

According to Kelly, 300 came to Samaná. This seems quite likely. About four thousand came to Santo Domingo under the aegis of a Philadelphia philanthropic society. Many of them died of typhoid fever, many others chose to go back to the States, because they did not approve of the moral standards of the people. Only those who settled in Samaná preserved any identity of their own and are known, according to one writer, 'for exceptional honesty, cleanliness and diligence'. Their names persist: Barrat, Shepherd, Phipps, Wilmore, Green, Anderson and many others.

Both Kelly and George maintained that their great-grandfathers were English, by which they meant English-speaking. Their grandparents and parents had all spoken only English at home, but now they themselves spoke Spanish with their children. The few accounts of these people all say that they sing archaic songs and use a form of English which has died out elsewhere. I could detect little or nothing of this. The English I heard the older people using in the street may have been a little drawling, but it was surprisingly accurate and owed nothing, as it were, to Harriet Beecher Stowe. All services in the church, Kelly said, were conducted in English until very recently and, even now, the harvest festival is held in both languages.

The church itself has a peculiar history according to Kelly, who said that it was sent from Philadelphia in 'kit' form in 1824, by a Wesleyan pastor, Jacob James. Nobody knew how to erect it and it was not put up until 1901. This was nonsense. In front of the church were two graves. One was that of Jacob James, 'Pastor of this church for more than 50 years. Born 1820. Died 1889 . . . and to his beloved wife Louisa James died 1905.' Next to them was Harriet, the British wife of a Wesleyan missionary, W. T. Cardy. She died in Samaná in 1839, 'having a husband and two young children to lament their loss.' Unluckily, the present Pastor was ill in hospital, 'as all the water had been lost from his body,' said Kelly, 'because of something he ate.' I was never able to clear up the mystery.

Before we left, we went to look at Columbus's fortification near where the Battle of the Bay of Arrows took place. Not much remains to be seen – only a base on a promontory overlooking the long bay. A more tranquil place could not be imagined. It was no wonder that Columbus described this island as 'the most wonderful landscape that human eyes have ever seen.'

When we got back to Santo Domingo, election fever was mounting. I dined with some friends, a typically mixed couple in that he came from Colombia, while she was Dominican. Both, however, had German connections. They discussed where they should retire. He wanted warmth and peace. She wanted more culture – music, theatre. The issue was further complicated by their having adopted twin girls in addition to their own daughters. The twins were very black in an otherwise white family. Santo Domingo was best for them, he maintained, where nobody cares a damn what colour anyone is.

The political situation seemed appropriate to this discussion. The history of the Dominican Republic was not one of stability. There were three possible presidents contending the elections. First, Juan Bosch, the socialist. He appealed to the anti-American feeling among the people. But who knew whether or not the communists were behind him? The present ruling party was represented by Jacobo Majluta. But this government was corrupt and had done nothing. Many of the projects started by Dr Joaquin Balaguer, an honest but right-wing former President, had been allowed, as I had seen, to fall into decay. Balaguer, now seventy-eight and going blind, was the third candidate. It was not an easy choice.

We left Santo Domingo rather gloomily. We had been so happy there and hardly expected to be so in Haiti. Hamish was sobbing at having to leave Yosa. We drove one last time round the cathedral square. The bells were ringing in a reggae rhythm.

Later, we learned that the voters of the Dominican Republic had elected Dr Balaguer. A people that can choose as their leader an elderly, purblind poet, albeit a little right-wing, must have a homeric sense of what is good for them.

21

Haiti

A CHAPTER OF TYRANTS

Jean Claude Duvalier had been driven out of Haiti about six weeks before we were to go there. Hundreds of Haitians were flocking back to their homeland from the United States. All Haitians need visas to return to their own country. (We did not.) As they could not get these in New York, they came via Santo Domingo, where there was a consulate. They came with vast piles of luggage and packages of amazing size and weight. The floor round the check-in desk was covered with innumerable bottles of shampoo and something called Rinse. There was a great deal of pushing and shoving and shouting and cursing. When at last we managed to check in, it was only to find the same scene repeated at the embarkation gate.

By now everyone had even more luggage, which they proposed to take on as hand baggage. There were absurd struggles with officials. One woman, besides huge cartons of shampoo, had a tricycle to which she had tied a mass of pans and metal cups. The man at the gate said she could not take it. She pushed. Those behind pushed. The tricycle and pans fell down the stairs with a wondrous clatter. The woman darted like a hurdler after it, grabbed it and raced across the tarmac towards the

265

plane. The officials were up to this. Halfway to the plane were men who rushed and grabbed the bigger objects from the passengers and stowed them in the hold. It was dreadful to see how much the dross they had brought meant to them, especially the women in their hideous pleated nylon dresses and their stiletto heels. Sometimes the screams of abuse turned to laughter, more often not. One woman on the plane sat in a seat that was not for passengers. She would not move. Somehow her way of sitting, staring straight ahead, no matter what was said to her, was so primitively obstinate.

It was calmer at the airport at Port-au-Prince, but as soon as we got outside we were plagued by tedious, pestering people. One particularly annoying man refused for a long time to get out of the car we had hired. How right we had been to regret leaving the gentle charms and seductive wickedness of Santo Domingo. I loathed Haiti at once.

It was immediately noticeable that the population of Haiti was effectively double that of the Dominican Republic, in that rather more people were crowded into half the space. Equally apparent to me, although this is stoutly denied by those curious people who like Haiti, the Haitians do not smile. They look and stare, but they show no sign of any emotion. It seemed to me that no one had any regard for anyone else. Their gestures are violent. They do not wave a car down if they want a lift, they whack it down. They give directions with their heads, jerking them to one side or the other. It is not hostility so much as an avoidance of contact. I could only surmise that after nearly two hundred years of treachery, brutalisation and betrayal by spies, they trust no one until they know him. It was uncomfortable, after months of happy-go-lucky encounters, to find that even Hamish, who would make instant friends with a polar bear, could form no friendship with a driver, a waiter or a guide.

Of course, it was a strange time to be in Haiti. Everything was in suspense. There was still a curfew at night, which meant that we had to be in our hotel by eleven o'clock. Everybody was waiting to see what would happen. Yet it could not have been that they were expecting very much. There is nothing in the history of Haiti to give anyone any hope.

As we drove around, the street names conjured up the gory horrors of that history. Boulevard J. J. Dessalines – the first president who, with two other future presidents, finally threw Napoleon out of Haiti after France's perfidious treatment of Toussaint l'Ouverture. Soon he pronounced himself ruler for life, as nine subsequent heads of state were to do. He went further, calling himself Emperor Jacques I. He did not bother with titles for others, declaring, '*Moi, seul, je suis noble.*' In fact, many of his ideas were sympathetic, in particular the division of the land seized from the French planters. He died within two years, murdered by the *mulâtres* or mulatto élite of the south.

Avenue Christophe. Poor Henry Christophe, born in St Kitts of freed slave parents, he it was who seized the north after Dessalines' death, representing the blacker elements of Haiti's population. He called himself King Henry I and created nobles, among them the Counts of Limonade and Marmalade. He was guarded by a special corps of police, called the Royal Dahomets (strong men from Dahomey), the first, but certainly not the last precursors of the Tontons Macoute.

Pétionville – a whole suburb for Alexandre Pétion, the third president but the first to die a natural death, Christophe having committed suicide, it was believed with a silver bullet, while the mob howled outside his palace. Pétion was also the first *mulâtre* to be head of state. The history of Haiti is partly that of an unending struggle between black and mulatto. If it were just that, it might be simple. The blacks outnumber the mulattoes and could dominate them. At the same time, there is a black élite and a mulatto élite. Both are determined that the mass of people will never deprive them of their privileges. It has always been that any black-dominated government has in it a number of the mulatto élite, and vice versa.

I was not sure which of the many Rigauds in Haitian history the rue Rigaud referred to. It might have been Numa Rigaud, the mulatto adviser to Louis Acaau, the black general of the Suffering Army, who, in 1843, led the only really big uprising of the peasant people against the two élites. It was interesting that even he should have a mulatto friend.

There may have been a rue Soulouque or Faustin, but I never found it. Perhaps neither group was proud of this alarming figure. He was black, but the mulattoes who, in the end, have nearly always had the real control of the country, chose to put him forward as president. They chose him because he appeared foolish, ineffectual and uninterested in politics or power. He would be their puppet – a situation which often obtained. Indeed, Soulouque succeeded three black puppets. This butt of everyone's jokes sat quiet and meek in the presidential seat. It may be that he overplayed his part, for after a year, in 1848, the mulattoes decided to get rid of him.

Soulouque sprang into life. During his year of sham docility, he had built up his own secret police force, the *zinglins*. They were the latest precursors of the Tontons Macoute. With their help, he embarked on a course of carnage, killing all those who had put him in power, all those who had ever mocked him, all those who had ever criticised him. Having purged the country of any who might oppose him, he crowned himself Emperor Faustin I. He created a peerage with 624 nobles. His court was preposterous, full of invented protocol. If Faustin laughed, his chamberlain would pronounce, 'His Majesty is laughing. Gentlemen, you too are invited to laugh.'

Oddly enough, once established, Faustin did some good in the country by promoting people from classes of society which had been hitherto considered incapable of anything other than labouring. Eventually, he was overthrown by a General Geffrard (a descendant of the general who fought with Pétion, Christophe and Dessalines for Haiti's independence), to whom Faustin had hinted that his loyalty was suspect. Geffrard knew that meant that his death was imminent. He deposed Faustin, making himself president for life; but he spared the Emperor's life, sending him in exile to Jamaica.

The horrors continued. The country sank lower and lower until, in 1915, the Americans waited for an excuse to provide another example of what Theodore Roosevelt called, 'a visit from the United States in the role of an international policeman.' Since 1911 there had been six presidents, one of whom, with the splendid name of Cincinnatus Leconte, had died when the National Palace was blown up. In March 1915, Vilbrun Sam took office as president. On 27 July, Sam ordered the butchering of 167 political prisoners. The crowd dragged Sam out of the French Legation, where he had taken refuge, and lynched him. The next day, the Americans landed and occupied Haiti until 1934. Nothing much altered, at any rate in the spirit of the place.

In 1957, there was a flicker of hope. A forty-four-year-old Professor Daniel Fignolé had ten years before launched a political party, the Worker Farmer Movement. He was the spiritual successor of Acaau, representing the mass of the people. He was not, however, worldly-wise or politically shrewd. The secretary-general of his party was an unknown doctor, François Duvalier. The odious Duvalier, whose name was still attached to the airport and a short avenue, shared many characteristics with Faustin Soulouque. He too was unassuming, often making himself out to be stupider and surely less ambitious than he was. Fignolé was an orator. He had a mass following. In the chaos following three or four transitory presidencies, Fignolé became president. He lasted nineteen days, was kidnapped and exiled. It was Duvalier, who had by that time distanced himself from the Professor, who organised this manoeuvre. The élites had struck. Thousands were massacred. The people were once more trampled down. Six months later Duvalier was president, presiding over a new reign of terror, until his death in 1971 – one of only six presidents to die a natural death in office.

Now we were witnessing another crossroads. The thirty-seventh president, the son of François Duvalier, had followed in the footsteps of twenty-four of his predecessors. He had been overthrown by violence. (Only two presidents, except during the American occupation, served their full term. Two were assassinated; one executed; one blown up; one killed himself.)

We went to Oloffson's, the hotel made famous by Graham Greene in *The Comedians*. It is still a wonderful gingerbread building on two floors, with long balconies and conical turrets. Many journalists from abroad were staying there, waiting to see what would happen. I asked one American what he thought of General Namphy, who had assumed power when Baby Doc left. 'I guess you don't get to be a general in any army by being a nice guy, but in Duvalier's army? Hell.' A photographer put it more simply. 'Haiti's fucked.'

At that moment, a tiny, dark man, dapper beyond reality in a white suit and carrying a cane, came up the stairs. His eyes darted everywhere. An arctic smile tweaked his lips. I did not need to be told who he was. Twenty years later, I recognised him from Graham Greene's description. He was Petit Pierre, the gossip-column journalist and Nosy Parker of *The Comedians*. His real name was Aubelin Jolicoeur. He went to a table and started to play backgammon with a young American. Somebody introduced us, asking if I knew him. When I said, '*Monsieur Jolicoeur est connu dans le monde entier,*' a wary look came into his eye. I wondered whether he liked or hated being Petit Pierre.

A few days later I saw him again. The arctic smile had a tinge of triumph about it. He had been made Secretary of State at the Ministry of Information. A friend had said that he had written some courageous articles, or rather that, 'the little *singe*, who everyone hates', had written some pieces, not of criticism exactly, but often pointing out what more could be done. That in itself constituted bravery. I wondered whether perhaps Graham Greene had somehow given him a kind of dignity, though I remembered of Petit Pierre, even, that 'there were occasionally passages in his gossip-column that showed an odd satirical courage – perhaps he depended on the police not to read between the lines.' Anyhow, I congratulated him and happened to add that I imagined he had won that previous day at backgammon, as the young American was not very good. '*Ah, oui. Moi, je suis comme un serpent. Je gagne toujours.*' Not always. I later learned, from Graham Greene as it happened, that he was soon sacked from the job.

We did not stay at Oloffson's, for the steps to it were too steep and numerous. Instead, we found a modern hotel, high up, overlooking the whole town and the Gulf of Gonave. It is the most perfect bay, with high mountains on either side, stretching out in long arms, embracing a huge area. The city below, on the flat land before the sea, was misty in the mornings and the evenings, probably from the smoke of innumerable charcoal fires. At night the lights, when there were lights, twinkled prettily. It was fine from up the hill, but in the first days I found it glum. Those people who should have looked so happy were not. They also appeared stupid. It was probably more that, when one spoke to them, they thought one was going to ask for something far outside their experience. They were determined not to understand. I felt so out of sympathy with the place that we decided to go on a journey to the north.

It was Good Friday. In Port-au-Prince, a mass of people were moving along the Boulevard J. J. Dessalines. Many of the women were in their best clothes – a white dress and a floppy straw hat. They carried little crosses made of wood or palm leaves. As soon as we were out of town, it became evident how intense the poverty was. We passed slums, half hidden behind slightly better houses. Nowhere in the Caribbean had we seen housing as bad as this. Once we were clear of the suburbs, we were in dull, dry country. All the trees which once covered the hills have been cut down. Even the few remaining trees are still being cut, but the scarcity of wood may be judged by the fact that a bag of charcoal in Port-au-Prince sells for $3 – supposedly a labourer's daily wage, though often a cane cutter will get less than $1. We passed some beaches and hotels that were drab compared with almost anywhere else.

270

The first place of any interest was St Marc, a colonial-style town occupied, so I read, by the British in 1790. It was dilapidated and decaying, whereas it could have been enchanting if restored. There were fine clapboard houses with wooden-pillared arcades on the ground floor, and a church of interest. In the square I felt a mild frisson of horror at the thought of the French murder by bayonet of all their black mercenaries during their attempts to suppress the Haitian rebellion.

At Estere, there was a crowd on the road. Several of the people wore red- and green-striped costumes and large hats, a little like a jester. They waved us down with imperious gestures. Surrounding the car, they shouted and a ragged band played, with a menacing drum beat. To the rhythm, they yelled, 'Dollar, dollar.' They thumped on the car roof and their shouting grew louder and louder. It was hard to tell if they were drunk. Hamish was much put out and wanted to hit someone. This scene was repeated in several villages. They were Good Friday voodoo parades, or rra-rra, all inimical and with no smiling faces; very different from the quiet, Christian parade in Port-au-Prince.

Then we turned inland and started to climb over the mountains towards Cap Haitien. We travelled for a while through a valley, the Passe Reine, full of mango trees and great, fat-trunked ficus. There were healthy plantations of plantain. This faint echo of prosperity made one realise how wonderful this country could have been. Then we were back again in the deforested, barren hills.

The buses in Haiti have wild names painted on them, usually with a religious connotation. I had seen '*Jesus pleura*', '*Le foi d'Abraham*' and one with '*Bon Dieu Bon*' on the front and 'God is Good' on the back. Others were secular: '*Amour d'Enfance*', '*La Vie est drolle*'. Ahead of us was one called '*Confiance à Dieu*'. Two men were clinging to the back. It started to rain in great tropical sheets. We signalled that we had room for one in the back of our car. One of them jumped down, but held onto the bus, which was going too fast. He ran like someone in a speeded-up movie, but fortunately managed to clamber back. The bus slowed and he dropped off again, this time safely. He got into the car laughing a fine open, natural laugh. I realised that this was the first person I had seen really laughing in all of Haiti. I had hopes that this cheerful man might teach me a lot, but his patois was so strong that we could understand little of each other.

We came down through the hills, many of which were steeply terraced and worked, to a fertile plain before we reached the sea. On the outskirts of the town of Cap Haitien, we came to a vast monumental group

271

dedicated to the heroes of the battle of Vertières of 1803. The central figure, in a cocked hat, I took to be Dessalines who, with Christophe, Pétion and Geffrard, defeated the French General Rochambeau, who had recently succeeded Leclerc – the man who had so cynically written not long before: 'Dessalines is at present the butcher of the negroes; it is through him that I execute all my odious measures. I shall keep him as long as I need him.' Instead, Dessalines butchered some fifty thousand Frenchmen.

General Leclerc was married to Pauline Bonaparte, Napoleon's sister. One of the houses in which she had lived while her husband tried to reassert French control over the island is now a hotel, called the Hostellerie du Roi Christophe. Christophe had used the house as a prison. I thought it would be interesting to stay there. It was a plain, stucco house built in the early eighteenth century, with a jungly, neglected garden. The man in charge was so unpleasant that we left and stayed in a far better place, perched above the ruins of the larger palace that Pauline had built.

Cap Haitien had little to offer apart from a few elegant clapboard houses. There was a cathedral, but its flat, stuccoed, classical front was dull. Its silver domes, however, could be seen from a great distance, a rare thing now. The poverty in the outskirts was appalling, as bad as anything in Bombay, even if there were no people sleeping in the streets. Here there were few beggars and no one pestered us. A man shouted '*Blancs*' at us. It was, I decided, not an insult, just a way to address whites. As in Port-au-Prince, there did not seem to be any sign of great elation at the overthrow of Duvalier. Perhaps it had not yet sunk in, or perhaps they had no faith in any future. It was noticeable that the rich houses and the large cars displayed with great ostentation the new flag. Had these people, two months before, been rubbishing Duvalier? I thought it unlikely. Everywhere was written the slogan 'Chak 4 ans', a demand for elections every four years. As I write, they have still had no elections.

The new flag, incidentally, was really a return to the original flag chosen by Dessalines – the French tricolour with the white torn out, so an even blue and red. Papa Doc Duvalier had changed it to black and red.

We had come, principally, to see the two extraordinary buildings which Christophe had put up during his reign over the north. We drove out of Cap Haitien, past what I thought, then, was the most depressing shanty town I had ever seen. After about half an hour, at the foot of the mountains, we came to the village of Milot. It is just a mud village of no interest; a fact which makes all the more remarkable the desolate ruins of the grand palace which rise beyond it. To one side of the palace forecourt is a Palladian chapel, its dome so brilliantly white that it might have been transported from El Oued in Algeria. The palace itself rises to four storeys above a grand, sweeping stairway. The plaster has fallen from the brick fabric, but the skeleton of this superb château, which he called Sans Souçi, convinces one that Christophe knew how to outdo the French in more than battle.

In its day, the rooms were panelled in mahogany, the floors were of marble and mosaic. Under the floors were channels carrying cold water from the mountains as a form of cooling for the palace; the water flowed on into fountains. Paintings and furniture from Europe filled the rooms. Here Christophe created his court. While the mulatto Pétion, who ruled the south, might mock the self-styled King Henry as an illiterate black, the truth of it was that Christophe had a certain taste and style. He even brought an English painter to run a Royal Academy of Art for him. Moreover, there lay behind the grandiloquence, which was never as comic as that of his imitator Soulouque, the purpose of demonstrating, as much to black people as to others, that they were as good as whites.

It must have been difficult, in his day, to reach Christophe's other building. Before the days of four-wheel drive, it used to take at least three hours to ride on a donkey up to the Citadelle La Ferrière. The road or track runs up through forest – at least here there are trees – until it emerges at a flat resting place. From there one can see this vast, blank-walled fortress, towering above the mountain. It is immense, bigger than any fortress one has ever seen, grey and implacable. From there it is still a twenty-minute stiff climb on foot or by donkey. I could not manage this and had to rely on other people's accounts of this grim symbol of tyranny, which defends nothing and would never have defended anything. One may take one's pick of whether the walls are ten or twelve or twenty or thirty feet thick. One may choose to believe there are 200 or 250 or 365 cannons littered about the terraces and battlements. One can see pictures of its thousands of cannonballs, piled up like giant's sweetmeats. Did ten, or fifteen or twenty thousand people die in the building of this place? It is simplest, possibly, to accept Alec Waugh's bald statement that 'nothing that has been said of it has been an exaggeration, that it is the most remarkable monument in the modern world.'

We drove back on Easter Day. At first, I felt less jaundiced about Haiti. While waiting for Hamish to climb up to the Citadelle, I had talked to some sensible young men. They had told me that General Namphy was 'army not Tonton'. They would, therefore, give him a chance. Nothing would happen in a hurry. Voodoo, they had claimed, was on the way out. It was encouraging that simple, country boys should have such clear and tolerant views. The land looked fresh after a little rain. Laundry hung drying on all the village bushes. People were washing in streams and rivers. They do this partly because there are streams and rivers and partly because there are no facilities of any sort. I noticed that there were no TV aerials, as compared with the Dominican Republic, where one sees aerials in very remote places. The terracing of the land was elaborate. Awkward, steep hills were worked to the summit, so that they look like enormous brown and green thimbles. On this special Sunday, everyone was in spotless clothes. The women wore either white or those vivid colours loved by black people everywhere – shocking pink, lilac, acid yellow, lime green and scarlet. Horses, I noticed, here play a big part in everyday life, poor Rocinante creatures. One of the more distressing signs of uneducated poverty was the obvious importance of having a large tomb. The tombs were huge – often, I feared, bigger than anything the corpses had occupied when they were alive.

At one point there was a landslide across the road. Two lorries trying to cross the road had slithered to one side, blocking the way and hanging on the edge. Men were trying to clear a path through the sludge and mud. There were two cars ahead of us, waiting. Boys and young girls offered to push us. One boy offered to sell me a large nanny goat for $30, which struck me as cheap. At last the men had cleared a passage. The two cars ahead of us were pushed through. It was all too easy, we saw, to slip sideways into the lorries. I noticed that neither of the cars stopped to thank anybody once they had crossed the difficult part, but rushed away. Our turn. We raced at the small gap between the lorries and the mountain of rock and sludge. Everyone yelled. Some pushed. We got through and stopped, to thank the pushers. At once, dozens of muddy arms thrust into the car demanding reward. I opened my wallet. One boy, probably the least deserving, grabbed two dollars. I pushed money at Hamish, to give on his side. A thousand arms. I gave another boy something. Hamish raced away. Behind us, they howled. We had to stop a mile or so later to wash the mud off ourselves, spattered by those myriad arms.

Soon we were through the pretty valley and back to the flatlands, travelling through rice fields dotted with white egrets. And we were back to rra-rra parties, which were more alarming than before. The people surrounded us, brandishing machetes. The men in the car in front had their windows open and people climbed in. At the fiercest party, we opened the window a crack and slid out our last dollar note.

It was Rocky Soderberg on St Kitts who had told us about the Caribbean Christian Center. I thought we might learn something there. It was devoted to all the evangelical churches and, had we wanted, we could have stayed there. 'Thou shalt not park,' said a notice outside, doubtless to show that the Lord has a sense of humour. The brochure revealed that it was not just parking that was forbidden. Dancing, smoking and drinking were also banned – the brochure had a picture of an eager, young black waiter bringing two Pepsi Colas.

The director was an enthusiastic, non-denominational protestant, called Emery Goodman. He was born a Catholic but, so he told me, he met the Lord in a Baptist church. The cliché about converts to Catholicism is that they become more Catholic than the Catholics. Emery certainly redresses the balance. He explained, with considerable indignation, that all religions in Haiti, with the exception of Roman Catholicism, were classed as cults. The ministry for foreign affairs was even called the Ministry of External Affairs and Cults. The Catholic church, he believed, was virtually in league with the satanism of Voodoo. He did not even have a good word for Radio Soleil, the Catholic station which had played a large part in the overthrow of Baby Doc. Emery asked if I knew that followers of Voodoo, on Good Friday, celebrated the death of Jesus Christ with parties. Had no one ever told them of the sequel of His coming to life and the Ascension? How could the Catholics be so linked with Voodoo? I said that perhaps Voodoo was comparable with the Albigensian heresy and the Cathars, on whose satanism the Catholic church had been extremely severe. But here we were in muddy waters. In any case, Emery, with his usual modesty, now took the blame on himself. 'It is the fault of the churches if they have not brought the message to the people – an abomination to the Lord that we have not taught the people the truth.'

On another occasion, I nearly got into a muddle with Emery about Genesis. He had declared a positive belief that the world was created 6,000 years ago. What about fossils, I asked? His answer would have pleased Edmund Gosse's father. 'The world, *as we know it*, was recreated 6,000 years ago. It existed before that and there was life on it. But 6,000 years ago, it happened exactly as it is written in the Old Testament – Man was created in God's image.' I asked if he had ever read Philip Gosse's *Omphalos*, the question being whether Adam had a navel? Emery laughed. I don't think he had ever given the matter any thought.

But it was Emery who showed me the aspect of Haiti which made me feel that all those people who find it amusing, those who feel that the artistic achievements and the poetic fantasies of the intellectuals excuse so much, are hypocritical beyond endurance.

Emery drove us through Simone City. This area is named after Papa Doc's wife. It was she who proposed its erection (building being too solid a word), not for any altruistic reason, but because she hoped to move there the inhabitants of a slum near the city, where their misery was visible. A few concrete shacks were put up, in an unsalubrious area, then a rush of tin shacks was allowed. Never, anywhere, have I seen such squalor. The widest road is uneven, rutted mud, the shacks along it fearful, black corrugated iron. The 'houses' are just lean-to, their corners not meeting. Inside, all is black from charcoal. Every so often, there is a gap between two shacks, wide enough for a man carrying a child, not wide enough for a donkey. These are the sidestreets and down these cracks, you could not call them lanes or even paths, are the poorer shacks.

Great swarms of flies move like a net thrown by a fisherman. There are no drains. The smells are almost physically solid, so that you can feel them on your face, like fetid gauze. When the rains come, they say that the water rushes through the shacks in torrents so fierce that mothers must clutch their children lest they be swept away.

One hundred thousand people live in Simone City. Never have I seen such people. It is not just that swollen-bellied children stare blankly at you; it is that every eye you meet is lacklustre with despair. In Calcutta, in the gutter, the people look at you with a sharp gleam of intelligence. Not here in Simone City. I wondered for a long time why.

I decided that this was the first place I had ever seen in the world where no one cares. In all societies where there is a great disparity between rich and poor, there is someone who cares. In India, charity is an important part of religion. In Haiti, the rich do not even pretend to care, they do not feel the need to pay lip service to the idea. The two élites play turn and turn about, while trampling as ever on the mass.

Until that moment, I had been worrying that I disliked the place so much, feeling that as a writer I ought to find out more, go to Voodoo ceremonies, to talk to intellectuals, to study primitive art. After Simone City, I wanted only to leave.

The next night I talked to a vivacious woman full of humour and lightly-worn perception. She spoke of the morning of Duvalier's going. It was, she said, an incredible sensation, more than just of a weight lifted, a debt paid, a sick lover's recovery – it was a new life. People's faces changed. They walked differently, stood another way. She came from a large family. Three of her brothers had been killed under the Duvaliers. One had dabbled a little in politics. The others had done nothing but be his brothers. There was nothing exceptional about her family. All families had had people murdered – for an incautious word, a reckless gesture.

We spoke, too, of Voodoo and how Duvalier had used it as his instrument. It had become no longer a religion but a political tool, with corrupt *houngans* (priests) who were Duvalier's men. The decline of it showed, she said, in ceremonies like rra-rra. The costumes are now tatty and the banners, once lovingly embroidered, are poor things. Everything in Haiti is debased – the art, the theatre. A visit to the National Museum confirmed this.

But now, what of now? She laughed. '*Liberté? Nous ne l'avons pas encore.*' Anyone, she said, could hold elections. It did not seem to me that she had any real hope; and she, of course, belonged to the élite.

We left the next day. Before going, I wanted to see Duvalier's tomb. Because the water table is so high in Port-au-Prince, nearly everyone is buried above ground. (There are exceptions, such as the political prisoners whom the Tontons Macoute forced to dig their own graves, just before Baby Doc left.) The Duvalier tomb had been shattered. It stood, an incongruous wreck, amid the pompous mausoleums of the rich Haitians. What happened to his remains? One story had it that his bones were scattered in the streets; another that Baby Doc had taken them with him, to keep them from the Voodoo priests, who might use them for strange practices.

As we drove away from the cemetery through an unfamiliar quarter, we found the road barred by some youths.

'Give us some money,' they said.

'What for?'

'We are cleaning the streets and we need money for paint, to paint the curbs.'

They were painting the curbs and telegraph poles in the restored national colours red and blue.

'Why are you cleaning the streets?'

'Because they are ours now and we must be proud of them.'

It was a spontaneous movement. It spread that day all over the town. Even Simone City had a tidier air to it. Young people were brushing that one wide, rutted road, which they have humour enough to call Champs-Elysées. Are they being deluded, I wondered, as they have so often been deluded before? I would imagine so.

22

Jamaica
THE GRAND FINALE

Another flight, another country. I had decided it would be the last. I had thought originally that I would go to Cuba. How, after all, could a Caribbean journey not include the largest island of the chain? But now it seemed irrelevant to the Caribbean I had seen. What I had been concerned with was a group of islands, each one quite different from the last, each with a vigorous spirit of its own; each hoping for a solution to its problems that would allow that spirit to flourish and remain independent from American domination; each very conscious of its neighbours, but quite unable or unwilling to join in any closer fraternity. Each one, also, had looked at Cuba and – in most cases by a firm majority – decided that that was not a lead they wished to follow. I decided that Cuba was a separate affair.

Trinidad had been the first island. I had compared the start of our journey to reading or even writing the first page of a new book. We had become so engrossed by our journey that time had flown by, as it does when one reads. One has to shake oneself to rejoin the actual world – but not quite yet. Rather as one looks to see how many pages of enjoyment one has left, I was, as it were, hoarding Jamaica. The

279

excitement of a new island, of a new chapter, had never dimmed. But Jamaica held something more. I had once, long ago, spent six months of great happiness there.

After Haiti, it was like coming home. Everyone had said, much as they had about Puerto Rico, that Jamaica, especially Kingston, was dangerous and evil. Our arrival was all muddle and jokes. I felt happy and relieved. We hired a car, intending to drive straight to the north coast to do nothing for a few days. Kingston looked very run-down, despite great skyscrapers, but on reflection, it had hardly looked up thirty years ago – just asleep. We drove past shanty towns but, however regrettable, they were nothing after Simone City. A little way out of Kingston, we had a puncture. Someone had said that her taxidriver had refused to stop anywhere on this road for fear of bandits. We were on a lonely stretch. It was getting dark. Hamish could not get the wheel off. A man was coming. 'What's the problem?' he asked. When Hamish told him, he explained that there must be a special key for the lock nut. The car-hirers had said nothing of this. We found it in the ashtray. The man then helped Hamish change the wheel. At first, when I offered him a tip, he refused. 'No problem.' Everyone said 'no problem' all the time.

Of course, Jamaica is not Saba. A friend later told me that he once had a puncture. While he was changing the back wheel, someone opened the bonnet. He asked what he was doing. The reply came, 'Is oright, man. You take de wheels, I take de battery.' Most of the horror stories are nonsense; my informant's taxidriver was probably hoping to get a larger tip for having brought her safely through the imaginary badlands. John Pringle once arranged a honeymoon house at Montego Bay for a young couple. They stayed only one night in Jamaica, making some excuse. It took a long time for John to learn the truth. The nightwatchman for their house had come on their first evening to assure them of how well he would care for them. He pointed to a house on the hill opposite. 'One man last week, they cut his head off. And over there, one month ago, two be raped in that house.' There was not a word of truth in it. The watchman was boosting his own importance so that the honeymoon couple would reward him well for their survival. We arrived in perfect safety in Ocho Rios and stayed in delirious comfort at the best-managed hotel on the island, the Sans Souçi – with no echoes of Haitian tyrannies.

It is a relief to find that one's memory has not deceived one. (Perhaps it had, a little, about the house I rented thirty years ago for $12 a week. It did not have quite the grandeur I remembered.) All through our journey

I had said to Hamish, wait till we get to Jamaica, then you will see a real beach, a real river, a real paradise. My faith had been occasionally shaken on the way. Nothing can be so majestic as the Pitons on St Lucia, no forest could be so dramatic as those on Dominica, the sweeping mountain views of Puerto Rico are hard to rival, the buildings of Santo Domingo are literally unique. Nonetheless, Jamaica is the most beautiful island of them all.

Perhaps it is the Englishness of the farmlands that appeals to me. Within ten minutes of the tourist coast, one can be in grazed parkland, made majestic by huge trees. Chestnut-brown cattle pattern the emerald pastures. These parks with their splendid Great Houses are the product of the much larger estates which existed on Jamaica. While plantations on other islands might have been thought large at 300 acres, here a planter (or more likely absentee proprietor) might own 10,000 acres. The Pringle family at one time owned 150,000 acres. There are still estates of 4,000 or 5,000.

But it is not just that. For many hours we wandered in the fringes of the Cockpit country, the nearly inaccessible mountain lands, where the Maroons, the wild bands of runaway slaves, sought sanctuary and fought off all attempts to subdue them. The road would wind through deep valleys. Every so often there would be a cluster of red roofs on a ridge and we would wonder how the people reached them, through the steep, thick woods. Then we would see them no more. Occasionally, there would be a few houses by the road, the planks of their walls often of different faded colours, like abstract paintings. The children would shout and the people smile. At one point, we went for an hour, climbing higher and higher, seeing no houses, no people – only forest, not dense but scattered with banana trees and mangoes and other signs of sporadic cultivation. Even this wild country is long-worked land. Then we came out on what seemed like the top of the world: to the right of us, the true Cockpit country, at first green, then beyond the first valley, blue and hazy, finally, higher even than us, faint hills in a muslin mist. Ahead were occasional roofs, nearly all red corrugated iron, one or two hipped, some small and flat. On the most prominent hunp stood a white house, far bigger than the rest, with a broad flight of some fifteen steps in front of it. None of these houses appeared to have any connection with another. This was not a village, just the homes of peasants with a house to match the size of the plot they worked. Some would have a car; others would be poor, too poor, but not so poor as to be wretched, nor so lifeless that they might not, 'peradventure' (as one said of something), claw their way out to a better life, for Jamaicans are nothing if not opportunists.

Then the rivers. There are those 365 torrents on Dominica; and the larger islands have real rivers, but there is something mysterious about the rivers of Jamaica. It is only here that anyone would think of rafting down the rapids, through gorges and great tunnels of bamboo. Jamaican beaches, too, are the only beaches that I can enjoy for more than an hour. There is no swimming in the world to equal those wonderful coves where the river water tumbles down, over natural limestone stairways with the look of abandoned, giant cascades, straight onto the beach. The cold mountain water mingles with the warm seawater, so that one can swim in and out of cold and warmth at whim.

The pattern of our life in Jamaica was vastly different from what we had become accustomed to on other islands. Hitherto, we had relied mostly on chance encounters in order to build up a picture of a place. Travel of this sort is, in many ways, a lonely business and to a certain degree I enjoy it for that. But it is not often that one meets an interesting person, as opposed to someone one is interested in. Jamaica, however, pullulated with interesting people and we suddenly recognised our need, after so many months, for more familiar company.

Of course, there were chance encounters. As we were driving one day we spotted a house with a red, orange and yellow roof a little below the road. As we came closer, we saw that the whole house was painted with figures and writing. A woman was standing in the garden. Hamish asked her if we might look at her house. It was an ordinary concrete bungalow, but every inch of it inside and out was covered with Rastafarian paintings and slogans and texts. The woman took us into the house and we gazed in amazement at the nine-foot high paintings of Haile Selassie on horseback, with dreadlocks hanging over his gold-braided uniform; of a liner filled with Rastas, sailing as much through the sky as the sea, presumably carrying the Rastas back to Ethiopia – one white man was falling overboard; of a four-legged man, the word 'Democracy' written above his head, 'Blasphemer' written across his forehead, his first lone eye was below his nose, in one of his three hands he held a book labelled 'Religion', in the second a gun labelled 'Politics', while his third drew a fully-clothed mannikin from his mouth-shaped stomach, labelled

282

'Christianity', between his legs another nose with an eye and, dangling upside-down, four more mannikins, at his feet a grave. Above was a wicker, false ceiling with more paintings, one of a lion with fire streaming from its penis, aimed at a startled, white bird. The texts, many of them concerned with food, were gibberish. Because of the madness of them, they were impossible to memorise. It was not till I got photographs that I could remember any, of which this is a typical example.

'When one realises that I and I existence was dated as far as one hundred billion years by anthropologist and archaeologist, one will note that I and I was preserved by some divine material because I and I was, and still is, a living masterpiece which is made up of solid properties, no colonial masters, imperial harlots or communists reapers have the opportunity to capture I and I under their portfolios. At this time all black people should arise and accept Rasta as roots culture, in this democratic society where neither principalities nor power have any access over. Rasta is no thief or robber but instead is [illegible] lineage of Rastafari King Selassie I.'

Talking to the woman was hard because she spoke so softly in a very strong accent, but also because what she said was on a par with the texts. It is possible that she was stoned. I understood that there was a man she lived with. He was out. She did say that they employed an artist and told him what to paint. She could not elucidate for me the differences between the various sects of Rastafarianism. I asked if hers were a peaceful branch. 'I am peaceful it is the right one,' she said with some ingenuity. She spoke so much of Ethiopia that I asked if she had been there.

'Yes, that where we from.'

'Have you been on a visit?'

'Yes, but I don't just now.'

Rastafarianism is a curiosity. It originated in Jamaica, under the influence of Marcus Garvey, who founded the Universal Negro Improvement Association in the United States. He preached a form of black nationalism and a return to Africa for all the descendants of African slaves. Garvey supposedly prophesied the crowning of a black king which would herald a day of deliverance for black people. After Ras Tafari was crowned Emperor Haile Selassie in 1930, a number of people assumed that he was the promised deliverer. It was probably Leonard P. Howell who first proclaimed that Haile Selassie was the living God.

By the sixties the Rastafarians in Jamaica numbered about twelve to fifteen thousand. Poor Howell, after various spells in prison for fraud, preaching violence and assault, and various other crimes, was eventually shut up in a lunatic asylum. Others pursued a more gentle course.

The actual doctrines of the Rastas are hard to pin down. In 1960, the Jamaican Institute of Social and Economic Research published a *Report on the Rastafari Movement in Kingston, Jamaica.* They concluded that Rastafarians:

> . . . held in common only two beliefs: that Ras Tafari is the living God and that salvation can come to black men only through repatriation to Africa. On all other matters the opinions of the brethren vary as widely as the opinions of the rest of the population. Some wear beards, others do not; and only a small minority wear the locks. Some are men of the highest moral fibre, while at the other extreme are men of crime and violence. Some smoke ganja; others abhor it. Some are excellent workmen, while others avoid work. In all matters except two, the divinity of Ras Tafari and the necessity of repatriation, Ras Tafarians are a random group.

The question of repatriation has faded over the intervening quarter of a century. It is now a token belief, rather as Jewish people, who have no intention of moving from New York or London, say at Passover, 'Next year Jerusalem.'

The Institute's report went on to give a detailed account of one section's teachings. They are typical, if not of every Rastafarian's beliefs, of Rastafarian cast of thought.

> The black race are the true Israelites, the House of David, and the Emperor, the Lion of Judah, descended from King Solomon and the Queen of Sheba, is their true head. Those Jews whom Hitler and the Nazis exterminated were merely false Jews of whom the Scripture has said, 'Woe unto them that call themselves Israel and they are not.' God is black (Jeremiah 8), Haile Selassie is black, Solomon and Sheba were black, and so are the true Israelites. The white men have worshipped a dead God, and have taught black men to do likewise. The white man's God is really Pope John XXIII, Pope Pius's successor, the head of the Ku-Klux-Klan . . .
>
> King James I of Britain, a white man, translated the Bible, distorting and confusing its message; but to those who, by virtue of Ras Tafari's divine power, have been given inspiration and prophetic insight, the false passages put in by the white man for his

284

own purposes are easily detected, and accordingly Ras Tafari brethren treat the Bible carefully, using only that part which they regard as the true Word of God . . .

The black race, having sinned, was punished by God their Father. Punishment was meted out in the form of slavery, conquest, and control by the white man. The four pirates, John Hawkins, Cecil Rhodes, Livingstone and Grant brought the Africans to the Western world as slaves under Elizabeth I, who has been reincarnated as Elizabeth II. Her former beloved Philip of Spain, has also been reincarnated as her present husband, Philip, Duke of Edinburgh. The golden sceptre which belonged to the House of Judah in Ethiopia and which carried with it the dominion of the world was stolen from Ethiopia by Rome – which then had world empire – and from Rome by Britain which inherited the Roman power. On the coronation of Haile Selassie I in November 1930, King George V of Britain sent his son, the Duke of Gloucester, with this sceptre as a gift to the Emperor. The Duke of Gloucester, who is said to have succeeded George V as Edward VIII, while in Ethiopia wandered off into the bush, eating grass, thereby revealing himself as the reincarnated Nebuchadnezzar, King of Babylon. The Emperor Haile Selassie, receiving the sceptre, simultaneously recovered the symbol of Ethiopian world power. In return, he is said to have given the Duke of Gloucester a small emblem for King George V. When the Duke returned to Britain and handed this to his father, the latter is said to have been stricken with paralysis and to have died shortly after, although it was some months before this fact was announced to the British public. The Duke of Gloucester then became King and, to fulfil prophecies, abdicated, knowing that he shall resume the throne after the reincarnated Elizabeth I to rule as the last King of Babylon and to witness its utter defeat. This is clearly apocalyptic, the Messiah being the Emperor and the instrument chosen for the destruction of Babylon being the Bear with three ribs (Rev. 13), that is Russia, which 'will come to stamp out the residue thereof so that Babylon shall be a desolation among the nations' . . .

The original God of the white man was Adam-Abraham, the leper, Anglo-Saxon blood-sucker and slave master. Pope John has inherited his role . . .

Sodomy is advocated by the priests of Babylon, notably the Archbishop of Canterbury . . . these are the ways of the white man and his God. The black man knows better . . .

I had breakfast one morning with Hector Wynter, a most fascinating man who was formerly the editor of the *Gleaner*. It was he who was responsible for organising Haile Selassie's arrival at the airport when he visited Jamaica in 1966. He held a rehearsal the day before, allotting the six different groups of Rastas separate places to stand. One group leader did not attend the rehearsal and, on the day, went to quite a different place, broke through the barrier and, with his followers, swarmed up the steps of the plane. Hector said that Haile Selassie burst into tears, whether from fright or from emotion he could not say.

The Rastas camped outside King's House during the whole of the Emperor's visit. Occasionally he would give a gold coin to one or two of them. Hector, one day, asked the Emperor when he was going to tell them that he was not God. 'Who am I to disturb their belief?' asked the Emperor. (This reminded me of an occasion on which I asked the Emperor what provision he had made for his country after he died. He replied, 'Ethiopia was not created for me. I cannot dictate what happens when I die.')

Today, the Rastas seem to have little influence and are regarded as largely harmless. Many have grown rich on the proceeds of growing and exporting ganja or marijuana – a trade said to be worth two and a half billion dollars. They build grand palaces and join the middle classes.

Another quite different group we came across were the German poor-whites of Seaford Town. About twelve hundred Germans emigrated to Jamaica in the 1830s. Their influence can still be seen in place names such as Berlin, Potsdam, Bohemia and Saxony, but the only recognisable group are the descendants of 251 Germans who arrived in 1835, at the prompting of a Prussian doctor, and settled on land, high in the western hills, given by Lord Seaford. They prospered for a while, growing sugar and bananas, but they were snobbish and refused to mix with the blacks. Gradually, inbreeding took its usual toll. Their numbers, which rose at one point to about five hundred, have now dwindled again to fewer than two hundred.

The village of Seaford straggles for a mile. The houses are no less poor than those round about. At the end of the village, raised on a promontory of land coming out from the hillside, is a small, stone church of indeterminate design with a sorrowfully large graveyard beside it. The people of the village are a kind of yellow colour, as if stained by something, but some of the children are striking by virtue of their startling fair hair. As with the inbred people of other islands, the whiter they are, the plainer they are. I could not fathom why there is something about inbreeding which multiplies ugliness and lack of intelligence as well as genetic defects, while the mixing of races makes for beauty, though not particularly for cleverness. Surely the pharoahs were not hideous and dim-witted? Perhaps they were.

Near the church was a small hut with some photographs and relics. A toothless young man of great amiability, called Derek Hacker, showed us the lists of people who arrived from Germany. The names were the same as those on so many of the newer stones in the graveyards: Eldermeyer, Widemeyer, Kameka, Somers. Derek said that he worked the same three acres that his family had had since 1850. He grew bananas, cane, yams and corn. It was difficult to believe that he made much of a living. In the graveyard, he showed us the graves of three Hackers killed in a road accident that year. Next to them lay a cousin, shot dead by marauders who came to steal their crop. The dead man's son had had three bullets removed from different parts of him.

The first stone church was built by the Jesuit Fathers in 1882. It was totally destroyed by a hurricane in 1912. The new church was built soon after, also by the Jesuits, but it is now in the care of Benedictines. Derek was most devout and took us with great pride to see the new altar – a dreadful, rustic affair.

'De Bishop him say it de prettiest altar he ever see and we must see no one do tief it,' said Derek. It seemed unlikely that anyone would steal it, as it was made of *lignum vitae* and Derek said it had taken six men to carry it in.

As we went about, I formed the opinion that the ordinary Jamaicans had a greater assurance than the people of the other islands. They had more certainty of who they were and of their rights. There was a feeling somehow that Jamaica has been worldly-wise for so long, that it is the most grown-up island of all. It seemed to me to have a style that was lacking on so many of the other islands. The average person was far more aware of what was going on and held stronger opinions on every subject. They were funny as well as tough. I wanted to buy one of those shirts which are, or used to be, made out of flour bags. There was none to be found in the market. One of the boisterous market-women, Madge, said, 'That Seaga say we cannot eat the flour *and* wear the bags.' I asked why the Prime Minister should say that. 'Because he is a fart. When Seaga farts, the whole of Kingston rocks, and many of the rural districts too.'

Jamaicans have none of that respect about which one hears so much in other islands. The actors of the television detective series *Dempsey and Makepeace* were on holiday in Ocho Rios, and we chanced to dine together. Michael Brandon had been in the market too. A man had tried to sell him some cocaine. When he refused, the man persisted.

'Look, I'm a cop,' said Brandon.

'Yeah, man, but it's good stuff.'

'I tell you, I'm a cop. I arrest people just for having stuff.'

'That's in the States, man. You're on holiday, you need some to relax.'

The Jamaicans are a wonderful mixture of roguery and enterprise. The opportunities are few in Jamaica, which may account for the popularity of smuggling. For a long time they used to ship ackee, a kind of fruit, to the United States. The Americans eventually banned its import, nominally on the grounds that it might be poisonous, but really because the tins were often filled with ganja. The smugglers changed to exporting vegetable oil, which was really ganja oil. Sniffer dogs in the States soon detected this, not because of the oil, which has no smell, but because the people packing it in boxes smoked so much themselves that the cartons smelled of ganja.

There are a great many Jamaicans in America. They started to go in large numbers during the administration of Michael Manley. This singular politician, in one of his impassioned speeches, said that there were five flights a day from Jamaica to Miami. If anyone did not like what he was doing, he should take one. Many did.

When the present Prime Minister, Edward Seaga, came to power, he asked them to come back. As an inducement, he said that anyone returning could bring his possessions, even a car, free of duty. Of course, every member of every family, from granny to the youngest baby, brought a car – and then emigrated again for a month and came back with five or six more cars.

It is interesting that, in the States, the Jamaicans are more successful than they are in England, where they are blamed for all the discontent. In Harlem, so I was told, they run many of the larger businesses. Indeed, they consider themselves superior to American blacks in the same way that they are sure that they are superior to the other Caribbean islanders.

This sense of superiority stems, I believe, from the general spirit of the days of the pirates and later of the plantocracy. Jamaican planters were ostentatious, vulgar and often brutal. At the same time, they were hospitable, sophisticated, humorous and eccentric. Taking their cue from the pleasure-loving planters, the emancipated slaves had streaks of hedonistic selfishness, fearless arrogance and spontaneous warmth of character, traits which have come down to present-day Jamaicans.

There is certainly no lack of the grand and the eccentric. We went to visit one old Great House. It was a majestic building redolent of the days of gambling and dissolution. There were grand Palladian windows, elaborate cornices separated a little from the open, shingle roof to allow air to flow, wonderfully polished floors of wild-orange wood on what was once an open verandah, for this wood is impervious to rain. The house looked over a great sweep of land, rather casually farmed, I thought, but splendid with huge trees, great clumps of swaying bamboo and groves of coconut. It had the decaying air of an Irish estate. The owner was reserved and serious. His family were away. As we drove back down the long drive, I remarked to Hamish that the romantic side of one's nature could not help regretting that life in such a house was now so sombre and respectable. When I repeated this to Jamaican friends, they roared with laughter. Did I not know, they asked, that the owner had a mistress in the lodge with three of his children and another girl in Port Antonio, not to mention a regular account with the brothel in Kingston?

Nearby, we stayed with Earl Levy, an entrepreneur, architect and hotelier. Earl comes from a family of Sephardic Jews who arrived in Jamaica 350 years ago. He is short, fair-haired, bespectacled and moves in a cloud of Brut. I liked him at once. Earl is a great believer in tradition. In his hotel, the waiters wear red jackets and white gloves and the guests, too, without exception, are made to wear ties and jackets for dinner. When I asked him whether this was not a bit formal in the tropics, more formal than one would find in any European resort, Earl said, with dignity, that it is only those who stick to the rules who survive. This was not to say that new formalities could not be added. Those red-coated, beautifully-trained waiters, as they set down one's food, gave that American, minatory benediction – 'Enjoy'.

Just down the road, Earl was building a gigantic castle. I can hardly imagine that another such building is going up anywhere in the world. A wide flight of steps leads up to the front door. On either side is an enormous concrete crocodile. One goes into a lofty, baronial hall, one hundred feet long and forty feet wide. After that comes a succession of spacious rooms – a yellow dining-room to seat thirty people, a pink, pilastered room hung with Piranesi prints, and many more – all with parquet floors. On the far side of the house is a terrace with a large circular pool, which Earl said was waiting for a statue of Neptune. It is a filmset folly, not a company's folly like Altos de Chavón, but one man's folly in the true tradition of the Jamaican planters.

Earl has a mysterious gift for getting things to work. On almost any other island, where poverty is intense, such a fantasy would be offensive. The people might protest. Not on Jamaica. The local police, before it is finished, have already borrowed it for their annual party. I have no doubt that when Earl has finished, this absurd creation will be a marvellous tourist attraction.

As we drove from the east of the island to the opposite end, this theme of the unusual kept recurring. Past Noël Coward's house, now a museum. The house is much as he left it. The pile of songsheets on the piano, I was told, diminishes according to the number of visitors. For some reason, the elegant, plain slab of his tombstone, set in the lawn with just his name and dates on it, has been surrounded by a dreadful affair like a birdcage. I only hope it would have made him laugh. Past Goldeneye, built by Ian Fleming, the creator of James Bond, the house in which Anthony Eden took refuge after Suez and his subsequent resignation.

At the far end of the island, we stayed with a deeply eccentric former officer in the Life Guards, Kenneth Diacre. He is a jovial, roly-poly man with vivid blue eyes. He has restored a small plantation house that he found crumbling in the forest, which he now calls Rat Hall. He also runs the Tryall Golf and Beach Club. He is infinitely hospitable and remarkably well read. He calls himself, with no great seriousness, the Comte de Liancourt and allows, perhaps encourages, it to be put about that he is the love-child of the late Duke of Rutland and a French lady of title. When I asked him where he was brought up he said, 'in France by the servants'. This engaging figure, although a newcomer, in some ways personifies the roistering, full-blooded spirit of Jamaica.

Up in the hills behind Ocho Rios, we, lunched with new-found friends, Valerie and Maurice Facey. They have a beautiful Great House, which they bought not long ago from an eccentric member of the Pringle family. This Pringle would go to see a friend off on a banana boat to

Europe and at the last second decide to go too. His servants, expecting him home for dinner, might not see him for four months. The Faceys, rather more conventional in their ways, have restored the house in perfect taste. They farm 2,000 acres, keeping 1,000 head of cattle and growing acres of those anthurium lilies so much admired in America.

What is particularly interesting about the Faceys is the proof they represent of the complete absence of colour prejudice that exists in Jamaica. When they got married more than thirty years ago, in colonial times, there was a fuss, for Maurice, like any other ordinary Jamaican, had slave ancestry. Today, nobody notices what colour anybody is. Unlike, say, Barbados, where the business people are white and the politicians are black, there is a complete mix, although it is true that the richer people tend to be paler. Hector Wynter had talked to me of the old colonial attitude to colour and how the pecking order went – White British, Jewish (Portuguese Sephardim), Black, Chinese, Indian, Lebanese. (Better, I suppose, than the 128 grades of colour in Haiti.) When he was young, Hector himself did not apply for a Rhodes Scholarship as he is black. Now, he said, it is a matter of attitude. If you go to a poor district and you own a car, they will cry, 'Hi, white man,' even if you are black. A pure white man can have a 'black (ie good) heart'. In Rasta talk, the opposite is a 'breadfruit'. Breadfruit is black outside when cooked, but still white (ie bad) inside.

If there is a criticism to be made of Jamaican society, it is that, like England, it has an Establishment. It is no accident that three out of five of Jamaica's Prime Ministers, albeit of opposing parties, have been related to one another and that the two founders of independent Jamaica, Norman Manley and Alexander Bustamente, were cousins.

Politically – and everyone in Jamaica is political – the island, perhaps not entirely by coincidence, appeared to be in a similar predicament to Britain. The current Prime Minister, Edward Seaga, is a shy man who appears arrogant. He is a secretive man who rarely smiles and trusts no one. He has a poor public presence. Every hitchhiker we picked up declared to us that Seaga was only interested in the rich. (The rich, when I told them this, were surprised.) He did nothing, they said, for the poor. Seaga's approach is often practical, but seldom popular. When oil prices went down, Seaga did not put the price at the pumps down, which he maintained would merely have meant more oil would be imported. Instead, he spent the profits on road projects which, he said, relieved unemployment and improved the roads.

Seaga's opponent, Michael Manley, is a man of such superlative charm that one person said to me, 'I never dare to go and see Michael, I know he will persuade me to believe something I know isn't true.' He is immensely popular, partly because he is an orator. Jamaicans love speeches. They do not necessarily mind even if they know a politician is lying. They accept enthusiastic rhetoric as meaning more, 'wouldn't it be lovely if. . . ', rather than a statement of fact. A good speech from Manley and they quite forget that last time he was Prime Minister there were crippling shortages, no electricity and no water and much violence. (Others who point this out forget that, if the price of water doubles, as it has done, people cannot afford it, so there is no difference. Either way they have none.) Nonetheless, many people are terrified lest Manley gets back, rather as they are terrified in England lest Labour should win.

It seemed to me likely that Manley would triumph in the next elections. Jamaicans believe in fair play. The electors seem to think two terms are enough. Moreover, they thought it unfair of Seaga to call the last elections at a moment when he was bound to win – partly because he had not rectified anomalies on the electoral rolls and partly because it was just after the Grenada invasion and people were afraid of Manley's flirtations with Cuba.

My love affair with Jamaica made me see only the happy side. I had come expecting many of the memories of thirty years ago to be shattered. I was amazed to find that the reverse was the case. The fundamental spirit which had charmed me then is still intact. The dramatis personae have changed, but their parts are the same. Much is immeasurably better. The people are better educated. The art is far more exciting and individual. The museum in Kingston is a delight, but the pictures in it spring from a natural artistry which has been released by independence. The walls of the humblest buildings are often covered with wonderful paintings.

The only music I heard when I was in Jamaica before was the calypso, borrowed from Trinidad, a popular, pasteurised rhythm, made amusing only by the saucy words of some of the songs. I never heard the mento, which had ribald enough verses, but which had an underlying, slightly lewd dance rhythm, slow and undulating, that distinguished it from calypso. It had not the appeal of calypso. Nonetheless, its beat suited better the second and fourth beat stress of rhythm and blues. It was out of a combination of mento and rhythm and blues that ska, rock steady and ultimately reggae grew.

In my pleasure, I forgot for a while the horrors that all the islands of the Caribbean are heir to. Where are the bauxite mines, once one of the most profitable of Jamaica's industries? Shut, because Manley tried to tax the investors too heavily, or so they say. Shut, I would equally think, because the United States has its own bauxite.

Then we went to an hotel of the latest kind. The guests pay for everything before they arrive. Once through the door they need never think of money again. Everything is free – food, drinks, cigarettes, windsurfing and other sports, sightseeing, entertainment, discotheque. They cost about $1,000 per week for each person, many insisting on couples (one adding heterosexual couples only). At first sight, it might be thought that people could take advantage of this system, drinking and eating with Rabelaisian greed. Evidently the guests soon tire of excess. On average, they consume only three dollars worth of drink and nine dollars worth of food a day. The hotel saves a fortune in staff. They need prepare no bills, keep no accounts for the restaurants or bars. There is hardly any 'front desk' work. Their only extra cost is in entertainment.

The usefulness of these hotels to the island is minimal. The guests see no point in going out when everything in the hotel is free. The employment is very small in comparison with an ordinary hotel. It is, in fact, the pinnacle of the tourist systems which make money for the foreign hotelier and benefit the community not one whit.

And, once again, it is not just foreign exploitation, nor economic impotence. One of the most encouraging enterprises I saw in the whole Caribbean was an agricultural scheme founded by some Israelis. Three years ago they started farming on some dry, unpromising land about two hours west of Kingston. Their experience in the desert was invaluable. They were now farming 6,000 acres. The executive director, Eli Tisona, waxed lyrical in his enthusiasm for their achievements. That year they had produced twenty-two million pounds of winter vegetables. The next year they expected to produce fifty million pounds from 2,500 acres.

Then there was the banana crop. They had nearly 2,500 acres for that, growing a variety called Ziv. They managed to get between twenty and twenty-five tons to the acre and were packing 300 tons a day. There were 400 acres of mango trees. And a 200-acre fish-farm, which would double in size next year. They produced a fish which they called Jamaican snapper. Mr Tisona said it was a freshwater version of the ordinary red snapper. It tasted better than the sea snapper, according to Mr Tisona. 'Less fishy,' he said. (Oh dear.)

All these wonders depended to a great extent on the Israelis' great skill with drip irrigation. This was expensive – about twelve hundred dollars an acre but, Mr Tisona explained, it would last fifteen years. I asked what happened about rain? Mr Tisona said that they had had a bit of trouble. Nine inches fell one week, but they had learned from that and could now control things. It was a wonderful scheme, already employing 3,500 Jamaicans, soon to expand to give work to 6,000. The workers told me how happy they were, for they were impressed by the Israelis' willingness to work side by side with them in the fields. This year they expected to make their first profit. Mr Tisona and I parted with mutual good wishes.

Three weeks after I got home, I heard on the radio that fifty inches had fallen in three days. The whole Israeli scheme had been washed away. Never before had it rained like that.

Now I learn that they will start again.

It was time to go. Hamish flew away to his love in Santo Domingo. I boarded a plane full of cricketers, the battered remnants of England's test team.

Index

Miami
FLORIDA
Key West

Matanzas

CUBA

Camaguey
Holguín

Guantanamo
Santiago
de Cuba

Cayman
Islands

Bahama Islands

300 km
150 miles
Peter McClure 1987

Cap Haïtien
Gonaïves
Gulf of St.
Gonâve Marc
Santiago
San Juan
Azu

Port
au
Prince
HAITI
Baraho

Montego Bay   Ocho Rios
                   Port
JAMAICA   Antonio
        Kingston

The Islands of
the Caribbean

GRENADA
                    Sauteurs
                        Green
                        Island
Gouyave   Tivoli
                    † Airport

St.
George's
        Grande Anse

0   10 km

DOMINICAN REPUBLIC

Cap Haïtien   Puerto Plata
                                Samana
        Santiago
HAITI   Sánchez
Port-au-Prince
        Lago de   ▲ Pico Duarte
        Enriquillo San Juan
                    Azua   Bani S. Cristobal
                                    † Airport
Jimani Neiba   Haina   La Romana
        Barahona   San
                    Domingo   0   50 km

COLOMBIA